Education in Ancient and Medieval India

(A Survey of the Main Features and a Critical Evaluation of Major Trends)

S.P. CHAUBE
A. CHAUBE

VIKAS® PUBLISHING HOUSE PVT LTD

VIKAS® PUBLISHING HOUSE PRIVATE LIMITED
E-28, Sector-8, Noida-201301 (UP), India
Phone: +91-120-4078900 • Fax: +91-120-4078999
Registered Office: A-27, 2nd Floor, Mohan Co-operative Industrial Estate, New Delhi-110044
E-mail: helpline@vikaspublishing.com • Website: www.vikaspublishing.com

SALES AND BRANCH OFFICES OF VIKAS® AND S CHAND AND COMPANY LIMITED

Chennai : Ph: 044-2363 2120, chennai@schandpublishing.com
Guwahati : Ph: 0361-2738 811, 2735 640, guwahati@schandpublishing.com
Hyderabad : Ph: 040-4018 6018, hyderabad@schandpublishing.com
Jalandhar : Ph: 0181-4645 630, jalandhar@schandpublishing.com
Kolkata : Ph: 033-2335 7458, 2335 3914, kolkata@schandpublishing.com
Lucknow : Ph: 0522-4003 633, lucknow@schandpublishing.com
Mumbai : Ph: 022-2500 0297, mumbai@schandpublishing.com
Patna : Ph: 0612-2260 011, patna@schandpublishing.com

Education in Ancient and Medieval India
ISBN: 978-81259-0435-9 Product Code: V7EAI69TEDU10ENAA0XO

Reprinted several times between 2005 and 2020
Reprint 2022

PRINTED IN INDIA
By Vikas Publishing House Private Limited, Plot 20/4, Site-IV, Industrial Area Sahibabad, Ghaziabad-201010 and Published by Vikas Publishing House Private Limited, E-28, Sector-8, Noida-201301

Contents

Preface

The existing complexities of modern life have left man — all over the world — bereft of spiritual contexts which his forefathers had developed, nourished and cherished and which in turn laid the foundation stone of modern human civilization. India, since times immemorial, has been well-known for its spiritual excellence and such seers have taken birth here who could enter into the unfathomable depths of spiritual consciousness. One has to make a deep study of our Vedas and Upanishads to recognise the nature of the consciousness which our ancestors could attain. Modern man is bogged down in the blind array of materialism and pragmatism, hence it is not easy for him to comprehend the essentials of our Vedas and other spiritual literature, although their comprehension is within his reach.

Agriculture was the principal pursuit of our ancestors during the Vedic and Post-Vedic periods. Nonetheless, they were quite alive towards affecting a harmony between their mundane and spiritual pursuits. They were of the firm conviction that the soul is much above the limits of the earthly body, castes, classes, times and places. In a way, their life was well-knit within a unique social system. The aim of our life, to-day, is entirely different from that of our forefathers as we now adhere to a different set of values. There is always a close relationship between "education" and "the place, period and the people" for which it is meant. The principal aim of education during the ancient days was to promote the physical, intellectual and spiritual development of an individual in such a way as to help him to affect a harmony between his worldly and spiritual life. The first part of the book presents the essentials of this system of education.

Vedic literature played a major role towards developing education during the ancient days in India. The Vedas were the chief source of education during that period. It is because of this basic feature that the contents and methods of education during ancient India have been based on Vedic literature.

In the second part of this book, a brief survey of education during the medieval period of Indian history has been made. Muslim rule during medieval days in India lasted for about 650 years of so. Education during this era mostly hung on the whims, caprices and interests of the respective Muslim rulers. The principal sources of the study of the nature of education in the Muslim period are some of the available biographies of the Muslim rulers and travel accounts recorded by some foreign travellers. The then existing system of ancient *pathashalas* seldom received any encouragement and patronage worth the name from the Muslim rulers, except in a very few cases which did not continue due to the historical vicissitudes of the period during which centres of ancient system were erased, burnt and completely destroyed at several places by the fanatic and fundamentalistic invaders. The ruins of Nalanda (Bihar) and of other seats of ancient learning bear ample testimony of these disastrous subversive events. During the medieval days Persian became the chief medium of instruction. Arabic was also compulsorily taught at places of education under the specific patronage of Muslim kings. Mosques, Maktabs and Madarasahs were the principal places of education during these days. At such places the religious and spiritual contents of studies prevailed. It may be noted that in spite of being deprived of the patronage of the government of the day, certain Hindu centres of learning also continued to exist even during these adverse times. In the second part of this book a brief account of these features of education of the period has also been given.

The sole purpose of this attempt has been to meet the curricular demands of the students of education at the graduate and post-graduate levels of our colleges and universities, as the subject of education during the ancient and medieval periods of India has been made a compulsory aspect of the courses of study for them. The authors will feel amply rewarded if this attempt on their part leads any one to proceed towards a more advanced study of the subject.

It is not for the authors to claim any originality in the preparation of this book. But certain evaluations and assessments of some features of the educational system as discussed herein are the atuhors' own perception of the same. It is hoped that they will merit the attention of the readers.

Sources of materials drawn towards the preparation of this volume are mentioned in the bibliography appended at the end.

S.P. CHAUBE
A. CHAUBE

SECTION I

Chapter 1

Philosophy of Life in Ancient India

It Originates in the Vedas

The Vedas, regarded as the oldest among the literatures of the world, are the original sources of the philosophy of life in ancient India. A study of the Vedas will enable one to get a thorough knowledge not only of the philosophy of life, but also of the whole fabric of ancient Indian culture. They constitute the vital force of Indian life. Consequently, the entire literature and philosophy of India, the Upanishads the Smritis and the Puranas, acknowledge the superiority of the Vedas. Not only have the various elements of religion been exhaustively treated in them, the glory of human life and thought ever since the beginning of this universe, also have been preserved.

As for the derivation of the word Veda, it is found in the four roots; 'Vid Sattayam'[1]. 'Vidlri Labhe'[2], 'Vid Vicharne'[3] and 'Vid Gyane'[4]. The root 'Vid Sattayam' is connotative of all those attributes and virtues which need to be cultivated in oneself, for the procurement of the means requisite for the satisfaction of the prime material and physical needs of human life as also for the full development of the human personality. The real greatness (glory) of human life consists of the cultivation of individual power. Hence, among the 'Ashramas', (stages or periods of life) 'Brahmacharya' (celibacy of student-life) was installed as the first and foremost one. During this first stage of life an individual amasses — through physical, mental and spiritual sufferance; endurance and devotion; material useful for the next stage of life; the Grihastha Ashram or the life of the householder. The first stage of life contains the keynote of human life and on it is based the dignity and the glory of the future life of the individual. As such, it has been regarded as the key apparatus for building life.

The root Vidulah Labhe connotes that element in the universe which enables the individual to meet his temporal life with the beatitude and supreme energy of benevolent and ultra-mundane existence. The enlightenment gained during the first stage of life helps the individual in the second stage of the householder (Grihastha Ashram) to develop a sort of emotional attachment with the world and thereby obtain a glimpse of the divine cosmic soul. That is why the wise and the learned while acknowledging the supremacy of the Grihastha Ashram over all others have regarded it as the scientific ordination of nature. In the Mahabharat, the sacred text-book of Indian culture, the nuptial sentiment of an individual who has passed through the Brahmacharya phase, has been called an enlightened resolve or a holy vow. Consequently, the individual in the Grihastha Ashram is seen striving particularly for material gains, which can also be dubbed as a desire for riches. But this desire, begotten of righteousness, is instrumental in helping him not only in gaining selfish ends but beatitude or salvation also. Therefore, the Grihastha Àshram is regarded as the key-pin or fulcrum of all the Ashramas. In the Vedas also the individual, or the householder, is bidden to earn and spend like a lord. In fact, the Grihastha Ashram implies life devoted to the systematic and harmonious development of all the faculties of the individual.

The root *'Vid Vicharne'* is indicative of the intellectual and mental development of the individual. When an individual, tired and weary of the enjoyment of material comforts gained through the cultivated inner power of the Brahmacharya state, begins to feel himself depleted of strength during the state of the householder, he needs to be replenished with power. During this state he is helped by his thoughts and ideas. "Hence, he has been bidden to go with the sacrificial fuel in his hands to the Guru, or preceptor, for the purpose of prudently redevoting himself to the rigorous life of the Brahmacharya and to attain self-realisation on the basis of his collected experience. The preceptor discharges his duties by enlightening the devotee's path of *self-contemplation* and by directing his intellectual and mental development by means of the experiences gained in his own life of dedicated seclusion. The word Veda with its root 'Vid Vicharne' has this particular utility in human life.

The root *'Vid Gyane'* gives to the human being a knowledge of his inherent supreme perfections and of his redemption. On being initiated into the fourth stage of the recluse, an individual can by his enlarged vision and by the realisation of the fact that God is Love, gain the unbounded love of the Almighty and thereby succeed in attaining the greatest heights of the final beatitude. The significance of the term 'Veda' with its root Vid Gyane in human life consists of this all-round development and sublimation of the human personality.

Hence, it transpires from the above discussion of the implications of the word Veda, that the Vedas themselves have ordained the four Ashramas of human life. It also becomes evident that by a complete observance of the obligations imposed by the four Ashramas, an individual can succeed in realising his ultimate goal.

It is an Aspect of Religion

The above discussion makes it clear that the Vedas, the veritable repositories of the spiritual knowledge of the Indians, embody in themselves the sublime religious feelings of human beings. One can well visualise the type of life led by those Indians who followed and incorporated the precepts outlined by the sacred texts in their every day existence. It is evident that the strands of numerous religions have been incorporated in the texture of life and thought in India. Hence, Indian life has always been tinctured with religious and spiritual ideas. The four aspects or the four arms of Indian life, are represented by the Rigveda, Yajurveda, Atharaveda and Samveda, or Religious, Materialistic, Conjugal and Spiritual instincts and pursuits or by Brahmacharya, Grishastha, Vanprastha and Sanyas Ashramas. Hence, the philosophy of life and the culture of India can be described as the counterparts of religion.

All this evidences that Indian life is the expression of religion and the principles of conduct propounded by the Vedas. The term 'Vid' is so comprehensive in its meaning that it is impossible to discuss it here in its entirety. The ordinary meaning of the word 'Veda' is 'to know'. What the individual has to know and what not is his *summum bonum* of education for life. In the Vedas we have a graphic account of this education also. It was for this very purpose that the four Ashramas of life were ordained. The Vedas have also planned out the four planes or levels of existence, viz. of knowledge, of action, of devotion and of wisdom, for the seeker of knowledge. In order to make the individual realise this the preceptor instructs the individual at the time of the 'Thread Ceremony' or his initiation into the Brahmacharya stage,— 'Thou art a Brahmachari' and thereby explains to him that the supreme goal of human life in this world is to realise one's identity with Brahma, the divine source of the universe. He further instructs him to continue in the process of self-development so that he may be able to retain this identity with the 'Brahma' throughout his life.

Knowledge, Action and Devotion are the means of the realisation of the Brahma and these are also the three pillars of religion, because religion is founded upon comprehensive knowledge, Action and Devotion. For the cultivation of knowledge, the first component of religion, the preceptor used to take resident students into his hermitage. Desiring that the mind of the student or the celibate, may develop and become like that of his own, the preceptor inculcated in the student the spirit of Brahma-realisation so strongly that never in his life could he stray from this goal. Further, again to enable the celibate to experience spiritual happiness, the preceptor made him realise that the human spirit can enjoy the bliss of association with Brahma only after having some beatific vision and after absorbing some of the traits.

The celibate while residing within the hermitage of the preceptor came to realise fully that the Brahma is the Great Reality and the world is an illusion. Wordly delusion cannot be dissipated until the darkness of ignorance is dispelled. Hence, for the realisation of truth, the knowledge of astrology and astronomy is essential. For the furtherance of his holy desire, the celibate enters into the presence of his preceptor as the very embodiment of politeness and humility. He carefully assimilates the precepts of the teacher, meditates upon them and finally, after recollecting and rolling these precepts over in his mind, he succeeds in gaining the knowledge of truth. The celibate has been depicted as regarding every spoken work of the preceptor as a precept. This indicates a specialty which has some significance.

The very word "instruction" (Upadesh) implies the elucidation of mystery. Hence, until the celibate contemplates upon and constantly turns over in his mind what he has heard from the preceptor, he remains incapable of realising the desideratum. The Upanishads while describing the process of absorption of knowledge led the celibate to contemplate upon what he heard from the preceptor, for it was only through contemplative recollection of the precepts that he could really understand them. Thus hearing, contemplation and recollection are laid down as the three stages of the process of self-development. Just as an individual succeeds in making all the parts of his body healthy, strong and perfect through physical exercise, in the same manner he succeeds in discovering the fugitive and mysterious light through deep meditation resulting from a through understanding of the terms: Hearing[5], Contemplation[6] and Recollection[7]. It is only through contemplative recollection that the soul of the celibate begins to scintillate with the dazzing brilliance of knowledge. And by means of this self-enlightenment he begins to feel the omnipresence of the Brahma in this triple aspect of "Sacchidanand"; attains the condition of Felicity and finally by realising the great truth enters into the state of Beatitude and enjoys the divine happiness of Redemption. It also dawns on him that joy and suffering are inseparable from human existence and that after the destruction of the human body the soul remains untarred by these.

It Accepts the Supremacy of 'Karma' — Action.

The outstanding characteristic of the ancient philosophy of life in India is that while no great significance is attached to physical existence in the world, yet the importance of action in this material world is not overlooked. The doctrine of action (Karma) occupies a very significant place in the Indian system of education. Yet this doctrine holds good in so far as it is helpful in attaining salvation. Action in its distilled form has been regarded not as a means of making the individual attached to the world but of bringing to him deliverance from the earthly turmoil by awakening him to the unreality of this darkling plain. Action or Karma should not be for the bondage of man and education. It should be for the redemption of mankind. This has been the ideal of the doctrine of Karma as also of the educational system of India. The principles of religious, material, conjugal and spiritual pursuits — representing the four aspects of Indian life embody the beneficent truth that material pursuits should be tinged with a spirit of religion and the activities of sex should be based on religious and economic consideration and should be such as to engender the spirit of active goodness, so that the ultimate goal of salvation may be realised.

Hence, after a critical analysis of the Indian philosophy of life, one arrives at the conclusion that the ultimate object of devotion for an individual is the Brahma and not this world. The material world is the laboratory of the human soul where the individual has to receive systematic education to bring about self-development. The Aryan culture of India lays the greatest emphasis on plain living and high thinking as the moral basis of this education for self-development. Consequently, the individual has been bidden necessarily to gain both kinds of knowledge, materialistic and spiritual.

Materialistic Education

This education embodies the various aspects of the knowledge of physical sciences. It is for a student that the developed social structure exists. The society is for the student, not the student for the society. All the social institutions of human society have been regarded as the fundamental elements facilitating the development and exaltation of the personality of the student. It is because of this that every impulse to action or Karma has been treated as the progenitor of the religious sense, as a voice of duty, not a complement to wishes; as a means of deliverance, not of bondage, nor of mere satisfaction of one's desires. The student engaged in the pursuit of material knowledge has consequently been treated as the fulcrum of the axis of the social structure, for in his development lies the well-being of society.

Spiritual Knowledge

Spiritual knowledge has been regarded as the means of attaining the final beatitude. For the realisation of the great truth, deep meditation in privacy is essential and hence the individual has been bidden to take recourse to severe penances once again.

The objective means and materials which are required in the pursuit of material knowledge, are not needed in the sphere of spiritual knowledge. The devotee of spiritual knowledge has been enjoined upon to keep aloof from material objects and to consume himself wholly in self-meditation because the main elements constituting divine or spiritual knowledge cannot be understood and realised through hearing or by means of intellect. These can be realised only through divine graciousness. In the Upanishads this fact has been well expressed by Yamacharya in his discourse to Nachiketa, "The Almighty manifests His Glory in the person of the really deserving individual". This principle holds good even in regard to the laws of this material world. The human eyes are not capable of seeing the dazzling sun by any means unless the sun itself sends forth its splendour. Hence, only that individual is entitled to spiritual knowledge who has brought about the sublimation of the religious sense; who feels the presence of the divine spirit in each and every object of nature; and who has crowned his self with inward glory by means of the right Yogic practices or processes of restraining passions, breath and sense organs by disciplining the body by means of Yogic postures, of cultivated retention and steadiness of mind, developing the power of concentration and of Yogic trance. Such a devotee of spiritual knowledge can in the real sense establish the great feeling of universal brotherhood.

To sum up, these are the essential elements of the material and spiritual education on which has been built the structure of Vedantic philosophy which apart from being exhaustive and all inclusive, is above the limitations of time and place. It is this very divine philosophy which has found varied expression in the excellences and the glorious achievements of humanity at large. It has again manifested itself in the form of the spirit of public welfare and universal brotherhood which scintillates through the immemorial teachings of divinities like Rama, Krishana, Budha, Jesus Christ, Gandhi and others.

Consequently, the religious spirit of Indian philosophy of life has embodied itself in all its magnanimity in the system of education. Equity, equality and universal kinship have became its essential adjuncts. The Indian system of education is pervaded with the desire for bringing about salvation and final beatitude along with the full physical development of the individual in the same manner as the philosophy of life is shot through by the spirit of religion. The Indian system of education caters to both physical and spiritual salutariness.

Some Outstanding Characteristics of Ancient Indian Education

The main characteristics, among others of the Indian educational system, are the inculcation of the spirit of plain living and high thinking, of brotherhood, equality, universal kinship, of cow-worship, social and public weal and the development of the sense of the constant omnipresence of Brahma, the Great Universal Being. The resident student during his stay at the preceptor's hermitage, situated in the very lap of nature; far away from the maddening world's ignoble strifes and invested with the fragrance of beauty, got education not only in the abstract principles but also in their practical application to life. Beauteous nature with its grandeur and the sweet, soothing atmosphere of the green herbiage, impressed his tender mind so much that he attached no value to the grandeur of majestic proportions around human habitations.

The vast canopy of the blue sky, the soft sonorous music of the rippling streams, the colorful sylvan heaths and the companionship with the silly innocent fawns — all this instilled into his heart such happiness that all the lesser passions were totally purged. And in addition to this the umbrageous protection of the preceptor tended to make his infant mind even forget the love of his mother and follow the path of duty. Apart from impressing the mind of the young student with the sweetness of his temperament, the preceptor also paid attention towards the general movements and conduct of the student. The parents of those days had implicit faith in the benign goodness of the preceptor. After six months of the student's residence, the preceptor carefully studied his actions and strivings. By this time such a strong intellectual tie used to develop between the student and preceptor that the former did not care at all for the finger of scorn raised by anyone and regarded the due observance of and obedience to the precepts of his teacher as his prime duty.

The Gurukulas, Rishikulas, and Acharyakulas of ancient time did not depend upon guidance from society, as is the case with the modern educational institutions. For the students the civic, social and political upheavals had no meaning. The divine rays of enlightenment were diffused not by the government officers or the secretariat, but by the hermitages of preceptors and ascetics.

The human beings of the world gained the knowledge of the principle of education for self-development at the holy feet of the Brahmans of India who had purged and purified themselves through sincere penance. According to the poet Tulsidas also, the preceptors who had attained the bliss of inward glory and happiness, had instructed even those who lived in royal palaces.

Summary

The Vedas are the original source of the philosophy of life in ancient India. The knowledge derived form the Vedas alone can give real happiness to an individual. Only he can acquire this knowledge who has lived a life according to the four ashrams - Brahmacharya, Grihastha, Vanprasth and Sanyas.

Generally the word 'Veda' means 'to know' but it is the Veda which inspires man to get the knowledge of Brahma (God). Realisation of God is the root of the system of the four ashramas. Knowledge, action and worship lead man towards this goal. Hearing, contemplation and recollection are necessary for this realisation.

The instruction to be received from the preceptor must lead to the attainment of real knowledge. The ancient seers of India, though not devoted to mundane affairs have not neglected 'Action' (Karma). They regarded redemption as the primary goal of knowledge and for this they advocated both the material and spiritual education of the individual.

Notes and References

1. विद सत्तायाम्
2. विद्लृ लाभे
3. विद विचारणे
4. विदृ ज्ञाने।
5. Shravan
6. Manan
7. Chintan

Exercises

1. Explain the special elements of the philosophy of Indian life in ancient India.
2. What are the main characteristics of Ancient Indian education? Explain.

Chapter 2

The Rigvedic System of Education

The Age of the Rigveda

The Vedas are the veritable bedrock of Indian culture, civilisation and education. The question regarding the date of the composition of the Vedas has not yet been finally answered. Nevertheless, it is generally accepted that among the existant literatures of the world there is no work older than the Vedas. According to Dr. Radha Kumud Mukerjee the Vedas do not mark the dawn of culture but rather its meridian. These Vedas do not simply embody the Indian philosophy of transcendentalism but also the teachings which aim at bringing about the all-round development of human life. The Vedas have been accepted in their original elemental form as the reservoirs of real knowledge and truth, gained and tested by the ancient ascetic sages of India who, like the modern scientists, had dedicated themselves to the life of severe penance for the realisation of the eternal principle. Hence, these ascetics have been called the great propounders of Mantras.

Of all the Vedas, the Rigveda has been regarded as the original one by European scholars like Winternitz, Macdonell and Griffiths as well as Indian scholars like Tilak. The discussions pertaining to the intrinsic and extrinsic qualities of the Vedas have made scholars accept an almost simultaneous origin of all the Vedas. It is borne out by a Sruti[1] that the Vedas were revealed by God for human benenediction through knowledge and for the realisation of the human spirit. It is the scientific process of knowledge, action (Karma), devotion and wisdom which makes human beings — superior to all other creations of the universe. Man is superior to other beings his actions and his religious conduct are based on intelligence. Hence, due to the predominance it gives to knowledge, the age of the Rigveda comes first in the history of education in India.

The Educational System of the Rigveda

The Vedas - The outstanding characteristic of the philosophy of life in India is that the ideal has remained unchanged all through. Consequently, the same idea has been presumed also in the Vedas, the original sources of knowledge. The commentators of the Vedas have given various interpretations of the term Veda, but Sayan, one of the profoundest scholars of the Vedas, has in his preface to the commentary on 'Krishna-Yajurveda'explained the term as implying that which shows the divine way of realising the adored object and avoiding the undesirable and the depreciable. The Rigveda also bears out this idea of the two periods into which Sanskrit literature has been divided. The first is Vedic and the second secular. In the Vedic age, there are the Vedas,Upvedas[2] (Atharvaveda, Dhanurveda, Gandharvaveda, YajurVeda); Vedangas[3] (Shiksha, Kalp, Vyakaran, Chhand, Jyotish, Nirukti); Brahmanas[4], Upanishads[5], Aranyakas[6], Darshan[7] Puranas[8]. In the secular literature are included the Ramayana and the Mahabharat, etc. along with the epic fragments, dramas and poems written in a poetic prose style.

The subjects mentioned in the Rigveda were taken in this intellectual aspect. These hymns were composed in verse and they included interpretations of God, soul, rebirth, action and its reward, the universe, the final destruction, rains, ashrama, regular and continuous self-study of the Vedas.

The Yajurveda has been written in prose and in this the cult of rituals has been well expounded. Within the scope of these rituals are included the sixteen practices relating to human culture, animal husbandry, music, mathematics, geography, astronomy, medicine, alchemy, architecture, mechanics, use of arms, horsemanship and military training, etc. Within the purview of devotion are included rectitude, love, mercy, philosophy, Bhakti or worship, asceticism, and Yogic practices, internment, etc. Acharya Yask includes in his exposition of the term hymn the above mentioned three types of education.

The Atharvaveda emphasises the importance of the principle of scientific education. This is why the Atharvadeda is regarded as embodying the spirit and methods of scientific knowledge. In the performance of the rites the scholar of the Atharvaveda has been accorded the position of Brahma because of his wisdom and scientific knowledge. The Yajna ceremonies of India which appear to be only symbols of certain customs and practices were in reality the practical experiments of the ascetic sages of India. The Rigvedic education system contained in itself the *summum bonum* of the eternal truths of the mundane world and symbolised the life realised by the metaphysician ascetics in the course of their life of ultra-mundane elevation by penance. The holocausts performed in the solicited presence of Brahma as well as the oblations by the priest chanters of Samveda were not mere vocal exercises but experiments in practical knowledge. The two forms of education in the Rigvedic system, which were based on the performance of the above mentioned religious rites, were oral instruction and deep self-study.

Subject of Study

The subjects of study in the Rigvedic age were the rules for the correct pronunciation of Vedic Mantras, details of religious ceremonies, grammar, astronomy, prosody and etymology. Along with these six subordinate branches of the Vedas, instruction was also given in logic which was was regarded as the touchstone for the religious knowledge gained through the Vedas and its subordinate branches. The definition of logic incorporates a scientific system for the periodic assessment of religion. The religion of truth is that which is obtained from the revealing principles of those men of the Vedic age who never went against the high principles and ideals of the Vedas and the scriptures. A religion different from them is no religion. The subjects of study in the Vedic period were thus those that helped the students in understanding the true spirit of religion.

Methods of Teaching

The methods of teaching were based on principles of human psychology. The sages in the Rigvedic age had adopted oral instruction and deep contemplation as the two methods of education in order to preserve the sanctity of the Mantras. The first was the means for rigidly securing the external form of the Vedic texts while the second for the preservation of the meanings and implications of those texts.

In the first system of oral instruction and memorising, the preceptor explained to the students particularly the Mantras of the texts along with the feet, the syllables of rhythms. Again for the security of the texts the students were given a good and regular practice or drilling in metrics, graded studies, the repetition of the Vedic Mantras, loud group studies. For correct pronunciation, instruction in orthography and grammar was always imparted. Correct pronunciation had great importance in the Vedic period. The above mentioned courses were planned for developing phonological studies. Consequently, the original form of the scriptures has been preserved till this day. It was also fully explained to the students that due to accentual and tonal distortions the word becomes harsh and unpleasant and thus prejudical to the speaker. Hence, even in the mechanical memorising system accomplishment was requisite as it was in the process of meditation and contemplation.

Meditation

There was provision also for the teaching of the methods of meditation upon the import and implication of the texts so that the wisdom contained in them could be preserved. This instruction was imparted by the preceptors only to the prudent and sagacious students who under the dexterous guidance of the preceptors and by means of self-study and deep meditation duly got hold of the hidden purport of the texts along with the meanings and significance of the words, hymns and stanza-forms. This was not possible through mere instructions. It is clear from the etymology of the word 'Mantra' that the correct realisation of the import of the 'Mantras' (hymns) was possible only through meditation along with the spiritual development of the student. Another purpose which was served by meditation was that the student not only experienced spiritual bliss resulting from the dawning of wisdom upon him but on being endowed with wisdom he became equipped to assume the mantle of a teacher in the midst of society. Thus by means of meditation the student also discharged his obligations towards the preceptor. In the Vedic system of education a student merely possessing knowledge of external facts was likened to a donkey who carries a load of sandalwood on its back but remains completely unaffected by the sweet scent. Hence, a student who simply parrots the texts has been condemned in the Rigveda. The importance of the practice of meditation was emphasised also for the reason that along with the progress and development of human culture those elements of religion were also secured which go to make up the texture of civilisation. That is to say meditation has been regarded as the very basis of culture and civilisation.

Centres of Rigvedic Education

Rigvedic education was given, as we have seen, through oral instruction and self-study or deep contemplation-cum-meditation. The family was the basic centre of education. The sages living in the family gave oral instruction to their sons. In this system of oral instruction stress was laid on the alphabet and syllables, accent, metres and euphonic combinations. It was because of this that the Vedas were also called Sruti, i.e., something that is heard. The students were not accorded permission to take recourse to meditation till they had satisfied the sage-preceptor with regard to their pronunciation.

With the passage of time the original form of the sacrificial rites was lost sight of and there grew around it a huge crust of formulae and ordinances. The oblation ceremonies became a symbol of the sage's genius which desired to attain still greater heights and consequently pupils other than the sons of the ascetic sages began to get admission into the family schools and the scope of these residential teaching centres began to widen. But, nevertheless, these teachings did not acquire the form of instructions. The entire management of these teaching centres was under the guidance of the preceptor and the pupils formed an essential part of the family of the preceptor. The pupils acquired knowledge of their social duties and responsibilities also in the home of the preceptor. It was against the background of the training in the common and social sense that the pupils were educated in the methods of spiritual knowledge. The family of the sage-preceptor himself inculcated in the pupils the social virtues and endowed them with religious enlightenment. By their services to the cow and to the land which was the source of material wealth they acquired not only physical fitness but also economic prosperity.

Brahman Sangh

The institution known as 'Brahman Sangh'[9] was established for the purpose of enabling the students who had mastered the six supplementary branches of sacred science and had perceived and realised the mysteries of the universe to carry on further investigations and propagate their findings and thus keep burning within themselves the desire to annex new citadels of knowledge. In this institution sagacious students got full opportunity for intellectual intercourse and to thoroughly absorb the obscure and abstruse elements. This 'Sangh' of the Vedic age was similar to the seminars of modern times and it was through this that knowledge was acquired and propagated.

Female Education

In the Rigvedic period female education was at its apex. The tongue (speech) which helps in the propagation of knowledge, Saraswati, the sustainer of human strength, have been celebrated as the embodiments of benign power. It is also mentioned that Brahma divided his soul into the two forms of husband and wife. It is because of this that woman has been called the complement of man for she is not only the symbol of man's power, but also of his knowledge, inner strength and action. Thus the woman has also been regarded as the perennial source both of mundane and ultra-mundane happiness. No sacrificial ceremony performed by man could be completed without the woman. While eulogising the prowess of motherhood the Rigveda goes on to say that the woman has the capacity of endowing the man, with whom she is pleased with the attributes of Brahma and Shiva[10]. Hence the woman has been revered as the fountain source of family life as well as the guide of the path to divine and heavenly bliss. The conception of education of woman, the inseparable counterpart of man in the Rigvedic age is well indicated by the observation in the 'Bajasaneyi Sanghita'[11] that only that girl is entitled to enter into the stage of the householder who is educated and has passed, through the state of celibacy (Brahmacharya). Even in the Purana in the parts dealing with the marriage system, we have such an indication of the vogue of female education. Besides, Surya[12], Shachi[13], Vak[14], some other female sages have been regarded as expounders of sacred texts. Still more, we have the mention of several female deities like Aditi, Usha, Indrani, Ida, Bharati, Sharddha, etc. as the incarnations of various elements. All this goes to show that in the Rigvedic age female education was also highly developed.

Education of other Castes

People of all the castes were entitled to education in the Rigvedic age. The second hymn (Mantra) of the twenty-sixth chapter of the Yajuraveda bears ample testimony to this[15]. All the available historical records pertaining to the caste system in the Rigvedic age testify to the fact that at that time every individual who had the mental capacity and the mature power of understanding was entitled to receive education. In order to make education available to all such people, the caste system in those days, was not regarded as a hereditary institution but as an occupational one. This is well borne out by the observation of the Sruti [16] that every one had the right to perform the Agnihotra[17] which had an all-pervading importance in the life of the Aryans in the Rigvedic age. These offertory rituals which were regarded as a means of national prosperity could be performed only by educated people. Hence every one had equal right to education. In the 'Srutis' the Shudras have been debarred from receiving education, but the word 'Shudra' is used not in the sense of caste but in the sense of one who is mentally so decrepit as to learn nothing in spite of the best efforts of the preceptor. Caste then did not imply as it does now, communities, but birth of parentage as is borne out by the observation in the second chapter of Yogadarshan[18] that persons of identical parentage constitute one caste. Apart from this it is very often mentioned in the Rigveda that not only the Brahmans were entitled to accomplish highest spiritual knowledge but also persons of other castes. According to Sarvapalli Radhakrishnan the Rigveda mentions a family in which the father was a Vaidya (physician), the son a Vedic poet, and the mother an ordinary grain grinder. Hence, it is clear that in the Rigvedic age persons of all the castes had a right to education on the basis of their mental and intellectural capacities. The 'Shudras' were undoubtedly given education through the device of mechanical memorising because high spiritual knowledge was imparted only to the deserving students.

The description of the society that we get in some of the Mantras of the Rigveda[19] is supposed to be based on the considerations of mundane and religious aspects of life. The total development of society is brought about by the progress both of the religious and worldly aspects of life. But knowledge was essential to maintain discipline and prosperity in society. Hence knowledge which can also be described in worldly parlance as a religion, was given precedence over everything else. The Brahman has been accorded great honour and high prestige in society because worldly functions discharged with the help of knowledge came to be treated as the means of the sublimation of mundane existence. The other castes have been accorded dignity in society in accordance with their occupations.

Summary

The Vedas

The Veda has been accepted as the oldest book by most of the scholars of the world. The Vedas are full of knowledge and wisdom. They are the preservers of the good and destroyers of the evil. They acquaint us also with the means of eradicating evils. Rigveda interprets knowledge, Yajuraveda, Samveda and Atharvaveda interpret the theories and principles involved in action, worship and science. All the four Vedas advocate that the aim of human life is to realise God.

The Rigvedic Education

During the Vedic period the curriculum was limited to the study of grammar, astrology and rhetorics, etc. All these subjects were taught at the homes of preceptors. As the number of students increased these homes took the form of Gurukulas. The method was mainly oral and self-study. Every one was entitled to receive education. The women, too, enjoyed this privilege. Women occupied a special place in society. The quality and the kind of duties were the basis of the prevailing caste-system. The concept of a born-caste had not yet evolved in this period. Gradually, the scope of the curriculum widened and it included literatures pertaining to the Upanishads and Sutras.

Notes and References

1. A Sruti means a testament, a scripture, a hearsay.
2. The science deduced from the Vedas, viz. the science of handiwork art, the art and science of archerey, the science of music, the Yajurveda consisting principally of religious rites.
3. The six subordinate branches of the Vedas, viz. rules for correct pronunciation of Vedic mantras, details of religious ceremonies, Grammar, Prosody, Astronomy and Etymology.
4. The Theological portion of the Vedas as different fromthe Mantras or hymns.
5. Those portions of the different branches of the Vedas containing discourses on divine knowledge.
6. Texts relating to forest life.
7. Philosophy.
8. Texts dealing with Indian mythology.
9. Assembly, corporation or monastery.
10. The two of the triad of Hindu mythology, Brahma is the creator of the universe and Shiva is the destroyer. The Vishnu is the feeder.
11. Collection of the hymns of one Veda, a scripture.
12. The wife of Sun
13. Name of God Indra's wife
14. Godness Saraswati
15. यथेमां वाचं कल्याणीं भावदानि जनेभ्यः
 ब्रह्म राजान्याभ्यां शूद्राय चार्यालस्वायचारणाय।
16 पञ्चजंनः मम होत्रं जुषध्वम् समान प्रसवात्मिका जाति न्यायादर्श, अध्याय 2, सूत्र 5
17. The ceremony consisting of offering oblations to the consecrated fire.
18. Yogadarshan, one of the six systems of Hindu philosophy.
19 ब्राह्मणोस्य मुखमासीद् बाहू राजन्यः कृतः।
 उरू तदस्य यद्वैश्यः पद्भ्यां शूद्रो जजायत्।।

Exercise

Discuss the nature of education during the Rigvedic period.

Chapter 3

Education during the Post-Vedic Period (The Period of the Upanishads)

Development of the System of the Family-Priest

The period of the post-Vedic education is taken as extending between 1400 B.C. and 600 B.C, marking the end of the Rigvedic age and the beginning of the religious textsof the Jains and the Buddhists. The ideals of education in this period continued to be the same as those of the Rigvedic age but certain changes had crept into the ways and methods. It has already been observed in this context that the aim of education of the Aryans was the attainment of redemption or salvation through detachment from worldly bondages. The pupils in the Rigvedic age took residence in the homes of the preceptors to achieve this ideal by means of rigorous living and offertory rites where a huge crust of ceremonies took the place of penance which implied deep self-meditation. Devotion also, instead of being intuitive or esoteric, became exotic, and consequently the form of offertory ceremonies expanded along with the progress of the post-Vedic educational system.

The need of competent priests was felt for the performance of these ceremonies, Consequently priesthood was established in the four forms of Hota[1], Adhwaryu[2], Udgate[3], and Brahma[4]. In the beginning these priests used to be those who had undergone some measure of contemplation and meditation and hence the scope of ceremonies in the offertory rite expanded on the basis of contemplation. But later on, these very ceremonies came to be regarded as the be-all and end-all of the offertory rite and the spirit of devotion and contemplation began to disappear. The scholar of the Rigveda was given the high position of Hota, the host[5], while that of Yajurveda the position of Adhwaryu. The priest well up in the symphonious texts of Samveda occupied the position of 'Udgate', whereas the scholar of Atharvaveda, was elevated to the exalted position of Brahma, because of his erudition and scholarship in Atharvaveda and his through knowledge of the general canons of all the three Vedas. In the society of the day the position of the priest was regarded as a very exalted and dignified one and the dignified status of the 'Purohit' was accorded to him. The homes where ceremonies were performed under the aegis of such priests had some similarity with the modern scientific laboratories, for apart from discharging such functions they also served the purpose of temples of learning where teaching work was carried on. Priesthood also had four ramifications in accordance with the four aspects of knowledge, viz. knowledge, action, devotion and wisdom. Hence, a coherent knowledge of the Veda was not only essential but compulsory for every priest and the Regvedic educational institutions were called Hoti, Adhwaryu, Udgatri and Brahman according to the subjects taught there.

The students of the Hoti institutions studied the Rigveda which is composed in verse, those of Adhwaryu studied the Yajurveda which is in prose, while Samveda was studied by those of Udgarti. For the facility of the last group of students Samveda, which consists of seventy-five principal and original Mantras and of a a lot of others derived from the other three Vedas, was divided into two parts, primary[6] and secondary[7]. These students were required to undergo regular drilling in symphony and intonation of the verses. It was essential for the Brahman students to have knowledge of the other three Vedas along with that of the Atharvaveda so that the offertory rites could be thoroughly examined. Consequently, the proclivity of the students also changed. The old tendency towards contemptation and meditation disappeared and the attention of the students became riveted to the banal externalisms of the offertory ceremonies. Instruction through such ceremonies also became mechanical like the old cramming method. The science of metrics or prosody which was the prime need of the Hota and other priests found its full development in the Vedangas. These Hotas and other priests also helped the development of the

Pratishakhya literature in which there is a detailed discussion of the etymology of orthography, intonation and pronunciation of the Vedic words.

Thus along with the development of sacrificial rites various dogmas and doctrines also came to flourish. Various physical sciences and handicrafts also developed at this time along with the outfit of the offertory ceremonies. The study of physical siences like mathematics, conics, astronomy and astrology as well as human physiology and anatomy was begun at this time. Although the development of the Vedic cult of rituals hampered the progress of spiritual meditation, yet it went on flourishing due to the upsurge of various useful secular subjects of study. The school of Brahman literature also bloomed under the inspiration of this expanded cult of ritualism. It was as a sort of reaction against the progressively materialistic tendency of the poetry of this school that the literatures of the Upanishads scintillating with the spirit of pure contemplation made its appearance. Thus in the post-Vedic period the cults of ritualism and gnosticism were roughly explored both in their gross and subtle aspects as a result of which gradually there came into existence such a literature which embraced every aspect of Indian transcendentalism. It is essential to glance over this religious literature as background to our study of the post-Vedic education system.

Brahman Literature

The Brahman-texts were next to the Vedas in importance during the post-Vedic period. These Brahman texts have been so called because they are a collection of the canons and ordinances relating to offertory and other ceremonies laid down by the Brahmans well conversant with the Vedas. The subjects dealt with in these tests are ordinances and aphorisms, the former implying the precepts relating to the performances of the offertory rites while the latter are the elucidations of the Mantras. In the Dharmsutra[8] of Apastamb it has been observed that the Brahmans are the propounders of ritualism, as also that the word Brahma is symbolic of the Veda and Brahman is simply the amplification of the above. In the post-Vedic period the language of the Vedas had become somewhat different from the spoken one because of the grossness of the cult of ritualism. Consequently, the interpretations of the Mantras became complicated and beyond the comprehension of commonalty. As such these came to be well-nigh forgotten. The

Brahman texts, therefore, gave authentic elucidations of these Mantras. In these explanatory portions we have fables, stories and descriptions of the heroic deeds of kings, all written in a very figurative and rhetorical language. In the extant Vedic literature the Brahman texts are frequently mentioned but many of those texts are not available now. The following are the important texts among the available ones-

Rigvedic Brahman	Aitaraiya, Kaushitaki
Samveda	Tandya
Yajurveda	Taitariya and Shatpath
Atharvaveda	Gopath

These Brahman texts contain all the main canons and ordinances pertaining to ritualism. The Brahmans by the amplifications and elucidations of the religious ordinances not only raised the cult of ritualism to its acme of perfection but also established their own sway in the spiritual field. These texts were responsible for a considerable amount of social progress.

Aranyankas

The Aranyaka texts written in prose-cum-verse are the addenda to the Brahman texts. These have been called Aranyakas because they embody the wisdom and teachings of the recluses among the priests, pertaining to methods of learning and teaching and to the various rules and regulations of ceremonies. These texts also describe the institution or caste and Ashrams as well as expound the mysteries of rites. According to these Aranayaka texts the whole universe is pervaded by the spirit of oblation but the heavenly bliss gained through ritualistic ceremonies being impermanent does not create any sort of abiding spiritual happiness. The doctrines of knowledge[9] and action[10] do not by themselves enable one to gain spiritual happiness. Hence, according to these texts a harmonious combination of the two alone can bring spiritual bliss. It is clear now that as in the Brahman texts the system of offerings and rites, etc. was evolved for the householders, so in these Aranyaka texts were propounded the practices of sacrificial cows and holocausts for the forest-dwelling ascetics. The language, style of these texts like rest of the Brahman texts is very sweet, simple, succinct and racy.

The Upanishads

The period of the Upanishads follows hard upon that of the Aranayaka texts. The Upanishads embody the highest form of Indian transcendentalism. The great German scholar Schopenheur, Max Muller, Macdonell and other erudite scholars of Europe have lavishly eulogised the transcendentalism and theosophism of the Upanishads which emobdy the eloquent teachings of the ascetic sages, who remaining detached from worldly illusion and had sublimated their souls through deep penance, and have not remained merely a conscience page in the history of human civilisation, but have laid such a deep and strong foundation of religion and humanity on which can be raised an exquisite structure of world civilisation. Schopenheur while giving expression to his feelings with regard to the Upanishads has eloquently observed that the religion propounded by the Upanishads will in the future be the religion of the world.

The scholars have given varied interpretations of the word Upanishad, but the basic implication of the word is that which enables one to gain theosophical knowledge or that which takes one nearest to the Brahma and destroys the sufferings resulting from ignorance of that knowledge, the gaining and propagating of which makes one worthy of coming into proximity with the Brahma. It is evident from the above examination that the Upanishads were written to establish a system of education which would incorporate the lofty ideal of self-sublimation and give a body and form to the highly developed spirit of metaphysical contemplation. This education was imparted secularly to the Brahmacharis who were endowed with genius, religious faith and a spirit of devotion, in order to enlighten them on the deep transcendental mysteries.

It is also evidenced by certain accounts in the Upanishads that these came into existence only to quench the intellectual thirst of those who were not satisfied with their studies in the teaching-homes of the preceptors in the Brahman-vedic period. In the period of the Upanishads the tide of ritualism of the period of the Brahmanas once again turned towards the cult of gnosticism-cum-devotional contemplation of the Rigvedic era. As a counterblast to the cult of ritualism and formalism the Upanishads openly declared that salvation could not be achieved through these inane offerings and practices. It is possible only through esoteric devotion. In refutation of the doctrine of ritualism it has been observed in the Mundak Upanishad that the persons busy in the performances of oblations are not better than calves (young ones of a cow). In the Vrihdaranyaka Upanishad the performers of oblations have been dubbed as the beasts of the deities. Hence, true knowledge unvitiated by ritualistic formalism has been regarded as the sole means of salvation. 'No salvation without knowledge' is the declaration of the Upanishads. The merging of the human soul into the cosmic soul implies salvation and consequently it can be said that the Upanishads mark the culmination of the gnosticism of the Rigvedic age. The intellectual fermentation which the Upanishads embody was the upshot of the desire to realise the mysteries of mataphysical contemplation and led in its turn to the development of the Vedangas. The purpose of these Vedangas was to help the students understand the correct implications of the term Veda. The exposition of the Vedas by Yask and the grammar of Panini helped a great deal in understanding the etymology of words as also in the formation of the mellifluous Sanskrit language.

From the above discussion it becomes clear that in the post-Vedic period gnosticism and ritualism were the two main tendencies in the field of education. For the purpose of ritualism only Samaveda and Yajurveda were written. The detailed discussion of this system of education was made in the Brahman texts. In the second half of the post-Vedic period Indian education once again turned towards gnosticism which in its transcendental aspect found full expression in the Upanishads. Hence, the best methods of the study of Vedas came into light and along with this a graphic account of post-Vedic educational system was also prepared. This is particularly connected with the system propounded by Upanishadic literature. In this well-organised system a high ideal of life was set before the human beings and to achieve the ideal a suitable outline of knowledge was given. Consequently, Upanishadic literature can be said to be embodying the highest and the most perfect form of Indian education. The modern philosophy of education appears to mainly support the principles of the Upanishads.

Aims of Education

The basic concept of the education system propounded by the Upanishads was that real education brings one face to face with true knowledge and thereby enables one to attain self-realisation or redemption. The knowledge of other physical sciences — being beyond the scope of true gnosis — is included in the category of illusion and ignorance because their study does not enable one either to get rid of worldly delusion or deliverance from transmigration or the process of births and rebirths. True knowledge comes only after the realisation of the Brahma for, as it has been emphatically proclaimed in the Upanishads, an individual realises the Brahma or attains Beatitude only after having conquered all doubts and illusions through a knowledge of truth[11]. This blissful or beatific vision has been put forth in the Upanishads as the goal of human life. This, in fact, is the *summum bonum* of the systems of devotional penance and self-meditation adumbrated by the Rigveda and the Upanishads.

Upnayan

The Upnayan[12] has been given great importance in the Vedic system of education. It has been repeated often in the Rigveda, but in the beginning it was not compulsory and persons started their education even without it. Later on in the post-Vedic period, the importance of this ceremony increased. The etymological meaning of Upnayan is 'to take one near', i.e., taking one to the preceptor for education. In the Atharvaveda we have a detailed account of this ceremony. In the age of the Sutras, Upnayan was considered to be of prime importance for the Dwijas' implying the twice-born. One was not called a Dwija' unless after being given birth to by his parents he had undergone the initiation ceremony through the preceptor. The preceptor commenced the work of teaching the initiate after acquainting him with the Servitor or Guru Mantra. The pupil was thus given a 'spiritual birth' by the preceptor. The foundation for the development of human life was laid by the Upnayan ceremony which is observed even today in a slightly chastened form by the followers of semetic religion. Nobody can be called a Christian without being baptised, nor a Muslim without the 'Kalma' or confession of Mohammedanism. In like manner any one who had not undergone the initiation ceremony was in those days deprived of the right of gaining education or performing religious rites. The initiate received the protection of the preceptor. The preceptor by making a pious resolve before a sacrificial fire, established with the pupil material a spiritual contact and became responsible for his all-round progress and spiritual development. The preceptor asked the pupil, "Whose Brahmachari are you ?" The pupil replied "Yours" and thereby dedicated himself heart and soul to the preceptor and set himself to concentrated study and fixed duties.

This contact between the preceptor and the initiate based as it was on pure spiritual and moral consideration, remained unvitiated by the artificial and mechanical methods prevalent in modern times. The initiate Brahmachari had for his physical make-up Kush[13], Mekhla[14], Mrigchhala[15], long matted locks of hair, Dand[16], and Kamandala[17], whereas the symbols of his inner life were hardwork, austerity and consecration which could be regarded as the external forms of true knowledge, action and devotion. In ancient literature, the, glory of Brahmacharya is so well depicted that in the Atharvaveda Brahma himself has been described as the supreme Brahmachari. The entire universe in regarded as the product of the penanced Brahmacharya. The supreme excellence of Brahmacharya is further brought out by the dialogue between Bhardwaj and Indra who appears as the questioner and expounder of texts respectively in the Chhandogya Upanishad, that the penance of Brahmacharya is an inexhautible source of mundane as well as ultraundane happiness. The panegyrists of Brahmacharya go to the extent of saying that in a country where there is even a single Brahmachari there will never be any danger of any sort of calamity.

In the period of the Upanishads every one had all sorts of facilities to make his life happy and merry. No student was bound down by any consideration of family and caste. The preceptor took a pupil under his tutelage only after knowing his name and gauging his inner qualities through a psychological examination. All the pupils enjoyed — like those who were high born, — the right of Upnayan and Brahmacharya. The significance of Upanayan in the life of student lay in the fact that the initiate pupil could by means of Brahmacharya, preserve all through life the halo of virility and the sense of dutifulness.

Subjects of Study

In the post-Vedic period the subjects of study were larger in number than those of the Rigvedic age which were mainly concerned with Rigvedic Mantras. The study of phonetics, prosody and grammar had evolved , but in the post-Vedic period a hung literature pertaining to the four Vedas also had come into existence. Secular literature developed alongside of the religious. This is well borne out by the dialogue between Narad and Sanat Kumar in Chhandogya Upanishad. Narad insists upon Sanat Kumar to instruct him, wherefore Sanat Kumar says, "Narad, relate to me in detail all that you know and come and sit nearby devotedly". Then Narad humbly submitted, "Bhagwan, I am well up in Rigveda, Yajurveda, Samveda, Atharvaveda and I also know verbatim the fifth Veda in its history-cum-Purana form. Apart form this I also have knowledge of Vedic grammar, philology Shradh[18], mathematics, astrology, theological teachings of the Upansishads, demonology, archery, astronomy, dancing, and music, etc.

"We have in the Upanishads the mention of a particular kind of knowledge which has been called 'Paravidya' which is different from the above mentioned sciences. This 'Paravidya' which implies a knowledge of things which are beyond the range of perception or comprehension symbolises the metaphysical knowledge of the Supreme Self and is superior to all others. It is only through this that the realisation of the supreme self, that is, the Brahma is possible. It has been called as such, because it aims at uniting the human soul with the cosmic soul, whereas other kinds of knowledge create a hiatus between the two and are consequently regarded as illusory. In the Kath Upanishad[19] even Vedantic knowledge is regarded as illusory or materialistic. Hence, we can conclude from the above that the scope of studies during the period of the Upanishad had immensely widened. Nevertheless, it was not possible for the pupils to study all these subjects. As such, a student could confine his studies to any one of the Vedas and its relevant literature. A student who had studied all the three Vedas was called in the Brahman texts as 'Srotriya' and in Kauk Sanghita as Trishukriya, i.e. one who has thoroughly studied the Vedas, which later on became Trivedi. The knowledge of the three Vedas was regarded as the means of real knowledge.

In the post-Vedic period the knowledge of the Vedic triad was given high importance, but alongside the system of specialised study had also advanced a great deal[20]. Consequently there had developed a number of schools imparting education in special branches of the same Veda. Mere bookish knowledge was condemned as dead weight on the tongue and only that knowledge which was zealously gained through the processes of hearing, meditation, contemptation and recollection was acknowledged and respected.

Methods of Teaching

The Rigvedic method of study through hearing,meditation, contemplation, and recollection continued in the post-Vedic educational system. In the Vrihdaranyaka Upanishad, these methods of spiritual education have been well analysed. In the first process of hearing the pupil listens attentively and devotedly to the words of the preceptor, then through meditation he makes a critical and intellectual analysis of these instructions and finally through contemplative recollection he tries to experience and realise fully the implications. Hence, in the process of gaining knowledge greatest emphasis was laid on the disciplined will of the pupil.

The great importance of the preceptor was due to the fact that he afforded guidance to the student in his path of knowledge. It was essential for the pupil to studiously listen to the instructions of the preceptor and then to realise the metaphysical truths, understand and absorb the facts gained through his own experience and self-contemplation. The literature of the post-Vedic period abounds in illustrations of the above system of education. Brahma after giving his son Bhrigu the outline of divine knowledge instructed him to realise it through devotional and continuous self-study of the Vedas. Bhrigu adopting this method worked continuously on these lines for four years after which he gained divine knowledge. In the Chhandogya Upanishad also Aaruni gives a similar instruction to his son Shwetketu. He made his son live for fifteen days barely on water and thus gave him a practical experience of the great truth that mind consists of material subsistence, life (energy or vitality) is aqueous and speech is symbolic of inner effulgence. Similarly, in order to explain to Shwetketu the relationship between the human body and the soul, the sage Aaruni instructs his son to fetch the fruit of the peepal or the holy Indian fig tree. Shwetketu brings the fruit and by examining it thoroughly obtains knowledge about the soul and the all pervading glory of truth as desired by his father.

Along with the above mentioned four systems, the method of question-answers also makes its appearance for the first time in the Upanishads. In this method metaphysical and spiritual facts were explained in a very fascinating manner by employing all the available material, viz. illustration , stories, fables, tales, biographical sketches. Socrates, the famous scholar and philosopher-metaphysician of Greece, had instructed his pupils through this system in the knowledge of truth.

The Daily Routine of the Students

A daily routine had been planned out for the students residing in the hermitages of the preceptors. With the help of this routine the pupils, while following the vows of celibacy remained tied to their systematic studies. The day-to-day education of the students trained them in practical spheres, conducive to their intellectual and moral development. As such, this can be regarded as an inseparable part of the whole educational system.

Education in Practical Life

Education in practical life had three aspects :-

1. Going about begging for alms.
2. Keeping ablaze the sacrificial fire, and
3. Looking after the animals.

Apart form this it was also compulsory for the pupil to work on the land. Alms-begging inculcated in the pupil the noble spirit of humility. Keeping ablaze the divine flame of the sacrificial fire not only helped his intellectual development but also invested him with a halo of inward glory. Service to animals and work on the land made him physically fit and morally immaculate. Hence, this education made the student the very personification of humility and invested him with spiritual radiance. In the period of the Brahmans and the Upanishads, patient, courageous and sober students unwittingly got hold of the secret of devoted servitude through this education in practical affairs. A number of examples pertaining to alms-begging, sacrificial fire, service to the sick and care of the animals, are available in the Atharvaveda, Shatpath Brahman and Aitareya Aranyaka. It is mentioned in the Shatpath Brahman that one Satyakam Jawal went on tending upon the cows of the preceptor till the number increased from 400 to 1,000. Work on the land and service to the cows were regarded as the sacred duty of the Brahmachari. In ancient India too these two were revered as mothers because they were the main sources of material and economic prosperity.

Intellectual Education

Hearing, meditation and contemplative recollection were the three aspects of intellectual education. The pupils gained knowledge by a harmonious combination of these three processes. Intellectual education was thus based on one's own perceptions. Hearing the precepts of the preceptor was sufficient for the purpose of education. In the post-Vedic period it was essential for both the preceptor and his disciples to follow all the rules and regulations pertaining to teaching and learning. For the pupils continuous and concentrated self-study of the Vedas was compulsory.

The student has been instructed to remain particularly alert in regard to the first two of the three processes of religious oblations, deep study and alms-giving. In the Shatpath Brahman continuous and regular study of the Vedas has been regarded as 'Brahmyagna'. By the performance of the BrahmYagna in the form of deep and regular self-study of the Vedas an individual becomes a lover of the Vedas. The student of the Vedas becomes self-satisfied and never dependent upon anyone. Every day he practices devotion for useful purposes and enjoys a sound sleep. He becomes a perfect physician of the soul and very often he also gains control over his senses. His power of concentration, intellect, and comprehension increases. He goes on developing his intellect and succeeds in discharging the obligations of his religion[21]. In the Taitriya Aranyaka the study of the Vedas has been regarded as the means of destroying sins. Regular self-study of the Vedas which is facilitated by his intellectual education, enables him to chasten and sublimate his soul. This was the prime object of intellectual education for the execution of which the practice of a fast which lasted for twelve years was established. This fast or mighty resolve was fulfilled only after concentration and regular study of the Vedas for a total period of twelve years by the student who observed during this period all the rules and regulations of the life of a Brahmachari.

Moral Education

Moral education pertains to the conduct and behaviour of the pupil into whose mind it was hammered right from the beginning that life implies rectitued. Education in morality is not possible through merely hearing the precepts of the preceptor. Hence the pupil, apart from leading the rigorously disciplined life of the Brahmachari, had to devotedly observe and follow certain practices in his practical life. Every preceptor was always solicitous for the probity of the pupil's character. For a good moral character, a pure and simple diet was considered necessary and intoxicating or exciting things were tabooed. In the second chapter of Manav Dharmashastra, it is observed in the context of the celibate's diet and moral duties that the celibates should avoid intoxicants, flesh, scented substances, sensual pleasures, coition, highly spiced and seasoned food, killing of life, massaging with oil along with all other cosmetics and beauty aids, moral depravations like lust, anger, avarice, infatuation, arrogance or jealousy as well as music, dancing, untruthfulness, nay all those things which were destructive of rectitude, and devote himself to the vow of celibacy. The student was always to avoid willful and wayward behaviour. "Shirovratam" was ordained for the student, according to which he had either to wear matted locks of hair or to shave them off. Shirovrat is also used in the sense of carrying on the head the fuel which is used in a sacrifice. The only idea behind the ordination of all the above maintained fasts and vows was that the student while remaining aloof from the beautification and adornments of the body might be always alert and prepared for the purity of the soul. The ideal life of the preceptor as well as his daily routine of rectitude inspired the young student to strictly observe all the above mentioned ordinances.

Duration of Study

Although in the period of the Upanishads the number of teaching institutions had multiplied due to the variety of subjects, still the period of study for the students generally extended to twelve years. Shwetketur had studied at his preceptor's feet for twelve years, Upkaushal had kept ablaze the sacrificial fire lit by Satyakam Jawal for twelve years, but Jawal had looked after the cows of his preceptor for a still longer period. Students who continued their studies for thirty-two years are also mentioned. In the Aitreyya Brahman we have the mention of such a pupil who remained at his preceptor's house for a very long time so much so that his father ceased hoping for his return, and distributed his property amongst his other sons. In reality one life is not sufficient for the study of the Shastras comprising boundless knowledge. In this context the fascinating incident of Indra and Bhardwaj described in the Chhandogya Upanishad is worth consideration. Bhardwaj remained all his life a zealous Brahmachari and devoted himself to the pursuit of knowledge. Seeing Bhardwaj's love for knowledge Indira went to him in cognito to test him. On being fully satisfied with his cross-examination of Bhardwaj, Indira in order to show him the palpable manifestation of knowledge took him to the four mountains which were the outward or external forms of knowledge and of the four Vedas. Indira asked Bhardwaj to take all that he could in one handful. Accordingly Bhardwaj took a handful of clay from the valley of one of the mountains. Then Indira observed, "Bhardwaj you have gained so far just a handful of knowledge and the remaining is still unreached". Bhardwaj was astonished to hear this. This story makes it clear that to annex the boundless fields of knowledge, not one but even several lives are insufficient. Hence, in the Upanishads emphasis was laid on the need of a long term for the work of gaining supreme knowledge. Even Indra himself in order to gain knowledge had lived a celibate's life at Prajapati's for a hundred and one years. In fact the duration of education depended also on the capacity and mental intake of the student. If a student was unable to complete his prescribed studies within twelve years he had to go on till he did so. History mentions some Indian students who, even in the time of Magasthenes (1300 B.C.) persevered in their studies for thirty-seven long years. Hence, the period of study depended upon the capacity, inclination and intelligence of the student.

Preceptor-Pupil Relation

In the period of the Upanishad, the relation between the preceptor and the pupil was very smooth and pleasant. The preceptor loved the pupil as his son and the pupil regarded it as his prime religious duty to serve the preceptor like an obedient, humble and polite son. In order to gain the tutelage of the preceptor, the prospective pupil presented himself before him with some fire in his hand, which implied that along with service to the preceptor he would keep ablaze the fire of his sacrificial altar. Although in the period of the Upanishads the cult of ritualism had been superseded by metaphysical contemplation and gnosticism, nevertheless the vogue of offerings and ceremonies continued unabated.

In the Upanishads, the ceremony of offering oblations to the consecrated fire has been regarded as a compulsory duty of the celibate, for this ceremony particularly in a ritual invested him with a great reanimating and revivifying power. Upon the importance of this ceremony there is mentioned in the Upanishads the story of Death soliciting her Lord Yamacharva for her pabulum to appease her hunger. Yamacharya gives to death everything of the world to devour but not the Brahmachari. Death devours all, but not being saturated she persists in her solicitations to her Lord. When Yamacharya tells her that he had given everything and nothing else remained, she demands the Brahmachari. In order to appease death Yamacharya yields and says that she could kill and devour the Brahmachari only on the day he did not perform the oblation ceremony. Hence, this ceremony was to the Brahmachari a shield for self protection against mortality and destruction. This ceremony was not only experimentation in knowledge, but a means of rising higher in the scale of service and penance.

When the Brahmachari went to the preceptor's hermitage with fire in hand, the implication was that he would keep ablaze the preceptor's consecrated fire, for in doing so he developed in himself unwillingly all those qualities which endow student life with excellence and also help in his spiritual uplift. On reading the Chhandogya Upanishad we come to know that Indra, keen on understanding the metaphysics of the Supreme Soul,along with Virochan, the king of the demons, went to Prajapati as ordinary pupils. Even in the Shatpath Brahman there is an ordination for the pupil to go as an ordinary student to the preceptor.

The duties and responsibilities of the preceptor have also been fully dwelt upon along with those of the pupils. The preceptor looked after the pupils as his own sons and was fully responsible for their upbringing, conduct, maintenance and welfare. On occasion the preceptor even attended upon the ailing pupil. Due to mutual regard and friendly attachment, the relations between the preceptor and the pupil became so cordial and affectionate that the pupil veritably became the son of the preceptor. Even such cases are mentioned in which some pupils were so much led away by the affectionate and filial treatment meted out to them by the preceptor that they forgot their own relations and went through their journey of life in the hermitage of the preceptor. Such pupil were called 'Antewasin'. Along with meting out fatherly love and treatment to the pupils, it was also the sacred duty of the preceptor to awaken the pupil to the realisation of the eternally true form of the Supreme Self. The preceptor considered it his prime duty to make the pupil, who came under his tutelage imbued with the spirit of tranquil contemplation and possessed with the social power of self-restraint and control over the senses, realise the mataphysics of the Immortal Brahma.

The preceptor who was thus bound with these duties, was nevertheless free to discard a pupil, whom he considered to be unfit after examining him. The preceptor could debar a pupil from gaining knowledge of the Vedas because according to Sankhya, the instructions of the preceptor do not bear any fruit when they fall on the barren ground of the mentally decrepit pupil[22]. The instruction which the great preceptor Vashishta gave to King Aj, became to him a source of distress instead of ridding him from woe. Hence, it was implicity enjoined upon the preceptor that he should give his metaphysical instruction to his son or to a pupil only after having thoroughly examined him for a month or even for a whole year. It was further enjoined upon him not to instruct an undeserving son or a pupil out of mere affection. In the period of the Upanishads, good conduct and intellectual acumen came to be highly revered. Consequently, the sanctity of spiritual and metaphysical knowledge has been preserved all through the ages.

In the post-Vedic period, spiritual education was often given by parents themselves to their sons. We have the instances in Chhandogya Upanishad of Shwetketu receiving education from his father Aaruni in addition to that from his preceptor and in Taitriya Upanishad of Bhrigu being instructed by his father Varun. In the post-Vedic period the importance of the Ashram system, Upanayan and other practices had decreased. In this context the name of Satyakam, the son of Jawal, is worth mentioning because he, of his own accord, started his studies in the old manner. Ashwapati Kaikaye had instructed old householders like Shala and others who were well versed in the Vedas, and awakened them to the true nature of the cosmic soul even without having gone through the initiation ceremony. The above examples make it clear that the Brahmacharya Ashram was not regarded as indispensable in the post-Vedic period. It was later on that the observeance of the four Ashramas became strict and rigid.

The Stately Position of the Preceptor

In ancient Indian life the preceptor held a position of great honour and stateliness and as such the sacrosanct temples of learning (Saraswati) were called Gurukulas. The preceptor was important in each of the four stages of life or the Ashramas which taken together completed the circle of human life. Although deep self-study was regarded as being of prime importance in the field of education, yet great importance and significance was attached to the preceptor for the reason that true knowledge cannot be gained without him. In connection with the process of self-study it has been observed in the Shuk Rahasya that self-study by means of meditation and contemplative recollection is useful only after the instructions of the preceptor have been attentively heard and absorbed[23]. Even the word Guru (Preceptor) has special implication, viz. of one who dispels the darkness of ignorance and gives religious instruction[24]. In the educational system of the Upanishads the honoured position of the preceptor is not only maintained but is elevated to the highest degree in the field of mundane existence. In the Kath Upanishad, Yamacharya Nachiketa rapturously describing the eminent status of the preceptor to the devotee of supreme knowledge says that true knowledge of the self is impossible without a competent preceptor[25]. Anyone who, being proud of his intellectual powers, essays to gain knowledge of the self all by himself is like a blind person guiding another blind man[26]. Hence, one who is keen to gain supreme knowledge should go to the shelter of a preceptor dedicated to the divine being. There is always the need of a preceptor in human life for cultivating a methodical and disciplined life as also for securing excellence in mundane and extramundane existence.

Consequently, a devotee of the knowledge of the Supreme Self has been instructed to go to the learned and devoted preceptor with sacrificial fire in his hands for the realisation of Brahma, even though he might have gone through the stages of the celibate and the householder and entered into the stage of the forest-dweller (Vanprasth)[27].

Along with these codes of conduct for the pupils certain rules and regulations were laid down for the preceptor also in order to prevent him from becoming wilful and wayward. In the Maitrayan Upanishad the son or the pupil has been regarded as the rightful claimant. The son or the pupil constitutes the reflection of the personality of the preceptor. Hence, there exists no doubt in regard to their moral and intellectual excellence. It has been enjoined upon the pupil that he should have high regard and great respect for the preceptor if he wishes to gain the highest knowledge. The pupil becomes worthy of entering into the world of knowledge revealed by the preceptor only when he cherishes the highest reverence and regard for his preceptor. The pupils those days were like the scientific investigators of today, always in quest of learned and devoted preceptors who in their turn remained solicitous for morally good and devoted pupils. In the Taitriya Upanishad, a preceptor expressing his desire for good pupils prays to God that Brahmacharis may come to him in the same manner as springs of water flow into the ocean or months and days merge into eternity[28]. It was on account of these pious wishes of the preceptor and the pupil that their souls merged into one another and became entitled to gain the beatific vision.

In reality the preceptor had been elevated during the period of the Upanishad to Olympian heights and was accorded the position of a Godhead. The statement of Kabir, the mystic poet, "Both preceptor and God are standing before me and I do not know to whom should I bow. Glory be to my divine preceptor who has signalled me towards God"[29] is expressive of the glory of the preceptor during the period of the Upanishads. Hence in the Shwetashchtar Upanishad, it has been pointed out to the devotee that by having intense faith in the preceptor who is like God, enlightement of the mystery comes automatically to the high-souled and lofty minded devotees[30]. The same idea had been expressed by Yamacharya in his address to Nachiketa, the great devotee of spiritual knowledge. Self-realisation cannot be gained without the divine grace of the preceptor merely through one's intelligence and scholarship. In the Upanishads we have the epithets "Srotriyam Brahmanish-tham" for such a preceptor, which elevates the preceptor to the position of Godhead. As a matter of fact only those who had amassed a rich fund of knowledge through the processes of hearing, meditation contemplative recollection and deep self-realisation, were given the honoured epithet of 'Guru' or Dev.

Institutions for the Expansion of Education

In the post Vedic period numerous institutions like Shakha, Charan, Kul and Gotra developed for the expansion of education. These institutions helped a great deal in the expansion of knowledge and hence a brief account of these is given below.

Shakha

The term Shakha in its original implications has been used for those three Vedas which had developed from the original Veda. The famous commentator of the Vedas has written commentaries on all the three branches of the Vedas, but later on the word Shakha or branch or ramification came to indicate different forms of the three Vedas which appeared in a form different from the archetype, in the various families of the sages. The original form of the Vedas for the preservation of which the study of metrics and the method of loud and group study was evolved could not be maintained due to the rising tide of preceptorhood and priesthood. Consequently, the original form maintained through oral instruction in the Vedic age began to undergo alterations during the period of the Upanishads. Sometimes the pronunciation changed, often a vowel mark was dropped, and tonal distortion took place and oftentimes all the three crept in together. In this way, different transcripts of the Vedas in varied forms were preserved in various families of the sages and each family made efforts to preserve and propagate its own transcripts as an independent branch. The scope of these ramifications did not remain confined to the Vedas but even the Brahman texts which were connected with the Vedas, were also divided into various branches and sections.

Charan

Usually 'Charan'[31] is regarded as synonymous with Shakha, which is wrong. Explaining the difference between the two, Panini has written that Charan is a group of those who study in a 'Shakha' or are its followers. In the *Math* Madhav-Bhashya of Jagdhar also 'Charan' has been similarly defined. The group of students who studied any particular branch of the Vedas, came to be called 'Vyuh', a text of the age of the Sutras, five Charans of the Rigveda have been described as Shaakal, Vaashkal, Aaswlayan Shankhayan and Mandukeyye. This list is incomplete as it does not mention many old Charans. Panini has mentioned 24 Charans in his Sutras - grammatical formulae.

Parishad

The word Parishad means developed on all four sides[32]. In the Upanishads this term has been used for the assembly of the learned and the wise where great philosphical problems were mooted and solved. Later on, it came to be applied to those places where learned Brahmans lived in a large number. In fact, Parishad was a group of various Charans for the purpose of discussions on tough spiritual problems and evolving new facts. The attitude of the Parishad was always liberal because the followers of the different 'Charans' were its members. Parishads are also mentioned in the Prati-Shakhya literature. In the age of the Sutras it is described as the cultural assembly of the learned in which obstruse religious, moral and philosophical problems were decided. These Parishads have played a very important part in the progress of education in the post-Vedic period.

Gotra or Kul

The basic meaning of Gotra or Kul is protector of stock or pedigree. Hence, the basis of Gotra was lineage or descent which was possible both in real and unreal forms. The Charans which were confined to the Brahmans, had at their root the various branches or familes of the Vedas. The scope of the Gotra extended to the ascetic sages, who were exponents of Mantras, and to all the various sects connected with these sage ascetics. The members of each Gotra regarded themselves as descendants of some particular ascetic sage and felt proud of themselves in following the particular educational system and principles associated with him. The Dwij (Brahman the twice-born) Kashtriya and Vaishya all claiming lineage with some sage or the other remained keen and alert to preserve the sanctity of their Gotra. Even in the progressive modern time, Gotra is regarded as something sacrosanct not only for the Brahmans but for other castes also. This is taken into consideration particularly in connection with marriages. Usually all the Brahmans are taken to be descendants of the seven ascetic sages - Bhrigu, Angiras, Vishwamitra, Vashishtha, Kashyap, Arti, Agastya, etc. but in fact, the ancestors of the Brahmans were eight and not seven, viz., Jamdagni, Gautam, Bharadwaj, Vishwamitra, Vashishtha, Arti, Kashyap and Agastya. These eight Gotras have been divided into forth-nine Upgotras (Sub-gotras) which on being sub-divided took the form of family units.

'Samavartan' Address

Samavartan address was also called the convocation address. At the time when the Brahmachari was fit to return home as a Snataka after completing his studies for the realisation of the mystery of the eternal principle operating in the universe and radiant with the mighty emergence of transcendental knowledge, the preceptor gave him his last exhortation full of great love and regard for the disciple. This exhortation contained golden instruction which helped him to make his journey of life happy and further enabled him to maintain social decorum. Each of the addresses was redolent of high regard, confidence, love, devotion, wisdom, detachment and mundane as well as extramundane salutariness. The address used to run as follows :

"O dear son, always speak the truth. Discharge the duties laid down by the Shastras'. Always remain busy in self-study, make offerings to the Guru according to his wishes, thereafter entering into the life of the house-holder. Try to preserve the sanctity of lineage. Never desert the path of truth, never desert the path of religion. Never turn your face from noble deeds. Do not show contempt for your own things, always remain inclined towards religious ceremonies."

"Treat your parents, preceptor and guest like gods. Do what is good and avoid evil deeds. You should imitate only the good things in your elders and not others. You should reverentially offer a seat-shelter and alms to any Brahman who may be superior to you as well as to other respectable and revered person who may come to your house. Charity should be given in all humility, that is, you should say to yourself. 'All wealth is God's. I have committed a wrong in regarding it as mine being led away by avarice." You should give alms saying to yourself 'Whatever I am giving is not much': You should do charity feeling all the time afraid lest it should be refused. You should do charity thoughtfully not promiscuously."

"While doing all this, if you are ever in doubt in regard to your duty and moral conduct, you should follow the example and conduct and behaviour of those Brahmans who are living there and are soft-natured, lofty-minded, high-principled, strict adherents to religion and efficient in counselling. Apart from this, if you are ever in suspense as to how you should bear yourself towards an inculpated person, you should follow the department of the thoughtful, upright, virtuous and pious Brahmans."

"This is the injunction of the Vedas, this is the admonition. This is the *summum bonum* of the Vedas and Upanishads. This is the instruction, you should practise in reality, these directions in this very manner.[33]"

It is evident from the above instructions that not only the religious duties have been brought home to the mind of the returning pupil but also the civic sense and social virtues which go into the making of a true and loyal citizen and a healthy and prosperous society. Along with the duty of preserving the sanctity of his lineage, the householder has been hereby instructed in all his actions and duties pertaining to cultural development, self-study, parents, elders, physical fitness and material prosperity, all of which taken together conduce to the all-round development of society. In fact, the right to education was his who had the ability to educate others after completing his own education.

The preceptors made their disciples realise that mutual give and take was essential to preserve the integrity of social ties. They made charity a religious duty solely for the reasons that there might always exist in society the element of mutual sympathy and the sense of a common ideal and further that the giver and the taker might be tied together by the bond of love and remain happy all through life.

The convocation address like the above-mentioned one had in it all the useful elements of the convocation address of modern times along with the scintillating spirit of spiritual love which is an imperishable and cherished possession of Indian culture.

Female Education

In the Vedic period women were revered as they were regarded as the fountain source of strength, man's imperishable treasure, and the great ordainer and dispenser of noble actions in mundane and ultramundane existence. But in the post-Vedic period they were deprived of all their social rights. They could not even participate in the social functions. Consequently, their intellectual development also stopped along with the social development. The sanctity of femininity had disappeared even in the period of the Brahmans, because at that time the birth of a daughter was regarded as inauspicious. But the tables turned again in the period of the Upanishads and the rights of women in religious oblations were reserved and as such they remained entitled to receive higher education in the Vedas.

In the period of Upanishads there existed a number of learned women. Women gave evidence of their deep knowledge and erudition by participating in the literary affrays arranged in the royal courts. The verbal bout between the sage Yajnvalkya and the eloquent debator Gargi in the court of Janak, King of Mithila, is now of historical fame. Gargi's arguments, scintillating with the brilliance and sharpness of intellect had astonished the court assembly. Yajanavalkya had begun to fret at her arguments. There is another narrative of this kind. When Yajnavalkya deserting the life of the householder was going to the forest he tried to distribute his property between his two wives. At this Maitreyi humbly submitted. " O my lord, will I be able to gain salvation through this wealth". Yajnavalkya replied, "Life-eternal cannot be hoped for through wealth"[34]. At this Maitreyi observed, "What will I do with wealth which cannot help me attain immortality"[35]. This argument does not only astonish great scholars but also indicates Maitreyi's dazzling wit.

The Upanishads also mention some such women who worked as teachers. Along with the knowledge of the Vedas, women learnt fine arts like music and dancing.

Education of Other Castes

The Vedic system of education had begun to disappear in the time of the Upanishads. During the Vedic age persons of the same family group followed different occupations according to their individual tastes. But now the outlines of the caste system having become prominent, rigidity and ossification set in. Birth and not occupation now came to be regarded as the basis of the caste system. Consequently, a host of social castes cropped up. The rights of the Brahmans increased tremendously. The Kshatriyas were out to suppress the tide of Brahmanical supremacy, although their own rights were not impinged upon. The social degradation of the Vaishyas and the Shudras set in. The big and independent agricultural classes (Vaishyas) of the Rigvedic age were breaking up into small functional groups[36] as a result of which castes like those of chariot-builders, carpenters, blacksmiths, etc. evolved. On account of the increase of the tendency towards traditionalism some of the above mentioned caste groups went down in social prestige. The Shudras had come to be regarded as untouchables and they were deprived not only of the right to participate in religious ceremonies but also of touching even the sacrificial milk. In spite of all this the caste system had not become strictly ossified and transfer from one caste to another and inter-caste marriage were in vogue. We have the mention of the marriage of ascetic sage, Chyavan to the daughter of the Kshatriya King Shayarti. Even in the religious ceremonies the sway and complete supremacy of the Brahmans had not come into existence, although they were given predominance because Shantanu's brother Devapi had, on being deprived of the royal throne, gained sacerdotal efficiency and performed several religious ceremonies at Shantanu's. In the Rajsuya-yajan[37], the Vaishyas and the Shudras were entitled to make jewel-offerings.

The system of education was bound to be affected by the above mentioned changed conditions. Now only the Brahmans were entitled to receive education in the Vedas, but the Kshatriyas also could receive education like the Brahmans. Many Kshatriyas could beat the Brahmans hollow in transcendental knowledge. A large number of Brahmans who had studied the Vedas used to go to King Janak to slake their thirst for transcendental knowledge. Even learned Brahmans like Balaki were highly impressed by the erudition of Ajatshatru, the king of Kashi. Prawahan Jaawal of Paanchal and Ashwapati King of Kaikaya had a profound knowledge of the philosophies. In the learned assembly conmenced at Paanchal, both Shwetketu and his father Aaruni could not answer any question put to them by the Kshatriya King Prawahan Jaawal as a result of which they had to become Jaawal's disciples. Chitra, the great grand son of Garg who was as Kshatriya sage, had an extremely profound divine knowledge and Aaruni had put himself under his tutelage also. A study of the Upanishads reveals that Kashatriyas, and not the Brahmans had the first and foremost right to divine knowledge. Just as Brahman texts belonged to the sacerdotal Brahmans, in the same manner the Upanishads, armoury of divine knowledge, were the texts of the Kshatriyas. But the number of Kshatriyas well up in divine knowledge was limited because the common subjects of their study were politics, science of warfare and archery, which they had to learn from the Brahmans.

In the literature of the post-Vedic period there is very little about the education of the Vaishyas and Shudras. The only thing we come to know is that agriculture was the main pursuit of the Vaishayas. Production and distribution of corn were their main functions. The 'Vaandij'[38] mentioned in the Rigveda is an indication of the term Vaishya. In fact, the importance of the Vaishayas lay in efficient distribution of corn in the society although when the occasion demanded they were prepared to take up arms. The education of the Vaishyas was primarly concerned with agricultural pursuits and small cottage industries. They remained aloof from the intellectual life and showed great keenness for pursuits relating to land. Their highest ambition was to become perfect villagers or at the most the Mukhya or the village headman.

Although the condition of the Shudras had deteriorated yet they employed themselves in tilling and cultivating the land, animal husbandry, handwork and handicarafts. They also showed interest and participated in music, dancing and instrument playing. The Brahmans themselves gave to the Shudras education in these subjects.

The proficiency of Narad in music and Vina-playing is all too well known. In the Brahman texts, the Brahmans are depicted as giving education in these subjects to their pupils drawn from occupational groups, like the Vaishyas, fishermen, snake-charmers, fowlers, etc.

Summary

During the Rigvedic period "Tap' and Yagna' were the two typical means of education. During the post-Vedic period, too, these two means remained with the difference that during the Rigvedic period it was 'Tap' which was especially emphasized, and during the post-Vedic period 'Yajnas' occupied the predominant place. Consequently, during the latter period the students had to spend much of his time in performing 'Yajna'. The aim of education in both the periods remained 'worship and devotion', but the means remained different. The simple process of the Rigvedic period had become complex. The preceptor enjoyed the same prestige in both periods, but the consequent egoism because of the 'Yajnas'performance had destroyed the previous detachment on the part of the preceptors.

During the Brahman period, the preceptors enjoyed a special prestige because of their specialization in the art of performing 'Yajnas' and the rituals. Because of the development of the various aspects of rituals, the number of subjects in the curriculum increased. It became rather impossible for a student to read all the subjects. So various branches of study like Upanishads, Aranyak and Pratishakhya were developed. The duration of study was twelve years. The students were careful when studying the branch of their own choice for acquisition of higher learning. Shakhas, Charans and Parishads were established. Here the more brilliant students used to study.

The Upanayan ceremony was made compulsory now. The four Ashrama and Varna systems were accepted during this period. Women's education and education of other castes took various forms. Various aspects of education came into the limelight. Various methods of education were also evolved.

Notes and Reference

1. One who throws articles of oblation in the sacrificial fire.
2. The priest who recites Mantras at a sacrifice.
3. Priest-chanter of the Mantras of Samveda.
4. Officiationg priest at a sacrifice.
5. A host (yajaman), one who performs the sacrifice.
6. Purvarchik.
7. Uttararchik.
8. A Jain treatise on Religion.
9. Yajna.
10. Karma.
11. Mundak 8-40
12. The ceremony of initiation or investiture with the sacred thread.
13. A kind of grass.
14. A piece of cloth which ascetics put round their waist, a girdle.
15. Deer skin.
16. A staff or stick.
17. An earthen or wooden pot used by ascetics and mendicants.
18. An act of devotion, the offering of water and food, etc., to the Brahman in honour of manes.
19. Mundak 1-1-5.
20. Chhandogyas Upanishad 8.7.11.3.
21. Shatpath 11, 5, 6, 3.
22. Sankha, Chapter 4, 29

23 श्रवणं तु गुरोः पूर्वं मननं तदनन्तरम्।
निदिध्यासनमित्येतत पूर्ण–बोधस्य लक्षणम।।

24 गिरति अज्ञानं गृणति उप दिशति वा धर्म सः गुरूः

25 न नरेणावरेण प्रोक्तं एस सविज्ञेयो बहधा चिन्त्यमानः।
अनन्यप्रोंक्ते गतिस्त्र नास्ति अणीययान हयतवर्यमणु प्रमाणात्।।

26 अन्धेनैव नीयमाना यथान्धा

27 तद्विज्ञानार्थं स गुरूणेवाभिगच्छेत।
समितपाणिः श्रोत्रियः ब्रह्मनिष्ठत्।।

28 तथापः प्रवहता भन्ति यथाभासा अहर्जरम्।
एवं मां ग्रह्मचारिणो धातरायन्तु सर्वतः स्वाहा।।

29 गुरू गोविन्द दोनों खड़े काके लागूं पाय।
बलिहारी गुरूदेव की जिन साहब दियो दिखाय।।

30. यस्य देवे पराभक्त्यिथा देवे तथा गरौ।
तस्यैते कथित्ता ह्यार्थाः प्रकाशन्ते महात्मनः।।

31 चरण

32. परितः सीदति अस्यां
33. तैत्तिरीयपोनिषद्–शिक्षावल्ली
34. अमृतत्वस्य तूनाशास्ति वित्तेन
35. किमहं ते न कुर्याम्। ये नाहं नामृतास्याम्।।
36. व्यावसायिक समूह
37. A sacrifice which only a Universal monarch is entitled to perform.
38. वाणिज

Exercises

1. Explain the characteristics of Rigvedic educational system and compare the same with the Vedic educational system.
2. Write short notes on - Brahmin, Aranyakas and Upanishads.
3. Describe the characteristics of education during the Brahman period.
4. What are the special features of education during the Upanishadic period ?
5. What was the place of women during the post-Vedic period of India ?
6. Why was the teacher eulogised during the post-Vedic period ?
7. Discuss the nature of education of women and the other classes.

Chapter 4

Education during the Age of the Sutras

Post-Vedic

The age of the Sutras is supposed to have begun seven hundred years before Christ and ended in the 2nd century. A.D. As it was impossible to preserve orally all the available scattered religious literatures of the period prior to the Sutras, it was deemed necessary to arrange and organise it so that its original form could be preserved. Apart from this reason another factor which operated was the rise of Buddhism which dealt a sort of coup de grade against the ritualism of the Brahmanical religion. The tenets as well as the language of Buddhism were simple and comprehensible to all and sundry. Hence, in order to re-establish the prestige and dignity of Hinduism it became necessary to consolidate its tenets and to make them simple and practicable.

The age of the Sutras thus came as a sort of reaction against certain external and internal circumstances operating in the field of religion. Consequently, in this period the work of organising, consolidating and preserving the old literature was well accomplished. The disorganised social structure of India was reshaped and put on the solid foundation of ethical principles while the diffused shreds of Indian culture were wrought into a rigid pattern. Thus, in this period not much new and original work was done, only the rehashing and consolidation of the old and existing practices, principles and religious ideas took place.

In the field of education also nothing new was added to the old principles which were simply given a more solid form. The assessment in the following pages of the educational system of this period depends upon the information available from the literature of this period.

The New Ceremony of Beginning Education or Learning the Letters[1]

Vadic literature does not contain anything regarding the ceremony of educational tirocinium or the beginning of one's education, but the later texts like 'Sanskar Prakash', 'Smriti-Chandrika' and 'Virmitrodaya' etc. deal with the significance of these ceremonies. The ritual known as 'Akshar Swikaran' - learning the letters was performed in the midst of a magnificent congregation and took place before the Upanayana and after the tonsure ceremonies — when the child was five years old. When it could not be solemnised in this way due to certain reasons, it was performed simultaneously with the Upanayana ceremony. After an invocation to the tutelary deities of the clan and of the family as well as to Saraswati (goddess of learning), Lakshmi (goddess of wealth and success) and Hari (Lord Vishnu) the preceptor made the pupil write the letters of the alphabet with a pen of silver or gold on a mound of rice spread on the floor. The pupil was put under the tutelage and protection of the preceptor and the ceremony came to an end with the offering of a remuneration to the preceptor. The child being young in age and immature in understanding must have been taught at the time of this ceremony only the letters of the alphabet because any sort of higher instruction would have been useless.

This ceremony did not have independent existence in the Vedic age and probably the Upanayana must have marked the beginning of education. The absence of a script might have been responsible for this. The knowledge of the alphabet became essential in the age of the Sutras because by that time the Sanskrit language of the Vedas had assumed a form very different from the commonly spoken one. However, in this period this ceremony had great significance and it was the first ceremony in the educational career of a child.

The Importance of the Upanayana Ceremony for the First Three Castes

The real beginning of education in this period was made after the Upanayana ceremony which was compulsory for the Brahman, Kshatriya and Vaishya castes. The Shudras had by then been relegated to the very end of the social ladder and as such heavy restrictions had been imposed on their education, which were conspicuous by their absence in the Vedic age. In the Taittiriya Brahman we have the mention of the chanting of the hymns in 'Agnihotra' by cartwrights who belonged to the Shudra caste.

Only those children who had acquired the age prescribed for Upanayana were initiated into education through this ceremony. The age limit minimum as well as maximum differed from caste to caste: it was 8 and 16 years for Brahman, 11 and 22 years for Kshatriya and 12 and 24 years for Vaishya children. The Upanayana could not be performed either before or after this age limit.

It is a debatable question as to why a higher age limit was prescribed for the Kshatriyas and Vaishyas than it was for the Brahmans. This might have been possibly due to the difference in the ideals and curricula of education for the various castes. Another reason for the lower age limit of the Brahmans might have been that they had to gain higher education for performing religious ceremonies and in order to do this satisfactorily they began earlier. Education in the Vedas did not have much utility for other castes and consequently a shorter period of study was adequate for their purpose.

Some scholars have attributed this difference in age-limit for Upanayana to the fact that the Brahmans wanted to show that their children were intellectually superior to others and became fit to receive education at a lower age. But according to A.S.Altekar who does not agree with this view, the reason was that the children of Brahmans usually began their education in their own homes unlike the children of other castes who had to go to the homes of the preceptors and it was not meet and proper for a child of five to leave his home. Even those children of the Brahmans, who had to leave home, could do so only after attaining the prescribed age. Thus this difference was actually based on considerations of circumstances and conveniences. In modern times also education depends on these factors. In comparison with the children in rural areas or those who are poor, children of the town and of rich people begin their education quite early in life.

According to Apastamb the age for Upanayana was determined in accordance with the aims and objects of education and different seasons were fixed for this ceremony for different castes. We give below an account of these:

Age	Caste	Season
7	Brahman	Spring
8	Kshatriya	Summer
9	Vaishya	Winter

In this manner the Upanayana ceremony was to be performed for every caste at the prescribed age and time. Those who violated this principle were regarded as pariahs and unholy persons unfit for religious ceremonies, education and social ceremonies like marriages, etc. They were reclaimed in society after expiation or atonement for which varied principles were laid down. It is, however, well established that both Upanayana and education were compulsory institutions of life. Hence, we conclude that through these religious restrictions compulsory education was planned out for all the three castes in the age of the Sutras.

Subject of Study

The subjects of study in Vedic schools during this period were comparatively larger in number. The Vedas and the Vedangas were thoroughly studied and great importance was attached to the study of grammar and associated literature. Panini's 'Ashtadhyayyi', Katyayana's 'Vartik', and Patanjali's 'Mahabhashya', etc. represent the rich grammatical literature that had grown during those days. For the study of the Vedas a knowledge of the Vedangas was essential. At this time it was thought that a thorough study of the Vedas was not possible without a knowledge of grammar, orthography, prosody, etymology, details of religious ceremonies and astronomy. The knowledge of numbers was given by India to the world, but the study of algebra and arithmetic had also come into vogue during this age.

In 476 A.D. Arya Bhatt gave a systematic and scientific form to the study of astronomy. The healing art had also developed, which might have been due to the impetus to preservation of life given by Buddhism with its cardinal tenant of Ahimsa or non-violence. Charak, the father of medicine, was the contemporary of Kanishka, the Buddhist king. With the passage of time, the Indian science of medicine spread to other countries and the Western people also learnt this probably through the Arabs. The study of philosophy and metaphysics, which had its origins in the vedic sanghitas, also developed and the six systems of Indian Philosophy - Poorva Mimansa, Uttar Mimansa, Sankhya, Yoga, Nyaya, and Vaisheskhik, were evolved.

It was not possible for any particular student in these schools of this period, to study the entire Vedic literature and as such Vedic studies were divided into several branches. This led to the system of the specialised study of a particular Vedanga and resulted in exaggerated importance being given to extraneous subjects than to the Vedas. The Vedangas themselves had developed under similar circumstances. Panini's grammar was also the upshot of this system of specialised study. The cumulative effect of this was that the practice of independent study of subjects correlated with the Dharm Sutras was adopted. Subjects like astronomy were given an independent and scientific basis and the compilation of Manav Dharma Shastra[2], which later on formed the basis of Manu's Smriti, took place in this period. Thus the scope of studies was fairly widened in the age of the Sutras.

Methods of Teaching

In the ancient Indian method of teaching, 'the individual' and not a group of student was the immediate concern and consequently the personal attachment between the preceptor and the pupil was of an abiding nature. The work of teaching was regarded as a sacred duty and not merely a business transaction. In the age of the Sutras also a definite code of ethics, principles and regulations both for the teacher and the taught was laid down, the violation of which was treated as a sin which could be rectified by expiation. Hence the preceptor started the lessons systematically and the pupil also studied with due observance of the code.

Teaching and learning based on mutual love and reverence were regarded as highly religious duties and the pupils took it as a sinful act to misbehave, as some modern students do, towards their preceptor. During his educational career the pupil listened reverentially and attentively to the holdy words of his preceptor and never once showed signs of negligence towards his studies unlike some derelict students of the modern universities and colleges.

According to Gautam, Dharma Sutra studies those days, commenced in the following manner :-

Before beginning his lesson, the pupil respectfully touched the feet of the preceptor, and then occupied a seat, as he was instructed, either in the direction of the North or the East. He touched his forehead with 'Kush" (a kind of grass) to ensure the sanctity of his mind and then practised certain exercises to attain the power of concentration. The pupil touched with his right fingers the left hand of the preceptor and begged him to begin the recitation of the Mantras. The preceptor chanted the mantra[3]. This had the effect of making the surroundings pure and peaceful. After the preceptor began the work of the day by chanting a portion of the first lesson in a very graceful but explicit tone, the pupil repeated the words with exactitude. This process continued for some time so that the pupil could thoroughly appropriate the expressions of the preceptor. When this was done the preceptor explained the portion and then proceeded to the next in the like manner. The whole lesson was revised along with the separate portions and thus finally ended. At the time of his departure the pupil again touched the feet of the preceptor.

The Rig Vedic Pratishakhya also which was composed about 500 or 600 B.C., has the description of a similar system. It can be safely affirmed on the basis of such a description that the system of instruction was oral and it was essential for the students to memorise the lessons. But the system of explanation and exposition prevalent since the age of the Rigveda, was given an added importance in the age of Sutras to facilitate a correct understanding of the Sutras.

According to 'Smriti Chandrika' the seven essential aspects of study were as follows :-

1. Servitude to the preceptor.
2. Hearing.
3. Understanding and absorbing.
4. Meditation.
5. Classification of doubts.
6. Discussion and argumentation.
7. Real attainment of wisdom.

Vachaspati Misra has suggested the following five processes for the attainment of metaphysical knowledge :-

1. Hearing the subjects.
2. Understanding the meaning of the words heard.
3. Argumentation.
4. Concordance of friends and class-mates.
5. Experience through practical application.

These can be favourably compared with the following three processes of knowledge as adumbrated by Dewey, the great master of the Philosophy of Education in modern times :-

1. A problem and its location	--	The word study
2. Suggested solutions and the selection of a problem	--	Argumentation and concordance.
3. Application	--	Experience through practical application.

Manu has summed up the above in the following manner :-

1. Realisation of some basic fact through the preceptor.
2. Realisation through individual effort.
3. Realisation through friends and class-mates.
4. Realisation through personal experience.

It is evident from the above that the old system of argumentation continued in the age of the Sutras also and that the method of cross-examination helped in the process of teaching.

According to Apastamb, experienced and capable pupils had to carry on the work of teaching during the absence of the preceptor. The monitorial system has thus been in practice in India from the ancient days and it was in vogue even at the famous university of Taxila.

Modern educationists also acknowledge the utility of this system according to which the preceptor got reliable assistance without any payment and the pupil an opportunity for self-development and for gaining practical experience of teaching. This also enabled the Indian educational institutions to practically demonstrate teaching methods.

In this method of teaching which was highly individualistic, the students got opportunities for education in proportion to their individual capabilities. Mediocre students could not keep pace with the bright and brilliant ones. Nevertheless in this system the preceptor could very well gauge the ability and progress of students and as such even the mediocres were not neglected. The preceptor began a fresh lesson only after ascertaining whether the previous one had been fully mastered or not. Due to the consideration of individual merits, only devoted and competent students got a long stay in the institutions.

Discipline and Punishment

The fixed daily routine for students, as adumbrated in the ancient Indian system of education created in them ipso facto a spirit of discipline. The life of the students was moulded in such a manner that principles of conduct and discipline were automatically inculcated in them. Hence there was at that time no trace of the modern complicated problems of discipline, nevertheless they did not overlook the importance of good discipline. In the Smritis we have accounts of admonitions and punishments meted out to delinquent students, who violated in any way, any of the prescribed rules and regulations. These punishments were usually spiritual, for example, observing fasts. This spiritual punishment not only made the student repent, but also provided him with an impetus to purge his inner self. It is evident that this method of punishment was based on the principle of self-reform and these punishments were more effective and useful than are the modern external or corporal ones which instead of bringing about a reform lead to an inverse in delinquency.

Apastamb never thought of corporal punishment and laid down that the preceptor should either remove the delinquent pupil from his presence or prescribe some sort of atonement. Manu was also of this opinion and regarded even verbal admonition and advice from the preceptor as quite efficaious. But Manu went a step further to suggest that if these methods failed to achieve the desired end, then some slight corporal punishment was not improper. Gautam also was in accord with this principle, but was totally averse to harsh physical punishment. He laid it down implicitly that preceptors who gave such punishment should be brought to book by the Sovereign. In giving corporal punishment it was always to be remembered that the student was not hurt on the quick and hence punishment could be inflicted on the back of the student with a small rope or a thin cane. This system obtained in all the educational institutions of ancient India. A student of Taxila who had developed kleptomania was given such a punishment. Apart from the prevalence of this system, life in the educational institutions went on in a smooth and disciplined way on account of the excellent and ideal relations between the preceptor and the pupil.

Tuition Fees

It has already been mentioned that the work of teaching was regarded as a sacred and religious duty in ancient India. The only way of redeeming the obligation of the preceptor was to take to teaching. It was expected of every student that after completing his own education he would become a preceptor and produce good students. In this way the utility of education was not a means of livelihood but of the expansion of knowledge. This also facilitated one in discharging his religious responsibilities for the system of education was thoroughly spritualistic and moralistic.

A preceptor who worked for emoluments was looked upon as a sinner. According to 'Smriti Chandrika' even the mention of emoluments was thought to be extremely derogatory for the preceptor. The entry of a new pupil into the home of the preceptor was like the birth of a new baby. The responsibilities of the preceptor tremendously increased with the entry of a new pupil, but nevertheless no hope of any reward or material profit could be entertained. In the Saur Purana those are treated as doomed souls who educate or are educated through money or prescribed fees.

On the completion of the studies offerings were made to the preceptor. It was the right of the preceptor to accept the right offerings and it was the duty of the pupil to show his reverence for the preceptor by making proper offerings only. The offerings made by well-to-do pupils were accepted. Since eatables could be included in the offerings pupils who were poor and destitute tried to procure offerings for their preceptor through hard physical labour. The Jatakas mention such students. The poor students undoubtedly had to render some services to the preceptor, as several students did at Taxila, nevertheless they were on par with the rich in respect of facilities and opportunities for education. Pupils who did manual work during the day received their education in the night.

As a matter of principle, the offerings were made only on the completion of studies, but rich students offered to the preceptor the total amount right in the beginning. We have several such instances in the Jataka texts. According to Milindpahna, Nagsen's father had given the 'dakshina' (honorarium) to the preceptor in the beginning. Preceptor Dron had also received his honorarium in the beginning for the education of the Kaurava princes.

Thus in ancient India no one was bound to pay a prescribed fees but teaching was invested with such a halo of dignity that the preceptor was not denied anything. As a result of this it was possible for centuries, to mould anew in the light of education, the lives of about 80 per cent of the people, and to maintain the high dignity of Indian culture in the world. The social thinkers of India were always solicitous of the fact that economic hardship should not interfere with the teaching work of the preceptor and as such every one in society looked to his economic needs and accorded him a very high and respectable status in society.

Co-education

Though co-education was not in vogue in ancient India, yet it was not forbidden. There are some such evidences in old literature on the basis of which it may be affirmed that the people were not averse to co-education. According to Bhavbhuti's 'Malti Madhav', Kamandki was educated with Bhurvasu and Devarat. In the ' Uttar Ram Charit' Aitreyi is described as receiving her education with Lav Kush. The description of the classes of Sujat, Kahob and Pramadavara shows the vogue of co-education. Even love-marriages between co-eds took place because they were not looked down upon. The society of the day was not averse to Gandharv[4] marriage, it rather approved of it.

Academic Session

On the Poornima[5] day of the month of Sravan, a special function called 'Upakarman' was arranged and this marked the beginning of the academic session of the Vedic education institutions. In this function both the preceptors and the pupils fully participated and after the worship of the Vedic gods invocation was made to the tutelary deities who presided over Intellect, Wisdom and Faith, the three stages of mental development. After this, offerings were made to the sacred memory of those great personalities of the past who had contributed a great deal to the founding and management of the various departments in the institution.

The work of the institution went on regularly for probably six months after the Upakarman function. The regular session was supposed to end on the Poornima day of the month of Paush[6] with the celebration of Chandsam-Utsarjanama[7] function. For the remaining months the study of the Vedas was stopped. Thus the regular academic session of the institution lasted for five or five and a half months, but during the remaining period the students carried on self-study. The study of a new chapter of the Vedas was begun in a new academic session. During the session the institutions observed holidays on Poornima, Pratipada[8] and other religious occasions.

Thus in those days winter and rainy seasons were thought to be the most suitable periods for serious studies. Along with the suitability of the seasons the peaceful environment in the institution was also necessary for deep concentration on the part of the students. According to the Dharma Sutra, stormy blasts, painful groans of the sick, the beat of the kettledrum, the howls of the dogs and jackals, etc. cause interruption in the concentration of the students and as such studies should be suspended at such times.

According to Gautam and Apastamb a new lesson should not be taken up till the return of those students who had gone on some tour. Teaching should not be carried on in times of social calamities or political disturbances.

Hence, it may be safely concluded from the above that in the Vedic institutions teaching remained suspended for quite a long time during the year. It also becomes clear that in these institutions there were good arrangements for uninterrupted work and that great significance and sanctity was attached to education and the educators.

Duration of Studies

The duration of studies was fixed in accordance with the subjects. Even in the Vedic age there was the practice of specialised study and in the age of the Sutras this was further developed. We gather from the Gautam Dharma Sutra that the period for the complete study of a Veda was 12 years and as such 48 years must have been required for the study of all the four Vedas. In all probability a large number of students could not have been in a position to devote so much time. There were several such students who dedicated their lives to devotion and study, but generally the ordinary students studied a particular Veda for 12 years. In the record of Megasthenes we have accounts of students studying for 37 years.

The duration of study depended usually on the mental capacity of the student. In the individualistic system of education the latent abilities of the student were fully exploited. A student who could complete his studies even before the stipulated period was accorded permission to return home although the study of the Vedas could be carried on till he turned grey.

Female Education

In the education system of the Sutras, female education was given the same importance as in the Vedic system. In the Gobhil Grihysutra it is laid down that the wife must be educated in order to be entitled to participate in the religious ceremony. According to the Purva Mimansa philosphy of Jaimini, the position of woman in a sacrificial ceremony is fixed in the same way as man's. In the age of the Sutras women who had mastered the teachings of the Vedas, put on the sacred thread. At this time girls of eight had like the Brahman boys, the right to Upanayana, for this ceremony was compulsory even for the girls. The interest which women took in studying the extremely dry and abstruse Mimamsa Philosophy is indicative of their abilities. The book Kashkritsni was written by a learned and erudite lady named Kaṣhkritsnim and women who studied this were called Kashkritsna. The discovery and introduction of this new word provides sufficient evidence to the fact that at time there were a large number of women who were genuinely interested in studies.

The feminine form "Upadhyayani" and Upadhyaya of the noun Upadhya, prevalent in the ancient literature proves that a large number of women took to teaching also. According to Panini there were some student-hostels in which only girl students resided and the supervision of these was entirely in the hands of women teachers.

Right up to the Maurya period women enjoyed quite a respectable position in society, but around 200 B.C. they began to suffer a setback. Consequently, female education also suffered and the importance of Upanayana gradually frittered away. The social degradation of women adversely affected female education. After the second century A.D. it became compulsory to marry off girls before they entered puberty. Yam, Yajnavalkya and other writers of Smritis denounce those who married girls after they had crossed the age of puberty. Hence, girls were married off at eight or nine and female education could not survive under such circumstances, nor did it.

In spite of all this, girls of wealthy families received education in literature, music and dancing, etc. in their own homes through competent teachers. In South India many women who had received higher education wrote poetry in the Prakrit language. We find an account of this in 'Gatha Saptashati'[9]. The poetesses whose compositions we have in this collection are Rewa, Roha, Anulakshmi, Madhvi Pahayi, Waddhwahi and Shashiprabha. Poetess Vijaya of Berar province who has been praised by Raj Shekhar was accorded a place next to Kalidas. Silobhattarika had also etched out a niche for herself in Sanskrit literature. Only recently a play 'Kaumudi Mahotsav' written by Vidya or Jijjaka, has been unearthed. Women wrote books on medicine also. A book on midwifery in Arabic was written in the 8th century A. D. by a woman named Rusa. The women were gaining proficiency in the fields of philosophy and argumentation also. The wife of Mandan Misra listened, as an arbiter, to the literary affray between her husband and Shankaracharya.

We have accounts also of women skilled in the sciences of war and politics. The queen of Masag herself faced Alexander on the death of her husband. Sugandha and Diddha have been immortalised as rulers in the history of Kashmir, Naynika of Aandhu and Prahhavati Gupta of Vaktak dynasties had managed the affairs of state during the infancy of their children. It was after the Muslim invasion that the vogue of female education completely died out and it remained so for practically 800 years.

Parishad

The system of Parishads for debating and deciding complicated religious problems was in vogue in India from time immemorial. In the age of the Sutras definite rules and regulations were laid down for organising and systematising the Parishads and their work. The Parishads were organised only in places where learned Brahmans predominated. Ordinarily a Parishad had 10 members whose selection was made according to the following pattern outlined in Gautam Dharma Sutra.

1. 4 members	-Well-versed in knowledge of the 4 Vedas.
2. 3 members	- Masters of Dharma Shastras
3. 3 representative member	- Representatives of the Brahma Charya, Grihasth and Vanprasth Ashrams.

The total number was thus 10. The arrangement was accepted by Vodhayan Dharm Sutra also, but with regard to the three scholars of Dharm Shastra, it was laid down that one of these should be versed in Mimamasa philosophy, a the second should have complete knowledge of the Vedangas and the third should be a profound scholar of Dharmastra.

Manu also agreed in regard to the names of the members in the Parishad but he distributed them in the following manner :-

1.	(a)	Scholar of Rigveda	1	
	(b)	Scholar of Samveda	1	3
	(c)	Master of Yajurveda	1	
2.	(a)	Master of logic	1	
	(b)	Scholar of Mimamsa	1	4
	(c)	Scholar of Niruvasta	1	
	(d)	Master of Dharmashastra	1	
3.	(a)	Representative of Brahmacharya ashram	1	
	(b)	Representative of Grihastha ashram	1	3
	(c)	Representative of Vanprashtha ashram	1	
		Total number of members		10

According to Manu a Parishad could be constituted only with three scholars of the three Vedas. If three suitable scholars were not available only one scholar of the Vedas could constitute the Parishad and his decisions were to be regarded superior to those of the other common people. Since the decisions of the Parishads were acknowledged in toto, any opposition to these was regarded as illegal and unconstitutional.

Parashara also shows a great deal of agreement with Manu's opinion. According to him a Parishad could be constituted either with three or four Brahmans well up in the knowledge of the Vedas or with five Brahmans having a deep knowledge of the Vedangas and Dharmasutras. A sage who had divine knowledge of the Supreme Self could alone constitute the Parishad and such a sage who was proficient in the Vedic system of ceremonies, could decide issues once for all.

We can draw the following conclusions from the above discussion of the organisation and constitution of the Parishad :-

1. In the age of the Sutras the Parishads were organised in a more or less uniform manner. The number of members was usually 10, but a Parishad could constitute 5, 4, 2 or 1 member only.
2. The members of the Parishad had to be masters of their subjects. They had to possess a thorough knowledge of all the values pertaining to knowledge or ritualism. This was essential for the efficient discharge of the Parishad's responsibilities relating to religious debate and conclusive decisions.
3. The presence of members having special knowledge of particular subjects shows that the system of specialised study had advanced much in this age. According to Gautam and Vodhayan Dharmsutras, it was necessary to have four members who had a special knowledge of the four Vedas. Although Manu did not deem as essential the presence of a scholar of Atharvaveda, nevertheless, there is abundant proof of the prevalence of the system of specialised study.
4. Along with the scholars of Vedas and Dharma Sutras there were in the Parishad representatives of students, householders and forest dwellers. There was no representative of the Sanyasi - ascetics or recluse hermits, - because they had no connection whatsoever with social life. At the time the Parishad was the highest organisation for religious discussions as also for finding solutions to various religious issues. The student representation on such a body some 2,500 years ago indicates the high esteem in which the student body was held. The significant and dignified position which the students were given in the ancient Indian educational system is not possible in the modern progressive and democratic times.
5. The Parishads were the highest organisations for finally deciding complicated issues and for evolving new values and their decisions were binding on all. Along with learned members

representing various kinds of knowledge and learning there were three representatives of the society also. Thus it would not be wrong to regard these Parishads, on the basis of their organisation and responsible functions, as the forerunners or purveyors of modern universities.

Thus the organisation, the high standard of attainment of the constituting members along with the membership from the student body and the society at large, all these things go to prove the great importance of the Parishads.

Sumavartan[10]

When after having passed through the Brahmacharya state, the pupil was to return home to re-enter into household life, the Samavartan ceremony was solemnised. This ceremony symbolised the end of the state of celibacy and the commencement of the life of a householder.

The Samavartan ceremony took place on some holy and auspicious day. On that particular day the Brahmachari shut himself up in a room before the break of dawn after having attended to the daily chores. The idea behind this was that the halo of splendour around the Brahamachari may not put to shame the rising sun. There cannot be any better way of recognising the importance and significance of students. When the celibate came out of the room at about midday his nails were pared and beard and hair were shaved and his staff and bowl, the symbols of his state of celibacy, were submerged in deep water. The preceptor gave him a good bath with cold water. The student now got the right to enjoy all those things which he had renounced during his celibacy. He put on a new dress as well as the earings specially made for this occasion along with other articles of comfort like, shoes, turban, umbrella etc.

Arrangement was made at this time for a special Havan[11]. After invocation to the tutelary deities of the clan and the family, and to the preceptor, the Snatak[12] took the vow to educate the pupils who came to him. After this the preceptor gave him 'Madhupark'[13] as a gift, which was given only to high and important dignitaries like the King, the preceptor or the son-in-law. Then the Snatak was taken on an elephant or a chariot, to the assembly of the learned and the wise and he was introduced to those intellectual giants. The preceptor made a proclamation in regard to the erudition and scholarship of the student and the asembly gave him its blessings.

After all this the student laying down his 'Dakshina' (honorarium) at the feet of the preceptor, returned home as a new entrant into the household. This is how the Samavartan ceremony was celebrated and is well indicative of the social status of the Sanatak.

Summary

Sutra Period and its Education System

The Sutra period extended before 700 A.C. During this period the Indian culture was systematised due to the rise of Buddhism and the preservation of the previously created religious literature. In education also the prevailing traditions were systematised. Below we hint at the various educational features as found in the Sutra literature.

Beginning of Education

It was celebrated by a special ceremony. At the age of five the child used to begin writing with a silver or golden pen on the grains of rice after worshipping gods. After this he had to live under the guardianship of the preceptor.

Upanayana Ceremony

The real education started from the Upanayana ceremony. Upanayana was compulsory for all the three Varnas except the Shudra Varna. For Upanayana the age for Brahman was 8, for Kahatriya 11 years, and for Vaishya 12 years. The maximum age for the Brahman was 16 years, for Kshatriya 22 years and for Vaishya 24 years. According to some this difference in age was because of the mental superiority of Brahmans. According to Dr. Altekar the Brahman boys were taught at home, whereas the other caste children had to leave their homes for education. Those who ignored Upanayana were not regarded fit for social ceremonies.

Curriculm

Ved, Vedanaga, Grammar, literature and astronomy were the subjects of study in the Sutra age. Mathematics developed in this period. Science also made a rapid progress. Vedic education was divided into sub-branches due to specialised study. Manav Dharma-Shastra was formulated.

Teaching Method

Teaching was a religious duty. The relation between the teacher and the taught was a private affair. The student sat at a place, touching the feet of the teacher and after getting his mind concentrated through Pranayama, a request to start the lesson was made. The teacher recited the Mantras in a serious tone and the pupil followed him. In addition to learning the lesson by rote, its analysis was also done.

Discipline and Punishment

The regular completion of daily work in schools was itself helpful in maintaining discipline. Those who ignored the allotted quota of work were spiritually penalized for the inner purification of soul. If the spiritual punishment failed to bring about the desired change, the student was physically punished but it was guarded that his soft portions were not affected.

Education Fee

There was no provision for charging school fee. Any educated person or teacher, who charged fee for imparting education, was regarded as mean. The custom of paying Guru Dakshina was in vogue after the completion of study. Guru Dakshina was costly as well as ordinary. Poor and unresourseful students paid Guru Dakshina out of their own labour. It was also the practice of the rich pupils to pay guru Dakshina at the time of starting education. Social thinkers of the time were themselves labouring for continuous and proper functioning of the teacher's work.

Co-education

We find some evidence that the system of co-education was much in vogue according to 'Malti Madhav'. Kamandki received education with Lava and Kusha. Love marriages were also performed and it was not regarded as ignoble in society.

Academic Session

The school work started with an Upkrama' ceremony on the full moon day in the month of Sravana and it was suspended with 'Chandsam' Utsarjan ceremony on the full moon day of Pausa month. The winter and rainy seasons were more suitable for study. The peacefulness of the surrounding was of primary importance. If the concentration of the mind was disturbed due to some unavoidable factors, the teaching and the learning work remained suspended. The school work was confined only to five or five and a half months.

Study Period

It took thirteen years to attain complete mastery over one Veda. Generally, students were devoted to the special study of a particular branch of a subject. But some of the students devoted their whole life for the sake of study. Students were permitted to leave the institution earlier than the time fixed for the course, if they attained full knowledge of the subject.

Women's Education

Women had equal rights with men in the Yajna ceremony. Upanayana ceremony was compulsory even for girls. Women also shared the job of teaching with men.They were called 'Upadhyaya'.Some hostels were reserved for women only. Some of these women 'Rama', 'Roha', Madhvi, Anulaxmi, Shashiprabha, Vijya, Shilobhattarika and Vidya have written books.

Academy :

It was a highly developed cultural institution. Generally its membership was confined to 10 people, but it could be reduced. Members were experts of special subjects and were representatives of the society. Religious discussions and imparting of justice were the responsibility of the academy. The students also had their representative in this institution. The judgment of the academy was accepted by all.

Samavartan Ceremony :

Passing his life under Brahmacharya Vrata, a Brahmachari after graduating used to return home. The Samavartan ceremony was performed on an auspicious day. The Snatak (graduate) gave up all the signs of Brahmacharya in his Kamandal, Danda, etc. by immersing them in water at the time of noon and after that the he was provided with all the comforts of life. Now he enjoyed all the things which were forbidden in Brahmacharya life. After the Havan ceremony he was taken on an elephant or carriage wearing new graments before the learned gentry where he was introduced to every one by his master who declared him as being a pandit. The graduate returned home after paying Guru Dakshina as he could.

Notes and Reference

1. विद्यारम्भ अथवा अक्षर–स्वीकरण
2. Holy writ for human beings.
3. ओउम् भूः ओउम् भुवः ओउम् स्वः आदि
4. Marriage by mutual pledge before respectable persons.
5. Full moon day of the fifth month of the Hindu year.
6. The tenth month of Hindu calendar.
7. छन्देसाम् उत्सर्जनम
8. The first day of each half a lunar month.
9. Collection of seven hundred verses.
10. Convocation.
11. Offering of clarified butter and other sacred articles to flames, a religious ceremony.
12. A student who enters into household life after having completed the period of celibacy.
13. A mixture of curd, butter, water and honey.

Exercises

1. Explain the characteristics of education during the age of the Sutras.
2. Comparing the education system during the age of the Sutras with that during the Vedic period, explain the subjects of study.
3. What was the nature of women education and co-education during the age of Sutras.

4. What was the importance of Upanayana in the educational system of the Sutra age?
5. Write short notes on - Parishad, System of Punishment, and Education fee.

Chapter 5

Education in the Epics, Grammatical Literature and Kautilya's Arthshastra.

In the age of the Sutras or thereabouts a lot of literature was written dealing with topics other than religious matters. In these books too, we get information about the practical form and shape of education in ancient India. An account of the education based process on such information is given below.

The Ramayana and the Mahabharata

A study of the Ramayana and the Mahabharata gives us a very clear idea of the highly developed culture of India although these epics do not contain much with regard to education. In the course of the discussion of the contemporary social conditions and the essential features of the life of the Kshatriyas, these epics make some cursory references to the education of the times. The pattern of education as it obtained in those days has been reconstructed from these gleanings and is described in the following pages.

According to the tradition of the caste system, each caste had its separate vocation or occupation. From the Mahabharata we come to know that the prime function of the Brahmans was to study the Vedic culture and preserve its sanctity; the duty of the Kshatriyas was to maintain the dignity and prestige of their caste. While producing wealth, doing charity and performing oblations were the main occupations of the Vaishyas. The methods of education naturally differed from class to class. The Brahmans had to make a specialised study of the Vedas in order to be able to give higher education to others. In the education for the Kshatriyas greater importance was attached to the knowledge of the sciences of war than to the study of the Vedas. So also the Vaishyas had to get more of vocational training than Vedic education. Yet the ordinances of the caste system were not so rigid and inflexible as never to be violated. Thus it was the duty of the Brahmans to take up arms for the protection of the helpless or to be prepared for war when the occasion demanded. Even the Shudras who doled out help and protection to the helpless were accorded high honour. Education was, nevertheless, compulsory for only the first three castes.

Although education was compulsory only for the first three castes and only these castes were entitled to take part in the religious ceremonies, nevertheless the Shudras could receive education and take part in rituals. In the social life of the ancient Indians, religious ceremonies had a very great importance and even Shudras participated in these and maintained a place for themselves in the intellectual and cultural life of the day.

In the national cabinet of ministers all the castes were represented by members who had attained the age of fifty. The number of members was determined by considerations of castes, nevertheless the criterion for membership was not the caste consideration but individual abilities and maturity of experience. A cabinet was constituted as follows :-

1. Brahmans	4 members
2. Kshatriyas	8 members
3. Vaishyas	21 members
4. Shudras	3 members
5. Other castes (Sukta, etc)	3 members

Thus the representation of the Shudras in the national committee was fixed and they could take part in the oblations, but not usually in the Vedic ceremonies. They could, of course, attend religious lectures and assemblies in which religious discussions were held. All this goes to prove with certainty that there must have existed some arrangement for the education of the Shudras.

Education of the Brahmans and Kshatriyas

Education of the Brahmans

Since Brahmans had to carry on the work of teaching, it was essential for them to have a through knowledge of the Vedas. The Brahman children had to duly observe the rigorous discipline of the Brahmacharya Ashram so well described in the Mahabharata. These students lived with the preceptor whose word was law to them. The daily routine of the students and the services rendered to the preceptor formed a part of education. The students awoke in the morning earlier than the preceptor, took their meals and retired to bed in the night after him. The students could not sit in the presence of the preceptor without the latter's permission. The students devoted themselves to their studies with the permission of the preceptor in the time left to them after rendering daily service to him. The students had to observe all the rules and regulations of the Ashram for 25 years. On the completion of their studies and after 25 years' stay in the preceptor's hermitage the student had to offer some suitable Dakshina (honorarium).

According to the Mahabharata, Bhishm, Dron and Dhomya used to educate the royal princes.

Education of the Kshatriyas

According to the Mahabharata the Kshatriya princes were given education in the Vedas, archery, fighting with mace or club, use of swords, elephant riding, mythologies, ethics and politics, etc. Pandu, Vidur, and Dhritarashtra had been educated in all these by Bhishm, whereas the Pandava and Kaurava princes were educated by Dronacharya. There is no account of the religious education of these desciples of Dronacharya who were highly proficient in all the sciences of war. Arjuna, the most beloved pupil of Dronacharya, was non-paralleled as an archer. Duryodhan and Bhim were specially skilled in club-fighting. The Pandav princes Nakul and Sahdev were excellent swordsmen, whereas Yudhishtir, who was the eldest among these princes, was an efficient charioteer. Two generations of royal princes, were educated in this manner by Bhishma and Dronacharya, but Abhimanyu who belonged to the third generation was educated by his own father Arjuna. Arjuna educated his son principally in the sciences of war in such a manner that Abhimanyu quickly mastering all the four branches of the science of war, became renowned like his own father.

According to the Ramayana, the kings were given education in reading and writing, in physical feats like skipping, hopping and swimming, jurisprudence, ethics and politics, and music, etc. Besides, the Mahabharata also mentions education in the science of medicine.

The royal princes had, according to these epics, to complete their education by the age of sixteen so that they could be equipped early in life to bear the burden of worldly responsibilities. This is borne out by the examples of Rama and Abhimanyu. It also goes to prove that religious instructions played a very insignificant role in the education of the royal princes.

Female Education

Female education must have been in vogue those days because we have in the Ramayana and the Mahabharata accounts of several erudite women. Shabri, who is mentioned in the Ramayana, used to live in the Pampapur hermitage and received high spiritual education form the ascetic sage Guru Matang. Suloma, the she mendicant, used to enter into philosophical discussions with King Janak. The Mahabharata mentions the case of a woman-celibate who had a religious discussion with Ashtavakra. The daughters of ascetic sages Shandilya and Gargya were also devoted to celibacy.

Some Prominent Hermitages (Ashramas)

Prayag

The Bhardwaj Ashrama which was an educational centre, was situated near the confluence of the rivers Ganga and Yamuna. In this hermitage Bhardwaj had accorded glorious reception to king Bharat and had got constructed for the purpose, a huge building for the King and out houses for his attendants and retinue. The fact that all this work was completed within the shortest possible time shows that the ascetic Bhardwaj was very popular and highly revered by the people of the adjoining places.

Ayodhya

Ayodhya was in those days a very renowned centre of Brahmanical education. There was an assembly of Brahmcharis, knows as 'Mekhil Mahasangh', which had once congregated before the king for mooting questions pertaining to common life. There is also the mention of an assembly of women known as 'Vadhu Sangh' which helped in the cultural upliftment of women. There were in the town, several student hostels which were called Ashramas of Awsath. The citizens of the town also attended religious discourses at these hostels. Several other educational institutions had been established by the people who themselves managed their affairs. Besides this there was a dramatic association of the people, which organised cultural functions in suitable nearby places.

Namish

The famous hermitage of the Ascetic sage Shaunik was situated in the Naimish forest. Thousands of disciples lived here and Shaunik was called the Kulpati or Patrarch. At Naimisharanya, the holy spot of Pilgrimage, sage Naimish performed a twelve year Yajna (a religious ceremony) to which he invited all the learned wise men.

The main items on the agenda of the ceremony were religions, lectures and discourses, etc.

The Hermitage of Kanva

There were a number of small hermitages along the banks of the Malini. Kanva was sole in authority over these. The whole environment of the jungle tract around the Malini used to be odoriferous with the blazes of the sacrificial altar and resonant with the chantings of the Veda Mantras. In these hermitages there lived eminent scholars of the Vedas, jurisprudence, philosophy, Smritis, grammar, etc.

The Hermiages of Vansishta and Vishwamitra

These hermitage have been mentioned but details and particulars cannot be found.

The Hermitage of the Sage Vyas

A few of the disciples of the great sage Vedavyas, like Suman, Vaishampayan and Jaimin were renowned for their erudition.

The Students in Hermitages

These epics contain accounts of students who were paragons of scholarship and were renowned for their achievements. Ved, Aruni and Upmanyu the chief of the disciples of Sage Dhaomya, are particularly mentioned in these epics. Aruni was known for his unparalleled devotion to the preceptor. Uttank, the disciple of Veda, has set before the world a unique example of teacher worship and established the importance of the teacher by the manner in which he tried to collect ' Dakshina' (honorarium) for his preceptor facing all sorts of extreme hardships. Kach had refused to marry Devyani, the daughter of his preceptor so that the holy relationship between the preceptor and the pupil may remain unsullied.

Grammatical Literature

Pannini and Patanjali are the two great names to be reckoned with in the field of grammatical literature. These Indian grammarians have in their discussion of the language and literature of those times shed ample light on the social econditions as well. Hence we get to know a great deal about the condition of education from this grammatical literature. We give below the pattern of education that emerges from the piecing together of these particulars.

Methods of Teaching

On the basis of the Sutras of Panini it may be said that the teaching of the Vedas was usually oral and the students had to memorise the lesson. The students were divided into categories according to the number of mistakes they committed in pronouncing the Mantras. Thus a student who committed one blunder was called 'Ekanvik'. This shows that the method of oral examination was in vogue.

There were some subjects to master which memorising was not sufficient and detailed expositions were necessary. Panini's grammar itself was such a subject. Although the need of understanding a subject for mastering it was accepted, yet memorising was the usual practice. Yask has emphasised the need of understanding in his Nirukta of Vedas, "Those who can simply pronounce or chant the Vedas are like carriers of burden. But he who understands the Vedas escapes from evil deeds and he ensures his happiness both in the mundane and ultramundane existence".

The Teacher and the Taught

According to the views of Panini and Patanjali the education of a student commenced after the Upanayana. They agree in their general ideas about the teachers, but there is a slight difference in their external descriptions. According to Panini the preceptors were all too zealous to educate their pupils to be good teachers whereas Patanjali opines that the pure duty and concern of the preceptors was to liberate the students from all evils. Whatever may be the case, both the grammarians agree on the point that the relation between the teacher and the taught was very close. Usually the pupils lived with their preceptors, but there were some day-scholars also who used to go every day to the preceptor's house from their own residence. As in the Vedic age the pupils often arranged for their meals through alms-begging. A staff and a bowl was still the symbol of their pupilship. In regard to the methods of teaching and learning the old system prevailed. The preceptor holding 'Kush' or grass in his hand commenced the lesson with all concentration on an auspicious day. The pupils worked laboriously and with clean bodies and with great attention they listened to the lectures of the preceptor. Most of the students spent their time in deep self-study. Modern facilities like lights were not available. As such the students studied during the night in the light kindled by burning cowdung cakes. Those students who were not laborious enough could not continue their studies. Quite a few students discontinued their studies for sundry reasons, like the rigorous discipline or the strict supervision of the preceptor. Such students were regarded as condemnable and were dubbed with abominable epithets like 'Khatvarurh'[1]. Students who changed over from one preceptor to another became the butt of ridicule and were called 'Tirth-kak"[2]. Thus discharging their obligations the teachers and the students remained busy in the work of teaching and learning.

Categories of Teachers

In the grammatical literature teachers have been put into different categories according to their qualifications and have been given different epithets :-

Acharya

Those who were profound scholars and original thinkers.

Guru, Shikashak and Upadhyana

Those who had similar qualifications and ways of thinking.

Brahmvadin

Those who remained busy with expositions and commentaries of religious literature.

Parivrajak

Those who in the last stages of their lives went about teaching and helping the expansion of education.

Parivarjak teachers were divided into two categories :

1. Those who remained aloof from human society were called 'Aranyak'.
2. Those who moved about with the villagers were called 'Naiktik'.

Panini has included in the category of Acharyas some of those teachers whose commentaries had generated new ideas and their disciples propagated those ideas. Among these Vashampayan and Kalap are worth-mentioning. All the above mentioned teachers had established their own hermitages.

Subject of Study

In the time of Panini ethical and religious literature covered a wide scope and was divided into the following four categories :-

1. That literature which was based on personal experience or which contained such matter as was realised through self-contemplation. This literature was called 'Drishtam' and Samveda was its glorious example.
2. That literature which was composed of the utterances of ascetic sages and learned scholars and which took the form of 'Sruti' was called 'Proktam literature' and included Kalp or that part of the Veda which treated rituals and sacred performances, and prosody etc.
3. The third type of literature was that which incorporated new findings, investigations and explorations. Kashakritsna's and Apishali's works are included in this category.
4. The fourth type of literature consisted of stories and narratives etc. for the commonality. Differentiating between legened and a story or narrative, Patanjali held that a legned was one which contained descriptions of the life of historical personages, whereas the characters of a story were usually imaginary or fictitious. Shishukandriya, Vasavdatt, Yam-Sabhiye and Sumanottar are placed in this category.

Besides these four types, there grew at that time a huge critical literature comprising of explanatory commentaries etc.

Along with religious and ethical literature there developed some materialistic literature also. Texts like 'Gaolakshnik', 'Bapas Vidhik', 'Ashwalaakshnik', etc. were written during this period.

Education of the Masses

In the time of Patanjail education of the masses was given a fillip by the development of the literature of the people. This was the period when history, Puranas, legends, stories and fables and dramas were written. The Ramayana and the Mahabharata with their mellifluous verses did not find much favour with the public. Even Patanjali himself had a discussion with a charioteer 'Soot' who gave an authoritative description of the plain and rarified form of words. The fact that an ordinary charioteer was allowed to enter into discussion with the great grammarian who was the very epitome of an age proves that education was prevalent among the masses.

Female Education

Although the texts of grammar do not give much information about female education, nevertheless Patanjali's 'Shakktiki' proves that there were women who used arms. Panini has also given a description of the women of the Vedic age. 'Bal Manorama' gives an account of women who were highly learned in the Vedas. The words 'Upadhyayi' and 'Upadhyana' used in 'Vartik' also suggest the prevalence of female education.

Specialised Education

The appearance of the work 'Natya' in grammatical literature is suggestive of dramatic literature and dramaturgy. Patanjali has mentioned some specialists of musical instruments viz. the Mridang players[3]. Particular words like 'Kathavachak', narrators of religious or other texts or stories, also indicate the prevalence of specialised studies. We get ample proofs about the prevalence of this system in the age of Sutras but on the basis of the above facts it can be affirmed that this system continued in this period also.

The Arthshastra of Kautilya

The Arthashastra of Kautilya gives a brief but vivid account of the educational system of the age of Sutras. A brief description of the facts gleaned from the Arthshastra is given below.

Duties of Students

The students must have in them a genuine love of knowledge and they should thoroughly understand and absorb the lesson given by the preceptor. They should remember the lessons, contemplate upon them and have critical discussions. The students should have unflinching faith in truth and should never shun service to the preceptor. According to Kautilya only students with this ethical and mental background could derive real benefit from the preceptor's teachings. Students devoid of these virtues could not possibly gain knowledge. These duties as detailed in the Arthshastra were similar to those of the Brahmacharis of old.

Primary Education

Primary education commenced after the tonsure ceremony. The Arthshastra mentions a few new subjects of primary education, like writing and arithmetic which were taken up in the very beginning. Real education started after the Upanayana.

Specialised Education

We have in the Arthshastra evidences of the system of specialised education of the Sutra age. Kautilya has mentioned Parashar, Katyayan, Bhardwaj, etc.as great masters of the science of economics. There is evidence also of the prevalence of several branches of economics viz. Parashar, Varhaspatya, Manava etc. even long before the Arthshastra of Kautilya.

Education of Royal Princes

According to the Dharamsutras, the age for Upanayana for the Kshatriyas was 11 years. The princes had to study only for six or seven years and thereafter enter the household stage at the age of sixteen. Obviously they could not have been given complete knowledge of vedic or philosophical subjects. Kautilya divided knowledge into four divisions :

1. Anveekshiki - Knowledge of philosophical subjects as also of those requiring deep contemplation.
2. Trayee - Knowledge of the three Veda (Rig, Sam and Yajur) and the six vedangas.
3. Varta - Knowledge of commerce, animal husbandry, agriculture and other vocational subjects.
4. Dand-Niti - knowledge of all the necessary things connected with the governance of a country.

The Royal princes had to gain education in Anveekshiki and Trayee also but Dand Niti and Varta had special importance for them.

Besides religious education the princes gained practical knowledge from able officers of the state about the land, commerce, animal husbandry, and agriculture. Thereafter they were educated in the subject.

The princes had to continue their studies even after their marriage and after having attained the age of 15. In the forenoon they had to take military training which included elephant and horse-riding and knowledge about the four divisions of the army. After midday they listened to lectures connected with history delivered by efficient scholars. History included subjects like Dharmshastra, economics, Puranas, exemplifications, stories, legends, etc.

Military Training to Women

Kautilya has emphasised that when the king gets up from bed early in the morning he should be greeted by women archers. In Kalidas' drama Shakuntala, the greek woman Sharghast makes her entry. The practice of having Greek women as bodyguards of the king prevailed for a very long time. Megasthenes has also mentioned such a woman bodyguard of Chandragupta who apart from carrying arms possessed great physical prowess. It is evident from this that at the time of the composition of the Arthshastra women were given military training.

Summary

The systems prevalent in the field of education of which we get some traces in the Epics, Grammar and Kautilya Arthashastra are briefly discussed below.

System of Education

Generally the education was oral. Some subjects needed analysis for proper understanding. Special emphasis was laid on the proper understanding of the subject. Writing and arithmetic were specially learnt at the primary stage of education.

Teacher

It was the duty of the teacher to prepare his disciples for teaching. Students lived in large numbers at the residence of the teacher. He regarded them as members of his own family. Some teachers were highly learned thinkers, while some were specially qualified in the analysis of religious literatures. Some teachers imported education by travelling from one place to another.

Students

The prescribed signs of a student were a Danda and a Kamandal. Students arranged their food by begging alms and laboured hard at the end of their educational career to pay Guru Dakshina. The students were devoted whole-heartedly to their studies and paid due respect to their teachers. They had a thirst for knowledge, capability of understanding a subject and keeping it in memory, power of thinking and unshakable devotion to their teachers. The students who travelled to many Guru Ashramas and suspended their studies due to disciplinary problems were not respected.

Education of Brahmans

Brahmans alone had the right of being Acharyas, so it was essential for them to be highly qualified. The reason was that they lived with the Acharya under Brahmacharya and were devoted to their studies. Expect the daily routine they served their teachers as well. The students finished their education following the rules of Ashrama up to the age of 25 years and after paying due Guru Dakshina.

Education of Kshatriya

The age of Upanayana for Kshattriya was 11 and that of entrance to domestic life was 6 years. Therefore they studied military science, Puran, history, the art of government and economics.

Military Education

Military education included archery, use of sword, fighting from a chariot, etc. Dronacharya and Bhishma turned their disciples into skilled men in war.

Mass Education

Stories, dramas, history and Puran, etc. are evidence of mass-education. The discussions of the famous grammarian Panini with a chariot-driver is testimony to this.

Subject of Study

Ved, Vedanga, Srutis, history, Puran, Vartik and other worldly literatures were the subjects of study.

Specialised Study

Parasar, Katyayana, Bhardwaj, etc. were the specialists of economics. The word 'Natya' indicates the specialists of drama present at the time. Patanjali has mentioned some specialists in instrumental music.

Women's Education

Shabari, Suloma, Sandilya and the daughter of Saint Gargi were learned and highly cultured. The word Upadhyani and Upadhyaya used for them clearly indicates the education prevalent in women. Military education was also imparted to women. The women-guards of kings were skilled in the art of weilding arms.

Main Ashram

Prayag - here saint Bharadwaj imparted education. He was highly respected in society. Ayodhya - Here we find many ashramas. Students from far and wide resided here and received education.

Naimish

Thousands of Brahmacharis lived here. Saint Shaunak performed the grand Yajna. Vashishtha, Vishwamitra, Kanva and Vyas' Ashramas were the main seats of learning.

Notes and Reference

1. Wicked.
2. Greedy crow.
3. A musical instrument of the tom-tom family.

Exercises

1. What was the nature of military education during the epic period in India ?
2. Describe the nature of the education of the Kshatriyas as given in the Epics, grammatical literature and Arthshastra.
3. We have evidences of the system of specialised education in the epics of the time. Explain
4. "During the epic period there was enough development of subjects pertaining to mundane affairs" - Discuss.

Chapter 6

General Features of Buddhist Education

Introduction

Buddhism

Hinduism, based on the religion of the Vedas, had become badly tranished with a lot of blemishes and shortcomings Buddhism arose as a sort of reaction against these defects, and as such it cannot be called a totally new religion. We find in Buddhism only a transmuted form of Hinduism. Even before Lord Buddha, Indian transcendentalism had appeared to be gradually leaning towards Buddhism. Those good souls who could not derive any inner satisfaction from Vedic ritualism brought the Upanishads into existence through deep self-contemplation. In the system of spiritual contemplation adumbrated by the Upanishads, the illusory nature of the world was fully brought out and the necessity of deep self-knowledge was greatly emphasised. Buddhism also had at its root the ephemerality and delusiveness of the mundane world.

Even in the Upanishads doubts had been expressed with regard to the efficacy of penance and sacrifices and in Buddhism also greater emphasis was given to spiritual knowledge in comparison with banal externalism and formalism. The only difference was that the pursuit of spiritual knowledge as described in the Upanishads, remained confined to the ascetics while through Buddhism it became feasible for the common man. Both the religions treat in a similar manner the concept of soul, sorrow, rebirth and salvation. In order to make people understand and realise these things Buddha made efforts to apprise them of the cause of sorrow in human life and gave them tangible ways of riddance from suffering, instead of discussing abstract metaphysical problems. The problem of Salvation had equal importance in Hiduism also, but Lord Buddha dealt with the ways and means of its attainment from a new angle. According to this method desire or avarice, worldly attachment and sorrow or suffering can be got rid of and knowledge, wisdom, mental peace and tranquillity and finally Nirvana or salvation can be attained. The basic tenets of Buddhism are concerned with this idea. For Buddha mundane existence was full of sorrow and suffering, and regarding ignorance as the root cause of all, he suggested ways and means of getting rid of these. Ignorance implied absence of true knowledge which the Upanishads also called delusory or spurious knowledge and regarded it as the root cause of all suffering. Due to the lack of real knowledge man remains subjected to the tendency of birth and he does not get redemption from the wheel of birth and rebirth.

Nirvana is attainable after the purgation of sorrows. Nirvana, however, does not suggest or imply the ending of life, because, as it transpires from his discourses, Buddha attained it even in his life time.

The Buddha had shown a way of purging sorrow and it was called the way of Nirvana. This way of Nirvana has been popularised as the Eightfold path in Buddhism. The following eight ways make the path of redemption easy and feasible both to the ascetic and the householder :-

1. Samma Ditthi	Right Views
2. Samma Sankalp	Right Intentions
3. Samma Vacha	Right Speech
4. Samma Kamant	Right Conduct
5. Samma Ajeet	Right Living
6. Samma Vyayam	Right Effort
7. Samma Sati	Right Mindedness
8. Samma Samadhi	Right Meditation.

In this manner Lord Buddha evolved a path for the common man which neither entailed discipline nor was it too difficult to traverse and anyone could attain Nirvana. Loard Buddha regarded the established practices of Hindu religion, viz. Vedic Mantras, worship of gods and goddesses, sacrifices, rigorous penance etc. as useless for the purpose of Nirvana or salvation. Hindu transcendentalism which was flourishing away from the common life in the lonely forests was thus made feasible for the common man. A new light shone upon the world and the whole Universe became bathed with this effulgence. This was a great gift from Lord Buddha to the woe-begone humanity.

The Buddhist and Brahmanical System of Education

Similarities and Affinities

The basic concepts of education were alike in the two systems. The centres of Buddhist education were also in peaceful surroundings far away from human habitations . Like the Brahmcharis of the Brahmanical system there were groups of Buddhist monks and their daily routines were more or less similar. It was the prime duty of both the Brahmacharis and the monks to go about begging for alms. For both there were strict laws against violence so much so that they were not allowed to go out during the rainy season or walk on the tilled fields. The rules of conduct were practically the same for both although certain modifications had been made . If in the Brahmanical system the Brahmacharis constituted a group of those who, following the rules of celibacy, dedicated their lives to the attainment of knowledge, the monks of the Buddhist system abnegating household life dedicated themselves to the attainment of salvation which required deep and real knowledge.

Differences

The prime difference between the two systems was that Brahmanical education had a sort of domestic aspect and was gained at the residence of the preceptor, whereas Buddhist education was gained in well-organised monasteries. The Buddhist educational institutions were well organised. Domestic life was an essential aspect of Brahmanical education, but in the Buddhist system all domestic ties had to be severed and the 'Bandhu Samaj' based on religion had to be established. In the first, greater emphasis was laid on the individual whereas in the second it was on the group.

The second main difference was that in the Brahmaincal system enjoyment of all the means of comfort and pleasure was tabooed for the pupil who had to cultivate strict mental and bodily discipline. Thus in this system student life was itself a severe penance. Contrary to this in the Buddhist system bodily adornment, cleanliness, regular meals, etc. were not forbidden, in fact the use of these was recommended. There was arrangement for medical treatment of the ailing students by expert physicians. The ideal of the Brahmanical system that "the lover of pleasures cannot get pleasures" was not fully accepted in the Buddhist system.

The third difference was regarding principles. The Brahmanical education was basically individualistic, whereas the Buddhist was democratic. This can be better explained by saying that whereas in the Brahmanical system the supremacy and dignity of the preceptor obtained all through life, in the Buddhist the students after entering a Sangh acquired a say in its affairs and the only difference between the preceptor and the pupil was of the level of spiritual knowledge. Thus there was a difference between the two systems in spite of some similarites.

The democratic system of the Buddhist Sanghs was later on abused and the inner atmosphere of the Sanghs became vitiated. The Sanghs began to deteriorate due to the absence of any organising and centralising authority and gradually the Buddhist religion itself began to lose ground in its birth place. The Brahman scholars like Sankaracharya and Madhavacharya once again attempted to re-establish the old system.

The Basic Organisation of Education

The Background

Buddhist religion evolved in the form of Sanghs which became the prominent centres of education. Buddhist education had no independent existence apart from the Sangh because it was concerned only with these Sanghs. In the Buddhist system religious and secular education was given only to the recluse members of the sangh and not to others. The Vedic education had evolved with the system of religious ceremonies (Yajna) and in Buddhist system, the Sangh took the place of oblations.

Hence, the system of Buddhist Sanghs incorporates in itself the educational system, because the practices and regulations of both were similar. We can determine the form of Buddhist education from these principles and practices.

Entry into the Sangh

There were rules similar to those of the previous system, for the student's entry into the Sangh. Like the Brahmachari the Buddhist monk had to go to the preceptor with the supplication that he may be taken under his tutelage. In the Buddghist Sangh the student was concerned with the preceptor and not with the monks of the Sangh. The preceptor had the full responsibility on himself in regard to the student, the Sangh had nothing to do with him. Thus, even in this system we find the presence of a personal relationship between the preceptor and the pupil.

Pubbja - Renunciation

The word Pubbja implies going out or renouncing. The future monk, according to this practice, renouncing all the family connection joined the Buddhist Sangh. Persons of all castes had the right to join these Sanghs and after joining all became one or had no caste. Even their previous clothes and general features changed. But usually persons of high caste only could join these. The future monks had to be not less than 8 years old. After receiving education in the Sangh from the age of 8 till the age of 12 a monk went through the 'Upsampda' ceremony at the age of 20. After this he became a full-fledged member of the Sangh.

The 8-year-old future monk went of his own accord, with his head shaved and yellow clothes in his hands either to some monastery or to some prominent monk and offering himself at his feet solicited entry into the 'Sangh'.

The monk made the future boy monk put on the yellow dress and asked him to take and pronounce loudly the three vows- 'I put myself under the protection of the Buddha', 'I put myself under the protection of Dharma', 'I put myself under the protection of the Sangh'. The monks after thus going through the 'Pubbja' ceremony were called 'Samner' and were thereafter given the following ten commandments :-

1. Don't destroy life.

2. Refrain from bad conduct.
3. Never speak a lie.
4. Don't eat at an inappropriate time.
5. Don't use intoxicants.
6. Don't speak ill of any one.
7. Don't use cosmetics, etc.
8. Avoid dance-shows, etc.
9. Don't take anything unless it is offered to you.
10. Don't accept costly things of gold and silver, etc. in alms.

These ten commandments were called 'Dassikkha Padani' and the Samner were duty-bound to adhere to them. The preceptor had upon him the full responsibility of the Samner, till he attained the age of twenty. It must be remembered that the child was admitted into the Sangh only with the permission of his parents and that those who suffered from any contagious diseases like leprosy, tuberculosis, scabies etc. or those who were slaves, officers of the state or soldiers, etc. were refused admission.

Upsampda

The Upsampda ceremony was performed in a different manner from that of Pubbja. The samner or Sraman (monk) after having devoted himself fully to his studies for twelve years and having attained the age of twenty presented himself before an assembly of all the monks of the Sangh. The Upsampds ceremony was based on group-consideration and only a unanimous decision or the favour of the majority enabled a monk to become a permanent life member of the Sangh. After the Upsampda ceremony the Sraman became a full-fledged monk and thereafter he had no connection whatsoever with his family or with the shackles of worldly life.

This was the main and essential difference between the two systems of education. In the Brahmanical system the Brahmachari returned home after completing their education and entered domestic life generally at the age of twenty-five. There were, of course, some students who remained Brahmacharis all their life. These were called 'Naishthik', but their number was very small. Contrary to this in the Buddhist system the monks did not return home after the completion of their studies but became permanent members of the Sangh and spent their lives as monks totally detached from worldly affairs.

Duties of the Preceptor

Both the preceptor and the pupil depended upon the sangh. The duties of the preceptor, who had upon him the entire responsibility of the pupil, were chalked out by the Sangh. It was enjoined upon the preceptor to educate his students like his own sons and to provide them with all the necessities of daily life, many be a bowl for alms-begging or clothes, etc. The preceptor also had to look to the physical development of his pupils and to tend the ailing students till they had completely recovered. In regard to the mental development of the pupils, the preceptor helped them gain wide and profound knowledge by means of his lectures, etc.

The Daily Routine of Students

The students rendered services to the preceptor, because this was an essential part of their education. The daily routine of the student was completed by discharging various duties. Getting up early in the morning the students made all the arrangements for the guru to attend to the daily chores. Cooking the food was also a part of their duty. The preceptor took his meal first and then the student washed his utensils and brought to him his alms-bowl, dress, etc. to go and beg for alms. If the preceptor permitted, the students also accompanied him.

The student had to return to the monastery earlier than the preceptor in order to make arrangements for his refreshment and retirement to bed. The student also prepared meals as desired by the preceptor and after taking his own bath arranged for hot or cold water as also a mud-plaster for him if he so desired.

If the preceptor asked him (the student), he got ready for a lesson. According to the prevailing custom the student put questions to the preceptor and the preceptor in reply gave him instructions. Apart from personal services to the preceptor, the student also looked to the cleanliness of the preceptor's residence, arrangement of things and the management of the kitchen. The student was completely under the control of the preceptor, he could not go out without the latter's permission. He could not accept anybody's service nor was he duty-bound to obey anyone else.

Preceptor-Pupil Relation

The relation between the preceptor and the pupil in the monastery was based on principles of love and equality. Each had his prescribed and well-defined duties which were discharged well and each remained attached to the other. The life of the preceptor was one of extreme simplicity and their wants were limited. The students who neglected their duties towards the preceptors were expelled from the monastery. But along with this the preceptor in order to obtain reverence from the students had to be men of great erudition, high character, and capable of exercising self-discipline.

The student on account of the deep personal contact could easily gauge the mental capacity of the preceptor. The student tried to redress the mental afflictions of the preceptor by means of religious conversations or in some other way. He also tried to rectify the wrong religious convictions of the preceptor. If the preceptor did anything in violation of the dignity of the monastery, it was the duty of students to bring it to the notice of the members of the Sangh and to ask for a proper punishment for the defaulter. It was also the duty of the students to demand the reinstatement of the preceptor after his expulsion as also to make efforts for desirable changes in his behaviour.

Thus the relation between the teacher and the taught was one of equality. The student had to serve the preceptor, afford him mental peace, and work for his reformation if there was a need. On the other hand, the preceptor was responsible for the physical, moral, intellectual and spiritual development of the pupil.

Nishkasan[1]

There were definite conditions under which the pupils had to leave the monastery. The preceptor had the power to expel a student when he realised that the student did not have the right regard, reverence and devotion for him. He could remove him from his discipleship. Besides, there were some other conditions also like the death of the preceptor, or embracing another religion, or leaving the Sangh or taking to household life, under which the education of the pupil was supposed to have ended and he had to quit the Sangh.

Number of Students and their Residences

In the Buddhist system a monk took upon himself the work of teaching one future monk, but Lord Buddha had permitted able and competent preceptors to take under them more students. The Sanghs were organised out of the cloisters and monasteries. In the monasteries students and preceptors lived together. Usually in fair weather the Buddhist monks lived under the trees or in the caves, but during rains or snowfall or other inclemencies of the weather they were permitted to live in the monasteries. The huge buildings which housed the monasteries were constructed either by the kings or by wealthy persons. In some buildings there was management for the residence of thousands of students. The ruins of the Nalanda university bear eloquent testimony to this. In the monasteries there were separate rooms for sleeping, dining, bathing, study, conversation, literary affairs, and for the reception of guests. There was such an arrangement in the Tetvan monastery constructed by prince Anaath Pindak.

These monasteries did not serve only a religious purpose, they were also centres of Buddhist education where education in fine arts and physical sciences, etc. was given. Along with the descriptions of universities we get accounts of separate student hostels.

Methods of Teaching

In Buddhist education great emphasis was laid on purity of conduct. For the development of the individual self a high mental and moral level was quite natural and with complete self-development it was possible to attain the state Bodhi-sattva. In primary education religious subjects were taught. Probably the students memorised the lessons by hearing them and repeating them to one another. Education in morality was also essential. They were acquainted with all the essential ingredients of religion by means of instruction in various systems of religious thoughts. The students delved deep into religious thoughts by entering into discussions with one another and thus equipped themselves for the future role of religious teachers.

The ways of education differed. There were those monks who lived in lonely sequestered places and devoted themselves to contemplation and tried to gain the highest knowledge by means of devotion and penance. Just the reverse of these were those monks who had a strong instinct for worldly life and they attached more importance to the study of physical sciences as also to the development of physical power. These two different types of monks lived separately so that they caused no hindrance to one another.

In the following pages are described the common methods of teaching in the Buddhist system.

Oral

The art of writing had become common by the time of Lord Buddha, but the method of oral instruction still continued in the field of education. This might have been due to the paucity or non-availability of writing materials.

In the Brahmanical system it was forbidden to write down the Vedic Mantras for it was against the religion, but in Buddhist system it was permitted to learn the art of writing[2], and to make it a means of livelihood[3].

Buddhism was a new religion, and it was necessary to propagate it, but successful propagation depended on the propagator's knowledge and answers. Lecture and argumentation had a significant place in Buddhism. Mutual argumentation and debate had a particular importance of its own in the scheme of higher education because it enabled the Buddhist monks to score over the Brahman ascetics and other religious thinkers in religious affray and thus impress the common people. Besides this they had to be proficient in the art of discussion in order to convince and satisfy through arguments those followers of Buddhism who had certain doubts. The effect of this, in the long run, was that the scholars became so fond of arguing and discussing things that they began to argue for the sake of argument only. In Buddhist literature, however, rules for such discussion are laid down[4]. Discussion should take place on some useful topic at a proper and suitable place like an assembly of learned people, royal palace or Parishad, etc. For subjects the following are mentioned:

1. Doctrine of Theory	'Sidhant'
2. Grounds or Theleology	'Hetu'
3. Citation or Exemplification	'Udaharan'
4. Parallelisms	'Sadharmya'
5. Heresies	'Vaidharmya'

6. Cognizable and tangible — 'Pratyaksh'
7. Inferences or analogies — 'Anumaan'
8. The Vedas or Tantras or Science of Futurity. — 'Aagam'

Illustrations and proofs were essential. The debater was to have a thorough knowledge of his subject and the capacity of expressing his view-point explicitly and in such a tone as to attract the ear of the listeners. Buddha had adopted the language of daily intercourse for his discourses. Hence efforts were made for the expansion of the regional languages. Sanskrit was not accorded any place in Buddhist education. The local languages of those days gained currency outside India along with the Buddhist religion which expanded there. Due to the preponderance of argumentation and non-availability of writing materials, Buddhist education remained oral.

Vidwat Sabha[5]

Morality was regarded as a part of education. The organisation of Vidwat Sabha in Buddhism was a means of moral education because in bi-monthly meetings of this organisations the monks of different Sanghs had to present their misconducts and misdeeds. It was essential for the monks to attend the Vidwat Sabha. Sometimes even an invalid monk was brought into the midst of the Sabha. If he was not able to come even in this position, the meeting of the Sabha was held at his place so that he could confess his wrongs if he had committed any, before all and there may also be evidence of his presence in the meeting: the meetings were convened on Poornmasi[6] and Pratipada[7] days. In these meetings only individual misdeeds were considered. Group misconduct was considered by learned people in other fields. Besides this there was arrangement for an annual meeting of the yearly Sabha where revered monks challenged the Sangh to inculpate them if it could. In this way Vidwat Sabha had great importance in the field of moral education.

Ekant Sadhana (Lonely Meditation)

Great religious importance was attached to the method of secluded living, contemplation and realisation of the Brahman ascetic. The Buddhist monks also lived, contemplated and meditated in solitary places but this was different from the way of the Brahman ascetics. These monks lived at such places from where they did not have to go begging for alms and from where they could render service to other monks who passed that way. It is worth noting that only those monks lived in secluded forests or caves and engaged themselves in spiritual contemplation who were desirous of getting rid of the obligations of the Sanghs or had lost all attachment with the world. For such a life only those were suitable who had gained experience in this kind of life by residing in the Sangh for quite some time. To some extent secluded living in a sequestered place was the only means of freeing oneself from the shackles of worldly ties.

Education of the Masses

As a matter of fact the Sangh was meant for those Buddhist monks who had renounced domestic life. These constituted its permanent members and the Sangh worked for their education only. There was no arrangement for the education of the Buddhist householder, however, the Sangh realised and discharged its responsibility to acquaint other followers of Buddhism also with the religious tenets and practices. The Sandh could not neglect such Buddhists because it was through the munificence of these householders that the daily physical needs of the monks were fulfilled. It was the duty of these monks to look to the education of the householders, and when they went about begging for alms they talked with them on religious subjects, disabused their minds of the doubts and misconceptions and thus kept alight the torch of faith. It is mentioned that king Bimbsar had instructed the residents of eighty thousand villages of his kingdom to adopt the teachings of Lord Buddha. But there was absolutely no arrangement by the Sangh for the primary education of the children of the householders and probably even the followers of Buddhism went to other educational institutions for their elementary education.

Below are given some facts relating to the education of the masses, as gleaned from the Jatakas.

1. In the Buddhist system religious education was given to the householders also in addition to the monks.
2. As in the Brahmanical system, Buddhist education was given outside the Sangh by Buddhist 'Sramans' in their own hermitages.
3. The two systems of education instead of being opposed, were

rather complementary to each other.

4. In the Brahmanical system after the age of Sutras, the honorarium had to be given to the preceptor before the commencement of education. This was the practice in the Buddhist system also.

According to Milind Panh, .the subjects of the Brahmanical and Buddhist education were as follows.

Subjects of Buddhist Education

1. Buddhist literature (Religious)
2. Practical knowledge of the constitution of the Vihars or Monasteries.
3. Maintaining of accounts of the charitable receipts to the monasteries.

Subjects of Brahmanical Education

The four Vedas, Puranas, history, grammar, versification, rhetorics, prosody, Vedant, sounds of animals, seismology, knowledge of omens and portents, Sankhya, Nayay Vaisheshik, systems of philosophy, science of Yoga, Music, Mantra, science of war, etc.

The Jatakas contain several facts about the contemporary condition of general and higher education at big educational institutions and these are reproduced below.

1. There were many such institutions in India where students from foreign countries came for their education. Of these Taxila was the most important, because the teachers here were very learned scholars who were renowned all over India. They were masters of their subjects. Thus from the educational point of view Taxila had great importance in the country.
2. Students came to Taxila for specialised studies after their primary education. Education here started at the age sixteen. Even in modern times students began their university education at this age.
3. Intelligent but destitute students were given financial aid by the state to prosecute their studies. Several students went along with the royal princes and their expenses were met by the State.
4. Tuition fees which amounted to one thousand current coins had to be paid up before the commencement of education. Those who were unable to pay the fees in cash had to do so through

physical labour and often students were given the option to pay the fees after completing their studies. The expenses of students who were totally incapable of paying the fees were met from the charity fund. The fees and charities, it must be remembered were not realised as remuneration for the preceptors but for the running of the institution which included the expenses over the messing, etc. of the students.

5. Usually the students lived with the preceptor and were educated by him, but it is also mentioned that even the outsiders who had married and were leading a family life were not forbidden from getting education. They were regarded as external students. This system obtained at that time when the preceptor got his daughter married to any of his good and competent students. Such students had the freedom to carry on their studies in the manner they liked.
6. A senior preceptor took upon himself the task of educating five hundred students with the help of some assistant preceptors who were called 'Pitthava Acharyas'. These assistants used to be appointed from amongst the bright and competent students. Some senior students used to educate other juniors even without being appointed as assistants.
7. On account of the different ways of paying the tuition fees, students who could not pay the fees had to work for the whole day and read in the night. Thus, the convenience of the students was always taken into account and arrangement for studies both in the day and in the night were made.
8. Higher education included particularly the study of literary and scientific subjects. Religious literature was included in literary subjects. The scientific subjects which are mentioned in the Jatakas were -

1. Magical and mystical formulas.
2. Huntsmanship.
3. Archery.
4. Medicine.
5. Sexual science.
6. Knowledge of the sounds of animals.
7. Hathi sutra.
8. The art of restoring a dead body to life.

It is to be remembered that this scientific and vocational education had its practical application also. In medical sciences, practical education was given and there were practical tests for these.

9, Books were also taught in these educational institution and the art of writing was also practised.The Jatakas mention that the religious text relating to Bodhisatva was given a finished written form and that the teachings were read from the book. This gives us an idea about the prevalence of the art of writing at that time.
10. The same kind of life was led by all the students whether they paid the tuition fees or not. Even the royal princes had to live like other common students. In the Taxila university there was no distinction between the high and low and everyone got the same kind of clothes, food, etc. The rules of the institution were alike for the royal princes and the students who did manual work. Nobody could possess and enjoy personal assets.
11. There were some who were not satiated mentally even after receiving higher education. Such students migrated to the forest and put themselves under some renowned ascetic and living in his hermitage dedicated their lives to the quest of the enternal truth. In some of the hermitages there were as many as five hundred such ascetic students. The hermitages were situated near human habitations also.

Monasteries

Monasteries formed the nucleus of the Buddhist educational system. The work of education was carried on by the Sanghs of the monks who lived in the monasteries. In some of the monasteries there lived as many as 1,000 monks. There were some common rules of the Sangh and the preceptors observed these and discharged their responsibilities. The new monks studied under the preceptor who had to take upon himself the responsibility of all the new entrants. Thus in the Buddhist system the small educational institutions remained under the control of a group organisation. The students were members of the bigger association and were entitled to take part in all its transactions. Hence, it can be said that unlike the Brahmancal system the Buddhist system though individualistic was, nevertheless, based on federal principles.

Female Education

Lord Buddha had not originally permitted women to join the Sanghs but later, on account of his step-mother Mahaprajapati who joined the Sangh with 500 Kshattriya women of the Shakya clan and also due to the solicitations of his dear disciple Anand he allowed the Sangh to take women also in its fold. The rules of the Sangh were very hard upon women. The women were tested for two years. They had to live separately from the monks. Although the daily routine for both was the same, yet the status of women was lower in the Sangh and they could not live alone with the preceptor. The arrangement of their education was that they were educated by one particular monk twice a month in the presence of another monk. Any woman who wanted to become a permanent nun had to obtain the agreement of all the members of the Sangh.

Such restrictions were imposed on women, nevertheless the importance of nuns in the Indian society and the Buddhist religion is self-evident. The Sangh rose in dignity and prestige due to the high spiritual knowledge and wisdom of several of the nuns. Among these nuns were generally women who had religious proclivity, but quite a few became nuns in order to get rid of the disgusting complexities of mundane existence. Several nuns form amongst these were renowned for their erudition. Sukka is worthy of mention in this context. Her religious discourses quenched the religious thirst of the people. These nuns were always ready to soothe the sorrows of the afflicted women and Nun Patchara was widely known for her benignity.

Buddhist literature does not say much in regard to the education of these nuns although there is a mention of these nuns taking upon themselves the work of educating the new entrants. This is proof in itself that there was arrangement for the education of the nuns and that these preceptor nuns must have had a through knowledge of the 'Dharm' religion of Buddha requisite for their preceptorship. Only then these nun preceptors must have been able to teach in the Sangh.

Even outside the Sangh, the women showed a strong tendency towards religion. Bisakha, Supiya, Ambpali, etc. were very religious minded and the Sangh in the propagation of the Buddhist religion and the spirit of service, friendliness and sympathy of these nuns contributed a great deal towards the mental and moral upliftment of women.

Vocational Education

The basic factor of Buddhist education was religion and the monasteries served this end. However, vocational education was not neglected at that time and it had an important place in the scheme of education. Even the monks had to learn sewing, spinning, knitting,etc. so that they could satisfy their needs with regard to their clothes. They also had to be acquainted with the science of house-building so that they could get the buildings of monasteries well - constructed. Those Buddhists who led a household life were educated in other useful vocations and crafts which helped them earn their livelihood.

Medicine :- The Ayurvedic system of medicine and surgery had advanced a great deal at that time. Charak, the father of medicine, had made his appearance in this period, while Jeevak, the son of Salvati, the royal maid-servant, was a famous physician of the time. He had studied the science of medicine for seven years at Taxila under some famous and learned teacher in medicine and returned home with the blessings of his teacher after qualifying himself at the examination. After completing his education Jeevak visited many cities and treated the ailing. He cured many irremediable diseases. We get an account of Jeevak curing a wealthy man of Rajgrih, and the son of a businessman of Kashi, by operating upon the brain and the abdomens of the patients respectively. After operating upon a particular part Jeevak used to apply an ointment which gave great relief to the wound. There are accounts in Milind Panh of other specialists in medicine like, Narad, Kapil, Angiras, Dhanvantari. The study of medicine was well planned. The students of medicine studied in a very systematic manner the causes and origin of the disease, its prognosis and diagnosis, cure and treatment, and methods of tending the sick, etc. under a competent teacher. Tuition fees was paid either in cash or through manual labour. Detailed and systematic instruction in surgery was also imparted. There was also the system of practical education in medicine. We can draw the following conclusions from the above.

1. At that time medical education was fairly advanced and consequently there were in the country numerous good and famous physicians.
2. The Vaidyas (Physicians) at that time were proficient in surgery along with medicine. They had knowledge of certain ointments and unguents which were very efficacious in healing wounds

and had great power as antiseptics.

3. Taxila was at that time the most prominent centre of medical education where there was a prescribed curriculum of studies and instruction was given in a very systematic manner and in accordance with time. The abilities and competence of the students were gauged by their success in examinations.
4. Although the remuneration of the renowned physicians was not fixed yet it was more than that of the physicians in modern times.
5. Facilities of transport for going from one place to another were not available in those days as they are today, still the renowned physicians used to go to far off places to treat complicated diseases.
6. The study of medicine was very systematic and well organised and the method of inparting practical education in medicine was also in vogue.
7. Treatment of snake-bite was also known. Other useful arts and crafts in which education was given were handicrafts, the science of building, arithmetic, sculpture and painting agriculture and animal husbandry, etc. The Buddha Vihars, Ṣtupas and the Buildings of Nalanda and Vikramshila universities built those days are eloquent testimonies to the achievement in the arts of painting and sculpture. In the vocational education also the preceptor-pupil relation was based on mutual love and reverence as it was in the Brahmanical system.

Summary

In order to do away with shortcomings which had cropped up in Hinduism, Buddhism developed. Buddha showed a new and easy path to the common man so that he could get relief from worldly troubles. In Buddhism we find a new way to attain salvation.

Buddhist and Brahamanic Education

Similarity

The basis of education in both the systems were the same. Buddhistic centres of learning were situated in peaceful surroundings too. In both the systems, the students developed themselves under the control of their teacher.

Difference

Unlike the Brahmanic system of education, Buddhist education was imparted either in Maths or in Viharas (monasteries). Like Brahmanic education the students in Buddhist education were not devoid of the comforts of life. The principles of Brahmanic education were centralised whereas that of the Buddhist system were decentralised.

The System and Principles of Buddhist Education

Sanghs were the centres of learning in Buddhist education. Sanghs alone had the right to impart religious and secular education to the Sarmans. There were special rules for admission in the Sangh. The relationship between the teacher and taught was personal. At the prescribed age of 8, the future Bhikshu left all the temptations of the world and was admitted to the Sangh. People from all the castes had the right to be admitted into the Sangh. The future Bhikshu wore only yellow clothes after getting his hair cut and recited the vows of 'Sharanatyam'. Later on he was called 'Samner' after the Pabbajja ceremony. The Samner had to compulsorily follow Das Sikkha Padani.

After the completion of 'Upsampada' at the age of 20, 'Samner' used to become full-fledged monks (Bhikshu') unlike that of 'Pabbajja', the system of 'Upsampada' was democratic. Having attained the requisite education and renounced all worldly ties, the monk used to lead a cloistered life.

The duties of the teachers used to be defined by the monasteries. The teacher was responsible for the pupils' education, physical development and if at all necessary, to make arrangements for the bowls for their begging. In the case of pupils, being ill, the teachers were to nurse them. With the aid of seminars and debates, the teacher used to import knowledge.

There was a prescribed daily routine for the pupils. Their duties included service towards the teacher, to make arrangement for his food, rest, etc. and to beg. Before doing anything, the permission of the teacher was solicited. The pupils used to learn by putting pertinent questions to the teachers.

The duties of the teacher and the taught were defined separately, but there was a bond of affection which placed them on an equal footing. The teacher was responsible for the well-being of the pupils. On the contravention of the prestige of the monastery, it was the duty of the pupils to get the teacher punished in a suitable manner.

Emphasis was laid on good conduct. Preliminary education was completely religious. The teaching work was conducted in convents and monasteries. The prospective monks were required to become capable of making permanent positions in the field of religion. Some monks used to meditate in isolated forests. Though the art of writing was known to them, yet oral teaching was prevalent. Seminars and debating societies were part and parcel of the contemporary educational system. Definite rules were formulated for debates. The language, used in ordinary conversations, was the medium of instruction. The conferences of the learned men were convened thrice in a month. All the monks were required to confess their immoral acts before the monastery authorities.

The touring Buddhist monks used to educate the general public (Grihasths) through religious discourses, but there wasn't any proper arrangement for the primary education of their children. Apart from religious discourses on Buddhist literature, constructive knowledge for running the monasteries was imparted. Foreign students studied in many Indian centres of learning. The state used to arrange for the education of brilliant and poor scholars. The students were educated in close communion with their teachers.

Women education was prevalent. Many learned women raised the status of their contemporary society. Though the daily routines for the monks and the nuns were more or less the same, yet some special restrictions were imposed on nuns.

In the field of professional education, medicine and surgery had an important place. Teaching facilities were also available in sculpture and painting.

Under certain conditions the teacher also had the power to expel a student. Expulsion was generally sought on the ground of bad conduct, insubordination and the lack of respect on the part of the student. A student had to leave the monastery on embracing any other religion as well.

Notes and Reference

1. Expulsion or going out.
2. Vide Mahavagg 3-5-9-9-.
3. Ibid 1,49,1
4. Saptdash Bhumi Shastra Yogachaya (Part XV).
5. The assembly of the learned people.
6. The full moon day.
7. The first day of the month according to Buddhist calendar in those days.

Exercises

1. Give a comparative account of the Buddhist and Brahmanical systems of education.
2. Narrating the duties of the preceptor and the pupil in the Buddhist education explain its effect on the educational system.
3. Describe the characteristics of the Buddhist education system.
4. What was the nature of male and female education in the Buddhist education system.
5. Give an account of any three Buddhist education centres and their importance.
6. Give a comparative account of Buddhist and Vedic education.

Chapter 7

Buddhist Education as Viewed By Chinese Travellers

With the expansion of Buddhism, the system of education naturally underwent certain changes. The study of subjects pertaining to mundane life, which was in vogue in the Brahmanical system, was taken up by the Buddhist instructions also, as it was necessary for maintaining the sway of the Sanghs. The knowledge of Vedic literature was necessary for the monks to obtain success in religious discussions and on all these depended the expansion of Buddhism. Hence, Buddhist education which was primarily religious was infected by a materialistic bias. In the beginning the Sangh arranged for the religious and moral education of the monks, but later on the monks studied both religious and secular subjects and the latter acquired great importance in the system of religious education. The main factor responsible for this material bias in Buddhist education was that the monks had obtained the sanction to leave the monastery and lead a householder's life. This became a regular practice with the passage of time and consequently the number of temporary members in the Sangh was many times more than that of the permanent ones. We have the account of King Bhartrihari leaving and then rejoining the Sangh seven times. Thus as a result of the presence of Brahmanical schools and the liberalism of the Buddhist religion, the aspect of Buddhist education began to undergo changes.

Those persons who were to lead a domestic life later on also went to the Vihar to be educated along with the Sramans and new monks. Previously, the Sangh looked to the education only of the monks who had to become members of the monasteries. The education of the masses had no place in the education of the Sangh except for the fact that the monks when on their round for alms-begging gave religious instructions to the Buddhist householders. In its developed form Buddhist education turned into a very liberal system of education.

Arrangement was made for the education of the masses and persons of all religions and castes were educated. Along with religious subjects instruction was given in subjects pertaining to mundane life and those monks who were well up in both were called 'Bahushrut', while the student who studied subjects of material life was called Brahmachari. The way of joining the Sangh was different for the children of the common people from that for the new monks. Arrangements for residence in the Viharas, for students of both the types were available.

Thus for the Buddhist Viharas the scope of service and sympathies widened a great deal and the Light of Learning and knowledge shot through these educational centres to the whole universe. But at the time of the expansion of education for the masses a new problem cropped up among the followers of the Buddhist religion. There were some such dogmatic and conservative custodians of Buddhism who did not want the slightest change in the basic principles of the religion, whereas there were others who did not want to check the growing influence of the religion upon the masses nor to neglect or desert those followers of their religion who were unable to strictly adhere to its basic tenets. Hence Buddhism split into two sects. The group of those conservatives who essayed to preserve the essential tenets verbatim came to be called 'Hinayan'. Whereas the group which favoured the co-option of the largest number was called 'Mahayan'. Later on these two branches were divided into further ramifications. The educational system of the Mahayani sect incorporated the study of numerous subjects and Pali alone did not remain the medium of instructions because Sanskrit also was now given a place. Thus there was a great deal of influence of the Brahmanical education over the later Buddhist system.

The Chinese Travellers

Three Chinese travellers came to India and travelled throughout the country. They recorded in writing their personal experiences and impressions and thus have left precious historical records of the time.

Since these accounts are based on personal observations, they are extremely veracious. All the three travellers have given descriptions of the practical form and shape of education. The accounts of these Chinese travellers, which are reproduced below, will enable one to understand the Buddhist educational system clearly.

Fa Hien

Fa Hien was the first to come to India. He came here in the 5th century B.C., travelled for fifteen years and visited about thirty regions or provinces. Everywhere he found the predominance of Buddhism. Fa Hien remained under the discipleship of the renowned Indian preceptor Kumarjiv who instructed him to study Indian culture besides Buddhism. He, therefore, studied Brahmanical literature at Patliputra. He spent six years of his travels visiting several Buddhist centres. He was so impressed and influenced by Indian culture that after his return to China a number of Chinese travellers came to this country although they had to face great ordeals.

Fa Hien has not mentioned Taxila in his accounts but it is manifest from his records that the Buddhist Sangh were at that time scattered probably all over the country and lakhs of Buddhist monks lived in these and practically all the rulers of the time were Buddhists in faith and creed. The prominent centres of education which Fa Hien has described are mentioned below :

Pataliputra

This was a prominent centure of Buddhist education at the time of Fa Hien and learned scholars taught here. About 700 monks of both the Hinayan and Mahayan sects lived in their respective Vihars. Monks came from far off distant places to receive higher education. Many Brahman Acharyas (teachers) were in the Mahayan Sect.

Shravasti

Lord Buddha lived here and gave his religious instruction for twenty-five years. Shravasti is renowned for the Jetwan Vihar. At the time of Fa Hien there had remained near Jetwan only one out of the ninety-eight Viharas, nevertheless this centre must have been an important educational centre also.

Rajgrih

The Vihar which Jivak had got constructed here was in good condition. There were also some Viharas which Bimbasar had built but the number of monks in these was not very large.

Vaishali

The Vihar which Ambpali had constructed and offered to Lord Buddha was present here intact.

Gaya

Here there were three Sangharams[1], the monks of which were strict adherents to their religion.

Kushinagar

Lord Buddha had attained Nirvana here. There were a number of monasteries which must have been centres of education.

Kanyakubja

Monks of both Hinayan and Mahayan sects lived here and they had separate monasteries.

Sankashya

Here also there lived innumerable monks and nuns of both the sects and they had separate monasteries.

Kashi

There were two Sangharams here in which innumerable monks lived.

Tamralipti

There were twenty-two monasteries and this was a renowned centre of Buddhism.

Purushpur

About seven hundred monks lived here.

Champa

Monks lived in the Buddhist Vihar of this place and it was an old Vihar.

We can get from the above an idea of the expended form of Buddhist education. A short account of the system of Buddhist education, subjects of study its organisation, etc., as described by Fa Hien is given below.

System of Education

Fa Hien found that in the whole of Northern India, barring the Eastern Frontier, the system of instruction was oral. He found in the Mahayan monasteries of Pataliputra and Tamralipi written copies of religious texts. There were arrangements for educating individuals as well as groups. The Buddhist monks met in the 'Religious Assembly' and discussed and solved various religious problems. Practically in all the Sanghs the methods of teaching were more or less similar to those of the Brahmanical system and the processes of hearing, meditation, and contemplation had great importance in the field of study. Fa Hien has also mentioned some other religious sects besides the Buddhists which, working as common organisations, made efforts for public weal but there is no account of the influence of such organisations in the field of education.

Subjects of Study

Till the time of Fa Hien Buddhist education was religious in spirit and content and the non-religious subjects had not been included. But due to the splitting up of Buddhism into two sects different educational systems were adopted. The Hinayan sect which imparted its own religious education was affected by this difference in religious thought. Fa Hien himself lived in Pataliputra for three years to study the Sanskrit language and the Brahman literature. Fa Hien himself transcribed the following books :-

1. Vinay, 2. One chapter of Parinirvan Vaipulya Sutra,

3. Sarvastivad, 4. Dhayiee Sahastra Gathaon Ka Sutra Granth, 5. Mahasandhik Abhidharm, 6. Sabhyuktabhidharm Hridaya Shastra. In all these books there was a mixture of stories and fables but Sanskrit was in vogue in practically all the Sanghs.

Organisation

Buddhist schools were held in Buddhist monasteries. In the beginning the Sangh depended upon alms for its needs and requirements, but later on the Sanghs came to be regarded as a part of society and they began to have permanent assets. These assets were collected by means of the munificence of rulers, moneyed persons and the populace. Its account were written on metal plates. Attached to the Viharas were buildings, lands, gardens, etc. and the Sangh had full rights over the total income derived from these. No ruler ever tried to usurp the property of the Sangh for it would have been regarded heinous. Some of the Sanghs had so much permanent property that there was no need for them of go for alms-begging.

Besides the permanent assets, kings and rich persons often invited the monks to dine with them and the common people also gave charity to the Sangh. A season was fixed for charity but charity was done at other times also and the Sangh accepted it. The Sangh had prescribed duties and had to work according to certain rules and regulations. Besides the religious and social work, the monks also had to do some penance and repeat the precepts.

Huan T Sang

Influenced by the Indian travels of Fa Hien, Huan T Sang began his travels in India in the seventh century A.D. Harshvardhan was the King when Huan T Sang came to India. Huan T Sang travelled practically throughout India and he had to face some hardships. Once he was looted by highwaymen. At another time when he was voyaging through Ganga he was arrested by pirates who wanted to offer him as a sacrifice, but the capriciousness of nature helped Huan T Sang escape. He gained a profound knowledge of Indian culture. He studied at Nalanda University for several years and after being awarded the degree of 'Dharmacharya - Doctor of Religion' he was appointed vice-chancellor of the university. He attempted to take to China Buddhist texts and other relics of Buddha, but several books dropped and sank into the river Indus while he was crossing it and all of them could not reach China. He requested Pragyadevi, a nun, to send them to him. He himself translated several Indian texts into Chinese. When Huan T Sang came to India Brahmanism was being revived, the Buddhist religion had split into two sects even in the time of Fa Hien. On account of the supremacy of Brahmanism, the Mahayan sect had greater importance in Buddhism. India had changed a great deal since the time of Fa Hien and Huan T Sang found a Brahmanical India in place of Buddhist India. Hence though he did not study Hindu culture, he could not remain uninfluenced by it and he got glimpses of the Brahmanical education also in the records of his impressions of the Buddhist system. The salient features of Buddhist education as described by Huan T Sang are given below.

Methods of Teaching

By the time of Huan T Sang there had developed numerous sects among the Buddhists. As a result of this, the monks had to remain prepared to meet criticisms in regard to the basic elements of Buddhism whereas previously they had to defend their religion only against the onslaught of other religions. Argumentation, therefore, became of prime importance in Buddhist education and in every institution of higher education training was given in delivering lectures, holding debates and argumentative conversations and discourses. In order to give encouragement to these arts, Buddhist scholars and logicians were handsomely rewarded and expert debators were accorded great honour. They were taken round on elephants and were attended upon by a number of servants. On the other side unsuccessful and incapable debators were severely dealt with and to put them to insult and shame their faces were besmeared with mud. The able monks were given all sorts of facilities in their work of exposition of the religious texts. These facilities were given in proportion to the number of texts in the following manner :

He who could annotate one text was relieved of the work of the preceptor.

He who could annotate two was given the title of 'Shreshth'.

He who was capable of annotating three had in his service a number of monks.

He who was capable of annotating four was given regular slaves to serve him.

He who was capable of annotating five was given an elephant for his conveyance.

He who was capable of annotating more than five texts was given a number of attendants along with the elephant.

Thus the criterion for one's merits in the society of those days was his ability in delivering lectures. This has a many-sided effect in the field of education. The work of the expansion of knowledge was carried on by learned assemblies which were convened from time to time. Huen T Sang had himself witnessed several such assemblies to which great scholars were invited from the length and breadth of the country. King Harshvardhan used to convene quinquennial learned assemblies in which the learned of other religions also participated.

Ethical education also was not less important . The observance of the codes of the Sangh automatically imparted practical education in morality and ethics. All the monks had to do physical labour and even the chief official of the Sangh had to contribute his 'Manual Work'. The only way for getting remission from this was to achieve proficiency in argumentation. The corporate life of the Sangh also afforded opportunities for ethical instruction.

Morality had great importance in Buddhist education. To test morality, assemblies were convened in which monks bearing good moral character were specially honoured, whereas for moral lapses they had to undergo severe punishments even to the extent of expulsion from the Sangh. The method of contemplation differed from sects to sects. The Mahayanis indulged in devotional contemplation and Hinyanis in mute meditation.

Generally there were no appreciable changes in the Buddhist educational system in the time of Huan T Sang and methods of hearing, contemplation and meditation continued to hold good.

The Sanghs made provision for both primary and higher education. There were several good teachers for primary education which equipped the students for higher education. Both religious and secular subjects were taught. The students usually commenced their education at the age of five or six with the Sanskrit alphabet. At the age of seven they were instructed in five sciences :-

(a) Grammar (b) spiritual or transcendental knowledge (c) architecture or mechanical skill (d) teleology and (e) medicine. Besides, these, there were other subjects also like astronomy, numbers, demonology, etc. yet in spite of these secular subjects education was primarily religious. Vinay, Sutras, Abhidharm, etc, were the popular subjects. Although students of other religions also received Buddhist education, nevertheless the Buddhist students predominated.

At the time of Huan T Sang Buddhism had split into various sects and offshoots and as such the subjects of study were not the same in all the institutions which usually taught subjects pertaining to the particular sect.

Centres of Buddhist Education

The monks of different sects lived in separate Sanghs and studied subjects pertaining to their own sects. We are describing below a few such monasteries.

Gandhar

The monasteries of Gandhar were in a rather wretched condition at the time of Huan T Sang, but at no time was this a prominent centre of Buddhist education and there were about one thousand monasteries at this place.

Kanyakubja

Sramans of both the sects of Buddhism lived here. At the time of Fa Hien there were only two monasteries here but as a result of the efforts of Harshvardhan the number of monasteries had risen to one thousand. More than ten thousand monks lived in these and this became the greatest centre of Buddhism.

Shravasti

Its condition had changed since the days of Fa Hien. There was only one monastery now in place of ninety-two. The Jetvan Vihar was completely destroyed.

Taxila

Some monks of the Mahayan sect lived here. Its pristine glory had rolled into dust and there remained only dilapidated ruins of monasteries.

Varanasi

Only three hundred Buddhist Sramans lived here and the followers of other religions outnumbered them. This was a prominent educational centre.

Sarnath

The Upwan monastery which was established in the time of Buddha continued to exist. It had eight departments and about three hundred Sramans lived here.

Nalanda

Nalanda was the best university of the time and from it radiated mighty effulgence of knowledge . The teachers of this university were widely renowned and about ten thousand students received education here.

Kapilvastu

Only one monastery remained here and there were about thirty monks. The ruins of about one thousand monasteries tell the story of its past grandeur.

Munghyr

Mostly Hinayan monks lived here. Huan T Sang himself studied here for a year. About four thousand monks lived in the different Vihars.

Anandhar

Huan T Sang remained here with a scholar named Chandraverma. At that time there were about two thousand monks here and more than fifty monasteries were in existence.

Udayan

This famous centre of education was in a dilapidated condition at the time of Huan T Sang. It is said that there were once fourteen hundred monasteries in which about eighteen thousand monks lived.

Mathura

The condition and position of Mathura was the same at the time of Huan T Sang's visit as it was when Fa Hien came here. About two thousand monks lived here and there were more than twenty monasteries.

Ayodhya

About three thousand monks lived in one hundred monasteries. Huan T Sang also saw here the old monasteries of the dead scholars like Shri Labdh Asang, Vasubandhu, etc.

Vaishali

Once upon a time it was a prominent centre of Buddhism, but at that time its condition was pitiable and only three or four monasteries remained.

Bolor

Thousands of monks lived in the various monasteries of this place but their character and religious knowledge was not of a very high order.

Nabh Sawan

The writer of the famous Buddhist text 'Katyamaniput' had received education here. At one time this was a famous centre of Buddhism but Huan T Sang found here only three hundred monks who belonged to the Sarvastivadin sect.

Sthaneshwar

About seven hundred monks of the Hinayan sect lived here in Buddhist Vihars.

Magadh

Monks of the Mahayan sect lived in all the monasteries here. In the province of Magadh more than ten thousand monks lived in fifty monasteries.

Mahabodhivihar

About one thousand monks of Mahayan sect lived here. The grand Vihar of this place had been constructed by the King of Ceylon and within its precincts there were three palaces and a number of rooms.

Vishok

About three hundred Sammatiya (a Buddhist sect) monks lived here and the number of the monasteries also was quite large. Formerly a renowned scholar named Dev Sraman Gop lived here.

Cheenbhukti

Huan T Sang lived here with the famous scholar, Vineet Prabh and had received education from him in Abhidharma for a year and a half. At that time there were ten monasteries here.

Matipur

Gunprabh the learned scholar, who lived in the monasteries here, wrote about one hundred books. Huan T Sang studied one of his texts 'Tatva Sandesh Shastra'. About eight hundred monks lived in the ten monasteries of the Hinayan sect.

Kapis

This was a rising centre of Buddhism. Huan T Sang lived here once during the rainy season. The monks of the Mahayan sect lived in one thousand monasteries of this place.

Kashmir

Huan T Sang was warmly welcomed here and he lived here and studied several sutras. Buddhism had an all pervading influence in the province of Kashmir and here more than five thousand monks lived in the hundred Buddhist monasteries. It was in Kashmir for the first time that 'Arhat Madhyantiki', the disciple of Buddha's favourite devotee Anand, had propagated the Buddhist religion.

Srudhnan :

The teachers of this place were renowned scholars. Huan T Sang also had received instructions in the Sraotantik branch from Jaigupta. At that time about one hundred Sraman, belonging mostly to the Hinayan sect lived in the five Vihars here.

Tiloshik Vihar

This Vihar was situated at a distance of about twenty miles to the west of Nalanda. The building of the Vihar was very grand and learned scholar of far off places used to assemble here.

Gaj

Seven thousand monks lived here most of whom belonged to the Sarvastivadin sect.

Pushkravati

Vasumitra was the renowned teacher of this place. A number of monks of Central India lived here.

Lump

A scholar of this place had travelled to China and had translated a Sanskrit text into Chinese. There were ten monasteries of the Mahayan sect here and the number of monks was very small.

Chola (South Indian)

In the land of the Dravidians about one thousand monks lived in ten monasteries. Huan T Sang had received here instruction in Yoga from a Ceylonese scholar.

Bejwada (South India)

The Buddhist religion was quite in vogue here and more than three thousand monks lived in the twenty decentralised monasteries.

Others

Buddhism was widespread in the provinces of Valbhi, Kanjipur, Konkan, Malwa, Bharoch, Maharashtra, etc. These places bear eloquent testimony to the nature and scope of Buddhist education.

I-tsing

Taking inspiration from his teacher Fa Hien, I-tsing came to India by the sea-route. He studied the Sanskrit language and instead of travelling he studied at Nalanda university for ten years. He gained a thorough mastery over Sanskrit grammar and lexicon and he compiled about four hundred Buddhist texts. On his return to China he translated fifty-six texts into the Chinese language as a result of which a new Buddhist sect came into existence in China. I-tsing mentions in his records several such places which he had not seen personally but nevertheless he visited all the prominent centres of Buddhism.

We find more new matter in the records given by I-tsing than in the descriptions of facts already mentioned by the earlier travellers. He has mentioned some facts about primary education which shed a great deal of light on the prevailing condition of primary education. While describing the rules and regulations of the Buddhist Sanghs regarding membership, etc he has given a comprehensive account of the Buddhist educational system. We shall discuss the systems of primary and higher education as they have been described by I-tsing.

Primary Education

In order to enable the students to remember their lessons, they were tested every day early in the morning. The teacher-student relation continued to be as of old. After receiving education in Vinay they were taught the Sutras and the Shastras. Under the religious literatures were taught, 'Buddh Charitra' by Ashvaghoshs, two texts of Matrichet and the Jatakmala and Shrilekha of Nagarjun. It was compulsory for students of both the Hinayan and Mahayan sects to read these texts.

Moral education was given no mean importance and great emphasis was laid on the observance of the rules of Vinay. The teachers remained solicitous for the conduct and character of the students and immediately warned them when they discovered any lapses. Expiation had to be undergone for any sort of dereliction.

According to the practice the education of the child began at six years and 'Sidhistu' was the first book to be taught. It contained the Sanskrit alphabet and took six months to finish. After gaining the knowledge of the alphabet, three hundred easy couplets or stanzas were taught. At the age of eight the student had to memorise one thousand Shlokas of Panini. From ten to fifteen years 'Dhatu' 'Kashika Vritti' was taught and the annotations of Panini's Sutras or Aphorisms which were written by Srathaditya and contained 18,000 Shlokas, had to be read.

As regards Teleology Nagarjun's 'Nyayadwara Tarkshastra' was given great importance. Philosophy and metaphysics were also studied along with this. The art of writing prose-cum-verse was also taught. The teaching and study of medicine had been divided into eight portions and different books were taught in each portion. Later on these were compiled into one. I-tsing has also mentioned the science of surgery.

Higher Education

After the student had gained knowledge of the above mentioned subjects, he was given special education which came under the scheme of higher education. In the higher study of grammar, literature was also included and the following poetry texts had to be studied :

1.Bhartrihari Shastra - The annotation of Bhartrihari's 25,000 shlokas were greatly admired and appreciated.

2.Bhartrihar's grammar-text - In this text there were 3,000 Shlokas and it included an annotation of 14,000 Shlokas which, it is said, Dharmpal had written.

3. Patanjali's 'Choorni'. - In this great commentary there were 24,000 Shlokas and three years were required for its study.

4. Vakya Padeeye - In this there were Shlokas and this also was composed by Bhartrihari. In this annotation 7,000 Shlokas were also included.

A student was called 'Bahushrut' after he had made a systematic study of these books and he was regarded as proficient in knowledge of grammar. In the Buddhist Sangh, attention was also paid towards the health of the student who had to do physical exercises every morning. Walking had prime importance in the scheme of physical exercises. At the time of I-tsing's visit Nalanda and Valbhi were the two prominent and important universities. In higher education special instruction was given in grammar, medicine, teleology, handicrafts and spiritualism.

Summary

On the division of Buddhism in two sections and the revival of Hinduism, the Buddhist education included the teaching of secular subjects together with religious ones. From the fifth to the seventh century, three Chinese travellers Fa Hien, Huen T Sang and I-tsing visited India. They travelled throughout the country and gathered vast knowledge about Buddhism. They visited famous Buddhist monasteries and have given detailed accounts of them. These foreign travellers were much impressed by the contemporary Indian culture. Their descriptions throw sufficient light on the Buddhist education. There were two stages of Buddhist education primary and higher. The general knowledge of the subjects used to be imparted at the primary stage, while at the higher stage students were given specialised training in various subjects. 'Religious education' was inseparable from education, but secular subjects like medicine, sculpture, art and painting were also taught. At the time all of southern and northern India was Buddhist. A large number of foreign students were studying in Indian universities. Those, having faith in other religions, were also allowed to study in Buddhist educational institutions.

Debates were a popular measurement of knowledge. Debating power was almost essential to establish the supremacy of Buddhism. Conferences of learned persons were often organised. The Buddhist monasteries were financed by permanent estates generally donated by kings, businessmen and the general public. The monasteries were the sole owners of these estates. The art of writing was known to them, but oral teaching was popular. The names of contemporary scholars and the centres of learning, as enumerated by Chinese travellers, are detailed below :

Centres of Learning

Patliputra, Shravasti, Rajgrih, Vaishali, Gaya, Kushinagar, Kanyakubj, Sankashya, Kashi, Tamralipti, Puruspur, Champa, Gangbar, Taxila, Sarnath, Nalanda, Kapilvastu, Munghyr, Anandhar, Udayan, Mathura, Ayodhya, Bolor, Nabhsawan, Sthaneshwar, Magadh, Vishok, Cheenbhukti, Matipur, Kapis, Pulash, Kashmir, Shrudhanan, Gaj, Pushkarawati, Lump, Bejawada, Chola, Kanipur and Valabhi.

Scholars

Mahakatyayan, Nagarjun, Dev, Vasumitra, Ishwar, Parshwa, Asang, Dignag, Kunarlabdha, Sthirmati, Narain Dev, Gunprabh, Vasubandhu, Gunmati, Dharmpal, Jai Gupta, Mitrasen, Chandra Varma, Pragyabhadra, Viryasen, Shantisen, Tathagat Gupta, Patanjali, Bhartrihari, etc.

In that age many books were written. Chinese travellers took away many books to their country and got them translated into their mother toungues. With the help of these books they spread Buddhism in China.

Notes and References

1. Name of Buddhist Monastery.

Exercises

1. Give an account of Buddhist education as described by Fa Hien.
2. What changes were introduced in Buddhist education in the course of time and why.
3. How did the division in the Buddhist community affect the education of the period.
4. Describe Buddhist education as viewed by Huan T Sang.

Chapter 8

Characteristics of Primary Education

It is difficult to know the exact form of the primary education in ancient India because no good material containing information on the score is available. Among the things which were unearthed, during the excavations at Mohenjodaro and Harappa and which symbolise the prehistoric civilization, are earthen pots with some inscriptions on them. Nobody has been able to decipher these so far. Nevertheless, this is sufficient proof of the fact that the art of writing was known to the people at that time. Some earthen pots of ancient India have inscriptions all over them in the Brahmi script. Through a seal belonging to the period around B.C. 450, one comes to know about the games of children prevalent those days. In a particular kind of game known as 'Akharika' a child used to make a mark in a shorthand script on the back of his companion. It can be said on the basis of this game of children that the people had a knowledge of reading and writing. It is quite possible that for the knowledge of the duties and obligations of the Vaishyas as detailed by Manu, the people of the business class had made some arrangement which also helped them in gaining knowledge of things pertaining to their daily life.

On the basis of the accounts of Megasthenes and other foreign travellers it may be said that even at that time there must have existed some arrangement for education. If any systematic education was not much in vogue it was quite possible that vocational education was gained by means of business and other connected transactions. It is not possible to say anything definite on this score. Nevertheless, it is a fact that people in ancient India knew how to read and write.

In the Brahmanical system religious and spiritual education of a very high order was given right from the beginning, but it was usually oral. Hence primary education did not have a separate identity. The children had from the very beginning, to learn correct pronunciation of Vedic Mantras and also to commit them to memory. Although people living in 1000 B.C. knew the art of writing yet they could not utilise or develop it because putting the Vedas which were revealed by Gods' words in black and white was regarded as a sinful act at that time.

With the rise of Buddhism in India expansion of education took place and attention was paid to primary education also. Cloisters and monasteries turned into schools. It is evidenced by the rock-edicts of Ashoka that in the 3rd. century B.C. a large number of people were well up in ordinary every day languages. This was the result of the efforts of Buddhist monks and nuns who moved in the midst of the communality and gave religious discourses in the language ordinarily spoken. Provision for vocational education was also made in India during the peaceful regime of the Mauryas. Siddhartha Lord Buddha and Lav-Kush had commenced their education at the age of six and this must have been the usual practice those days. In the beginning they were taught the alphabet and this ceremony was called 'Akshar Swikarnam'.

Thus primary education got an independent place in the Indian educational system even in the 2nd century B.C.

The social structure of India underwent a change in the 5th century B.C. The Shudras were no longer regarded as fit for primary education and women were put under great restrictions. Consequently, the expansion of primary education was impeded and whereas previously eighty per cent of the Indians were literate, now literacy narrowed down to only forty per cent. The condition of primary education deteriorated rapidly and the internal political upheavals as well as external invasions dealt such a blow against the system of primary education that only ten per cent of the people remained literate.

Ancient literature contains information only in regard to the Vedic educational institutions but no material is available with regard to primary education. Hence it is well nigh impossible to know how the primary schools were managed. All the available information in context is given below.

Organisation of Education

As regards the elementary vocational education, the children received this at home through their parents. In some localities of business-people, however, arrangement was made by this class for vocational education and separate and independent teachers were appointed for the purpose. Persons of other professions took their cue from this and, as evidenced by the narrative Upali, began to establish such educational institutions. In the beginning of the Buddhist age there were primary schools in villages besides the Sanghs and these were managed collectively by the villagers. When Buddhism split into two sects - Hinayan and Mahayan, then in the educational system of the latter the study of non-religious subjects came to be regarded as important and the Mahayani Sanghs helped a great deal in the expansion of primary education. The Chinese traveller I-tsing has described the condition of primary education along with the higher education of the Sanghs.

Although a few competent individuals looked to the management of primary education, yet right up to 400 A.D., it was on the whole managed by the villages. Society provided maintenance to the teachers who carried on their jobs independently.

After the 5th century A.D. some educational organisations patronised by the State came into existence. Students who had received higher education through these organisations became primary teachers and took to the work of primary education.

All the primary schools in ancient India were located in villages. Mr. Mathai has opined that these primary schools came into existence with the organisation of the villagers themselves. The village priest discharged the duties of the teacher along with those of the priest. The economic needs of the schools were met by the village-bodies and the teachers maintained themselves on the fees realised from the students or the produce of the land attached to the temple. In ancient India the primary schools were thus collective, and they worked as independent institutions with the spirit of common weal.

Methods of Teaching

In ancient days there was a total lack of text books and writing material. It took years for the completion of the manuscript of a book and as such primary education was given by means of natural resources.

The children of the people wrote with their fingers or thin pieces of stick on the laid-out mound of sand, while the children of some high-ups used wooden writing boards. The teacher wrote a letter on a big blackboard and the students copied it on their boards and pronounced it audibly. After the knowledge of the individual letter of the alphabet students were taught the combination of words, which took about six months. After this the student had to learn to read and write numbers. Instruction in arithmetic proceeded on similar lines. In the absence of the teacher the brightest student carried on the work of the monitor-teacher.

When the students had mastered the art of writing on the wooden boards, they were taught to write on the leaves of the palmyra tree. The teacher wrote a letter on the leaf with a pointed piece of wood and the student ran over it with charcoal ink and thus practised good writing. This continued for a long time and then only a student learnt the art of good writing (calligraphy). There were no printing presses those days. Hence it was necessary to emphasise good penmanship.

Subjects of Study

In the Upali narrative we have evidence of the fact that the art of writing was also included with reading in the scheme of primary education in India. Due to the lack of stationery or writing materials, oral instructions continued to hold ground in the primary schools. The primary education in India was religious as well as vocational and only subjects relating to religion and vocations were taught in schools. In the Vedic institutions education was confined to the correct pronunciation of Vedic mantras and only a simply acquaintance with reading and writing was given in subsidiary subjects. Vocational education was mostly given in families in the traditional manners. After some time such institutions were established in which general education in reading and writing was given. Such institutions have been described above. For meeting the requirements of daily life instructions in the three Rs was imparted. The art of writing had developed in India about 450 B.C. as is evidenced by the children's game "Akharika'. In the general primary education which was given outside the Sanghs instruction in reading, writing and arithmetic was given. The King of Kalinga had received similar instruction in his childhood. In the 'Singlovad Sutt' the duties and obligations of parents as well as teachers and students have been detailed which show that the child was given instruction in general knowledge, science, stories, etc.

The Rock-Edicts of Ashoka testify that the art of writing was in vogue and primary education was generally given in the language of every day conversation. This also proves that primary education had fairly advanced till then.

The influence of Sanskrit began to increase again after 250 A.D. and it was included in the scheme of primary education. The students were given instruction in the Sutras at a particular age. After 500 A.D. the every day language again showed an upsurge and the importance of Sanskrit began to wane till in the 9th century A.D. it was totally eclipsed. The every day language acquired complete sway in the field of primary education. Besides local dialects, subjects like accounting, measurements of land and book-keeping were also included in primary education.

A Critique

In primary education the students were given a sort of practical instruction in those subjects which pertained to their individual daily work. This education cannot be regarded as complete or all round because only a knowledge of the three Rs was possible in this system and the enlightenment of the student remained confined to the particulars of the daily vocation. The finer sensibilities of the students remained suppressed and found no chance of expression.

Along with this, students could not attain much culture and refinement. Learning by rote was another defect of this education which checked the students from exercising their own brains and thus hindered with the independent growth of their mind and intellect.

Yet if we seriously consider the hard circumstances under which the ancient Indian primary education did its work we will have to admire it. These primary schools held under the shades of trees or a thatch roof imparted instruction to the common people for centuries in useful practical education. Primary education in ancient India had some special features which we lack in the modern systems.

These special features are given below :

1. The work of these schools was directly concerned with life and the students who read here were fully equipped for meeting the requirement of every day existence.

2. The ancient primary education was individualistic and it could be naturally adjusted to the individual abilities and requirements. Consequently the students got opportunities of progress and development in proportion to their abilities. This is not possible in the modern system of education which is based on the consideration of classes.

The method of learning the art of good penmanship by running the fingers over an inscribed letter, shows that the Indian primary education was acquainted from very early days with some of the principles found in the Montessori system.

3. In the absence of the teacher, competent students were entrusted with the teaching work which provided them with opportunities for self-development and trained them for shouldering responsibilities. As a result of this training, they could achieve success in their lives.

4. In these schools practical instruction was given in the three Rs and knowledge of reading, writing and accountancy was not confined to books only. Such education was given in primary schools till recent years.

5. In these schools the teacher-student relation was based on affection and reverence. The real basis of this relation was the ideal of spiritual identity and the feeling of oneness and kinship which cannot ever be traceable in the modern schools.

Thus in spite of its several shortcomings the ancient Indian primary education has a great significance. Considering the serious defects and shortcoming in the field of education these days in spite of the facilities which are now available but were conspicuously absent in ancient times, it would not be wrong to give the old system high praise. It was because of primary education that the institutions of higher Vedic education could succeed in developing the culture of India. These primary schools were verily the pillars of the knowledge and culture of India.

Summary

Ancient Indian history bears testimony to the fact that there existed one other type of educational system in India, even in the pre-historic age. The game of 'Akkharika', prevalent in about 450 B.C., indicates that the people of that time were literate. Brahamin education included even primary education in higher education. Vocational education was not uncommon. Primary education was made popular with Buddhism itself. The minimum age for entry in primary schools was six years. In the third century, there was a good percentage of literate persons. Primary education, in no way, was being managed by the state. These schools were run by the collective efforts of villages. Teachers used to impart education and the contemporary society looked after their welfare. Generally, the priests were the teachers of these schools. Fees were also being paid. Due to the shortage of books and stationery, children used to write on wooden plates or Tar-patra. The knowledge of the alphabet was essential. Monitors were elected from students to perform some the duties of the teachers. Good handwriting was encouraged. Oral education was popular. It was necessary to recite Vedic Mantras correctly and have sufficient knowledge of the grammar. Education used to aim at the proper behaviour of the students. Students were given sufficient knowledge which might be useful in their domestic life. They were trained to fix up their routine. There were remote chances for the development of finer faculties in them. Cramming of the text books was the popular method. They were trained to run their families efficiently. Education was strictly personal and not according to any fixed standard. The method of good handwriting was on the lines of Montessori education system. The monitorial system used to afford sufficient opportunity for the personality development of brilliant scholars. The teacher and taught relations were based on mutual respect and affection.

Exercises

1. Describe the nature of primary education in ancient India.
2. Explain the evidences of primary education in ancient India.
3. Give a critical evaluation of primary education in ancient India. What aspects of the same will you like to incorporate in the modern primary education in order to make it more adequate and why.

Vocational Education in Ancient Days

Ancient Literature does not provide much evidence of the general features and organisation of vocational education in India. However, on the basis of the available material we can conclude that vocational education was provided for in some way or the other; otherwise the Indian society of the time would not have attained so much vocational efficiency and economic prosperity. Several goods produced by ancient Indian industries found markets in foreign lands. The people of ancient India were familiar with sea routes and they had contact with western countries. The commercial voyages described in the Jatakas are testimonies to these facts. To carry on trade by sea routes ships were needed and in India huge ships were built on a large scale. The ship traders earned huge profits through transhipment of goods to and from far off countries. Trade in leather carpets and cloth was carried on by land routes, also with the tribes across the frontiers of the country. Successful trading in ancient India gave great impetus to the industries and a number of things began to be produced through the cottage or home industries. Beautiful, strong and attractive earthen pots were made here, while the carpenters turned out fine articles of woodwork such as bed-steads, boats, ships, chariots, etc. Through cottage or home workmanships the demand for woollen, silken and muslin cloth was met. Fine ivory work has been crafted in India since ancient days. Embroidery, perfumery, gold work, jewellery and manufacture of arms and ammunitions were some of the chief industries of India.

The State extended its partronage to competent artisans, so much so that in the reign of Ashoka there was a provision for the punishment of those who tried to harm such men. The ship builders and the manufacturers of arms and ammunitions were given salaries and remunerations by the State. In age of the Sutras people gained special proficiency in vocational instructions. Hence, it is proved that the system of vocational education definitely existed in India. We shall describe below the organisation of this education on the basis of the material available.

Education in Medicine

The study of medicine was in a very advanced stage in ancient India. In the Taxila University students from foreign countries came to study Medicine, for it was renowned for medical sciences. The practice of medicine was a very respectable and lucrative profession. In the first century medical science developed in India and along with the science of curing diseases, the knowledge of the various methods of surgery also had an important place. Sushrut wrote a book in which he discussed various surgical ways and methods of healing minor wounds to abdominal operations, amputation of the limps, etc. The ancient Indian physicians were also acquainted with the methods of nasal surgery. Sushrut even suggested the study and dissection of the dead body for practical knowledge in surgery.

Charak wrote a book on Medicine in which he discussed the causes of disease, its prognosis, diagnosis and the prescription for treatment.

Along with the science of curing human diseases, the study of veterinary sciences was also in vogue.

Shalihoti of the time is regarded as the father of veterinary science and even in the fourth century B.C. there were a number of veterinary hospitals. The rise of Jainsm and Buddhishim gave an impetus to the study of veterinary sciences. In the period of Ashoka several veterinary surgeons worked in the State veterinary hospitals. Kautilya in his Arthashastra has mentioned the provision of competent veterinary surgeons in the military department for the treatment of elephants and horse. Many books dealing with the treatment of the diseases of elephants, horses and other animals were written.

India remained famous for centuries for its medical sciences. The Caliph of Bagdad had sent some competent students to Taxila to study medicine. He also invited several Indian physicians to his court and got several books translated form Sanskrit into Arabic.

Organisation of Medical Education

There was a particular ceremony called "'Upnayana' for commencing education. On an auspicious day a square altar was erected, rudiments for oblation gathered and then the teacher and after him the students performed the holocaust ceremony with clarified butter and honey. The teacher and student then went round the altar and the physicians (Vaidayas) and the Brahmans who were present there at that time were worshipped. The student took oaths in the presence of the fire to make his student and professional life an ideal one.

Medicine was studied from a humanitarian point of view and not as a means of livelihood, even then physicians had a good income. Students were retained in the institution to be tested and examined and a student who did not come up to the prescribed standard were also permitted to go through the Upnayana. Besides Brahman teachers, Vaishya and Kshatriyas also taught the Ayurveda. Thus people of all the castes could take part in the teaching of medical science provided they were fit in every other respect. There were regulations operating in the institutions imparting education in Ayurveda just as in the Vedic schools. The institutions remained closed on particular lunar days and in inclement weather.

Samavartan

The Snataks of Ayurveda were given instructions in regard to their professional obligations at the time of their departure after graduation. On the basis of the duties and obligations of the physicians which were prescribed at that time, we give below some facts about the physicians in ancient India :

1. The physician had in view the treatment of patients and not remuneration or fees.
2. He remained always alert in regard to the knowledge of Ayurveda so that he could take advantage of the latest methods.
3. The physician remained prepared for the treatment of the patient even at the cost of his own life.
4. The physician instead of being puffed up with pride for his

knowledge remained sweet tongued, truthful and morally upright. This was very essential for his professional success.

5. Service to Brahmans and cows was regarded as the sacred duty of physicians.
6. The use of intoxicants, greed for the wealth of other people and misconduct towards women were taboos for them.
7. Great emphasis was laid on moral development along with the professional knowledge.

Military Education

During the education of royal princes, instruction was given in Varta and Ethics of Government also. Manu had regarded the education in the Vedas, Varta, and Politics as essential for royal princes. Subjects pertaining to the use of arms were treated as meet and proper for all the Kshatriya princes. Some princes found the study of grammar extremely difficult and they received education in other subjects.

A new course of study was adopted to incorporate the subjects essential for the education of Kshatriya royal princes, but generally the books which were used in the Brahman schools, were included in the curriculum of studies for the Kshatriyas. For a knowledge of the ethics of government, politics, etc, the study of Kautilya's Arthashastra was deemed essential. In the education of the Kshatriya boys, the book 'Nitisar' written by Kamandak in the third century, was commonly used. In the sixth century other books on political science were written. The matter of these books was very interesting and probably Arthashastra and Nitisar being rather uninteresting had become dry texts. The Panchtantra, 'Hittopdesh', Sari Sagar, Ramayana and Mahabharata, etc were such books in which the ways and means of solving the riddles of social and individual life so very useful for the training of the Kshatriyas were discussed in a very interesting manner. Later on, during the medieval period all books written under inspiration from the heroic poetry of Rajasthan, were found to be extremely suitable and useful for the education of the Kshatriyas.

Manu had forbidden the Kshatriyas from taking to teaching work. Although teachers of other castes could give education to the Kshatriyas, yet it was the Brahmans who had the upper most hand in the field. The Brahman priests (Purohits or family priests) continued to give education to the Kshatriya princes in Rajasthan even in later times. Kautilya in his Arthashastra has laid down the principle that the kings should always have Brahman priests as their instructors. The Brahman teachers were generally able and men of character and the Kshatriya princes received higher education under them with profit.

If was probably after the Epic age (age of Ramayana and Mahabharata) that the system of Upnayana was evolved in the field of military education. In this system the future student observed a fast on some stipulated auspicious lunar day, performed holocaust or oblation and invited a Brahman to dine. The teachers chanted Vedic Mantras and made the student hold arms. According to the caste of the student, the Brahman student held a bow, the Kshattriya a sword, the Vaishya a spear and a Shudra a mace or a staff. The teacher had to know the use of all such weapons.

On the completion of the studies a special function was arranged in which the teacher after the due performance of the ceremonies fixed a dagger in the garment of the students. The dagger was regarded as certificate of merit and the ceremony was known as 'Dhurika Bandhan'. This practice continued in Rajasthan right up to the beginning of the 19th century although its name was changed to 'Khang Bandhayee'. Rajput stalwarts entered into military life after going through this ceremony.

This system of education instilled into the Kshatriya princes the spirit of dutifulness and social service and gave them an ideal education in other aspects and values of life. This education exercised such an influence over the Kshatriya princes that they not only preserved the glorious characteristics of their caste, but also remained famous in the history of the country. This educational system continued to serve its purpose for a pretty long time, but with the change in circumstances and conditions of life the needs of the time also changed. Since this system could not get itself out of the traditional rut and adopt progressive trends, it lost its importance in the field of military training.

Industrial Education

Industrial goods of high quality were produced in India even in ancient days. We have already described in the foregoing pages how these goods were exported to foreign countries. The basis of this industrial excellence must have been the industrial education of ancient India. Industrial education was given in the traditional 'family-school' manner. The old experienced men in the family imparted instruction to the young in the family although later on persons of other families were also accorded permission to form these family schools. The artisan-teacher treated these persons of other families in the same way as he treated members of his own family. As in the Vedic educational system the teacher-student relation in this education was also individualistic. The teacher treated the student as his son. When any student went to such an artisan teacher both of them had to take certain vows to which they adhered strictly. The main vows are detailed below :

Prescribed Regulations for the Students

1. The student will not desert his teacher except for very compelling reasons, till he has gone through the prescribed period of study and has completed his training.

2. The student who deserted the teacher of his own accord will have to return to him and undergo punishment for expiation. If the relations had connived with such a student action as provided by the ordinance would be taken against them.

3. If a student was able to complete his studies earlier than the prescribed period he would still remain with the teacher and engage himself in industrial work because the credit for his earlier completion of studies went to the teacher whose competence and proficiency helped the student. The teacher could extend the period of study for a student who was unable to complete his studies within the prescribed time-limit.

Prescribed Regulations for the Teacher

1. The teacher shall treat the student as his own son and shall be responsible for his maintenance and residence.

2. The teacher shall not withhold from the student anything that he knows and shall gladly give the student the full benefit of his industrial knowledge and experience.

3. The teacher shall impart education in toto within the prescribed time-limit. The teacher who dilly dallied with his work was regarded as condemnable and immoral.

4. The daily work prescribed for the student shall be in the interest of the student. The teacher shall not derive personal benefit from the industrial knowledge and bodily work of the student.

Thus knowledge was individualistic in the old system of industrial education. As a result of the close contact and constant association with the teacher, it was possible for the student to gain the experience of real industrial knowledge. Along with this he was greatly influenced by the personality of the teacher which naturally impressed itself on his industrial work. In ancient times industry was connected with a particular part of the society. The student living in the midst of the teacher's family took part in the social activities of the surrounding areas and thus became acquainted with all the social conditions and circumstances under which the old industries developed.

Evidence of the above described industrial education is available in two inscriptions discovered during investigations.

In ancient times there were some such industrial guilds which arranged for and controlled various industries. These guilds were called 'Sreni'. The planning of industries, the constructions, production and distribution of articles, etc., was managed by these Srenis. There was a separate Sreni for each industry and industrial education was given at the residence of the Artisan where a number of students collected for the purpose.

Sreni (Guilds)

In ancient India there were local industrial guilds known as Srenis for the management of industries, but it is difficult to determine the time of their inception. In the Jatakas eighteen such guilds are mentioned but we get appellations like 'Dyers association', 'Carpenters' association', Blacksmiths' association, 'Coblers' or Tanners association. These associations and guilds have been described by Kautilya also in his Arthashastra.

The membership of the Srenis was hereditary and the young descendants succeeded the old ancestors after their death. The new members had to pay some fees too. The income accumulated by the Srenis was spent in charities, etc. The guild had the power to inflict pecuniary punishment on anyone who violated any of the regulations. The guilds acquired an unduly great influence in the field of industry, so much so that a ruler acknowledged this. The king put a 'Sreshthi'—head of the Sreni, next in importance to the Purohit. With the passage of time the powers of the Srenis increased so much that they controlled the appointment of artisans, their period of work, wages and the managements of the products, etc. Along with the increase in powers the obligations of the Srenis also multiplied and their prime functions were to inculcate the spirit of brotherhood among the artisans and to look to the interest of the members. Industrial education in India made much advancement through the excellent management by the guilds. Consequently, the industrial products were of a very high standard.

In India, industry was regarded as a form of corporate religion and not only as a means of livedlihood. There were prescribed rules pertaining to the religion of industry, violation of which could prove prejudicial to the mundane and ultra-mundance existence of the artisans. In this way, the work was carried on by means of a religious and not purely materialistic incentive to the artisans. The caste system was another factor responsible for the industrial property of India. The influence of the caste system might have been baneful in social life, but in the field of industry it was beneficent.

Industrial education in ancient India was totally separate from the cultural and those students who were well up in industrial knowledge were totally clean of cultural education. Knowledge of mythology, Ramayana, etc, was automatically gained in the family schools either by reading or through oral information, but the study of philosophy and literature was not possible there. The medicants and saints used to pay frequent visits to the villages and through their instructions the student-artisans, got to know something about religion and morality. The social functions of the villages also provided instruction in other useful aspect of life. After the eighth century literacy went down and the artisans who worked with their hand began to be looked down upon. As a result of this, workmanship became purely industrial in its bias. Whatever may be the case, as far as workmanship is concerned the importance of the industrial education of India is very clear.

Summary

Ancient works have a negligible description of vocational education in India. In addition to business tours, the Jataks contain description of sea passage business. Engravings on the articles of the pre-historic era provide sufficient clue to the fact that there were high class manufacturing centres in India and its articles were in great demand in foreign countries.

Medical education had an important place in the vocational education of India. Foreign students used to study medical sciences in the Taxila University. Medical education included surgery in a developed form. Veterinary science was also known to them. 'Sushrut' and 'Charak' have written books on medicine and surgery.

Indian physicians and surgeons were invited to foreign countries. The Caliph of Baghdad got many Sanskrit books on medicine translated into Arabic. A person was allowed to study medicine only after the performance of a ceremony known as the 'Upanayan'. A student had to take a solemn oath before the fire that his life would be exemplary. The main objective of studying the medical science was the welfare of society and not profit making. Medical education was open to every one and generally teachers used to be Brahamin, Kshatriya and Vaishya. The graduates of Ayurveda were given lessons on their duties.

The second important vocational education was military education. The arrangements for this was only for the princes and the sons of Kshatriya. The teachers used to be Brahamins. It was also necessary to complete the rites of the Upanayan ceremony to undertake military education. After necessary offerings to the fire (Havan), the students took weapons according to their caste. After graduation a dagger used to be attached to the students dress as a certificate of having completed their education. This custom was known as 'dagger taking' and later on as 'sword taking'. The influence of military education is still distinct in the Kshatriyas in connection with the prestige of their caste.

The industrial education was the third type of vocational education. This was open to family members, but members of the other families could also take lessons. The teacher and taught relation was founded on affection and respect and both were to abide by certain rules. Liviing in close contact with the artisan teacher, the students used to gain practical experience about the work. Being in the family of the teacher, the pupils collected relevant information about the industrial society, by participating in social functions around them. Usually co-operative societies used to run these family institutions. The powers and duties of these societies were well defined.

Industry was given the status of religion in India and therefore, having religious inspiration, the industries of India were producing articles of high quality. Persons in the field of industrial education were debarred from cultural education, but they used to take lessons on moral and ethical education from their priests and also by participating in social and religious functions. Ancient India had an important place in the world, in the field of industry.

Exercises

1. Giving an account of the principal industries in ancient India, explain their importance.
2. What was the arrangement for medical education in ancient India ?
3. Describe the nature of military education in ancient India.
4. 'The Indian vocational schools in ancient days were hereditary and maintained some family traditions'. Elucidate.

Chapter 10

Ancient Universities and Centres of Education

Varanasi

Varanasi was very important in the period of Vedic education. Aryan culture was confined for a long period to the western provinces. In the age of the Upanishads, Varanasi came to be counted among the cultural centres, but it had still not gained much importance in the field of education. The royal princes of this place used to go to the Taxila university for their education.

After sometime Varanasi also became important among the centres of education, and people from distant places began to flock here for their education. At the time of Lord Buddha it was the biggest cultural centre in Northern India and it was here that Buddha started propagating his religion for the first time at Sarnath. As at Taxila, here also education was given in the eighteen arts and crafts and in the Vedas. Sarnath was a prominent centre of Buddhist culture and education. Emperor Ashoka made commendable efforts for the development of Sarnath.

Varanasi had a very high place in the field of Brahmanical education. The erudition of the scholars of this place was renowned throughout the length and breadth of the country. Shankarcharya had also consulted the scholar of Varanasi for the confirmation of his tenets. Here competent teachers imparted instruction in their individual capacities, because as in Nalanda and other centres of Buddhist education, here also there was a lack of well-organised educational institutions. The impact of

Muslim domination was felt here also, particularly on education, but nevertheless Varanasi retained its position as an educational centre.

Taxila

Taxila, the capital of the Gandhar province was the great centre of ancient Indian culture and education. In the very hoary past, Taxila was an established centre of Brahmanical education. In connection with Taxila it is mentioned in the Ramayana that Bharat had colonised it in the name of his son Taksh. Whatever may be the origin, Taxila remained popular even in other far off lands for thousands of years and innumerable foreign students came here for their education.

We do not have any solid proof of the existence of a well-organised university here. Teaching was carried on by thousands of competent teachers in an individualistic manner and the fame of Taxila was based on their erudition.

Due do its geographical situation Taxila had to face various vicissitudes during its long and glorious existence. Several inroads were made upon it, and as a result of the changing political conditions the educational system was also affected and the form of education kept on varying. The Zorastrians (Parsis), the Indo-Grecians, the Kushans and the Shakas invaded Taxila and established their sway over it in the sixth, second and first centuries B.C. respectively. And yet Taxila managed to preserve its own existence anyhow in spite of these invasive upheavals. Education was however affected by the different cultures and as a result of the Sanskrit and Persian influence the national script 'Brahmi' could not be retained at Taxila and instruction in Grecian languages was also started.

The eighteen arts and crafts which were taught at Taxila included the Greek arts also. Taxila was famous for higher education and students went there at the age of sixteen. They received instruction in military science, in astronomy and astrology, medical sciences, Vedant and grammar, etc. There were a number of such scholars at Taxila who had perfect mastery over their subject and under them the student prosecuted specialised studies. Panini, who was the greatest of the grammarians; Jeevak, who was renowned for his knowledge of medicine were educated here. The study of medicine took seven years and Jeevak had remained here for this period to complete his study. Chanakya, the author of Arthashastra and the famous political philosopher had also received higher education in this university. Taxila was famous for its teaching in the Indian sciences of war, but instruction in methods of Greek warfare were also given.

Taxila continued for centuries to enlighten, with its store of knowledge, the people not only of this country but of others also. The torch of knowledge kept burning in spite of the invasive eruptions and political storms but in the end the Huns put it off for ever by their depredations.

Nalanda

The ruins of the ancient Nalanda Vihar are still to be found in the Bihar province, seven miles north of Rajgrih and 40 miles south-west of Patna as faded symbols of its pristine glory. In the beginning, Nalanda was a small village but somehow it turned into a university of international repute. We mention below some of the main feature of Nalanda :

1. Nalanda was a resort of the followers of both Jainism and Buddhism. Jain literature mentions that Mahavir spent forty rainy seasons here. Lord Buddha also gave several religious discourses here. Nalanda made much progress in the time of the Mahayan sect.
2. According to the Chiense traveller Heun T Sangh five hundred traders had purchased the plot of Nalanda Vihar for 10 crores gold coins, and had given it to Lord Buddha. Several kings got Sangharams constructed here. Heun T Sang has mentioned six such kings -Kumar Gupta I, Buddha Gupta, Baladitya, Tathagat Gupta, Baju and Harsh. The kings of Pala dynasty also contributed a great deal towards the progress of Nalanda. In the ninth century Balputra Dev, the king of Swarna Dwip, was greatly impressed by the erudite scholars of Nalanda, and after expressing his high regard for Lord Buddha and treating worldly glory as useless, he dedicated six villages to the Nalanda Vihar.
3. Nalanda was the birth place of 'Sariputt', the beloved disciple of the Buddha. When Ashoka saw Sariputts' cenotaph here, he got a Vihar constructed. Ashoka is regarded as the first to establish the Nalanda Vihar.
4. Renowned scholars lived here and good and intelligent students came here to study. Nagarjun and his disciple also enhanced its prestige by their august presence and lived here for sometime.

The various monasteries of Nalanda which were built by various kings, were surrounded by a boundary wall in which there was an entrance gate, close to which was the residence of the Janitor or Gate Pundit who examined the students on their entrance into the university.

The excavations of Nalanda show that practically all the buildings of the Vihar were grand, beautiful and artistic. Soon after entering through the gate one saw the eight pavilions where the students were given group lectures. Besides, there were three classrooms of small measurement in which the students received their lessons. The Nalanda Vihar is the perfect embodiment of the highly developed architecture of India. All the buildings were constructed according to a well laid out plan. The main building had very tall sky-scraper sort of attics. The building consisted of several storeys and its domes and minars must have been very high. In the elegant courtyard of the university there were several big tanks of water in which the beautiful blue lotuses bloomed along with other flowers and added beauty to the lovelines of the surroundings. I-ting has mentioned ten such tanks in which the students bathed and sported.

Arrangements for the residence of students were also there. The hostels for the students were two storeyed and the rooms were of two types, single-seated and double-seated. In every room there were arrangements for book-shelves and hooks for lamps as also a square stone-bench probably for the students to lie on for rest and sleep. To facilitate the water supply there was a well in every building. There was the system of common messing as is borne out by the large ovens discovered in the excavations. Great facilities were probably offered to the monks of higher stratum. The monk-students did not have to pay anything for their boarding and lodging. Nalanda was perhaps the most famous centre of education in India at the time of Heun T Sang.

The Teachers

The number of teachers at Nalanda in Heun T Sang's time was about 1,510, and they were divided into three categories on the basis of their abilities. The teachers of the first category were those who had the ability to discuss and annotate fifty Sutras and Shastras. There were ten such teachers and Heun T Sang was one of these. The teachers who could deal with thirty such texts were put in the second category and at that time their number was five hundred. In the last and third category were those who were capable of dealing with twenty such texts and they numbered one thousand.

Sholbhadra who had studied all the Sutras and Shastras and could discuss them well was the head of the institution. According to Heun T Sang none else could equal Sholbhadra in abilities and as such all the scholars of the university revered him. Many other teachers of the university were renowned for their scholarship, Chandrapal, Jinmitra, Dharampal, Nagarjun, Sthirmati, Gyanmati, etc., had extremely extensive knowledge and the fame of the university verily depended upon the erudition of these learned scholars.

Free Education

The university was wholly and solely responsible for the maintenance, messing and medical treatment of the students. No fee was charged for tuition. The students thus had no other worry on their heads except to study hard and it was this freedom from pecuniary and other worries which, according to Heun T Sang, was the true basis of their glorious achievement. Thousands of students and priests remained here. Sraman Lee, the biographer of Heun T Sang has numbered the 'Newcomers' and the residents at ten thousand. According to Dr. Altekar the number of students in the university in the seventh century A.D. was about five thousand. In the time of I-tsing the Sangh managed and looked after the residence and messing, etc. of about three thousand students.

The Nalanda University had extended its scope to foreign lands from where good and intelligent persons came to gain knowledge. Students from China, Mangolia, Tibet and Korea, etc. came here to slake their thirst for knowledge. In order to maintain the high ideal of the University the students were put to a very hard admission test in which about twenty per cent could successfully compete. Only successful students got admission into the University and yet the total enrollment in the University was ten thousand. The foreign students who came out a cropper in the admission test returned to their own lands.

Besides higher education, there was also provision for secondary education in the University. The new monks of the Sanghs, the Brahmcharis and others must have been young in age at the commencement of their education. Admission tests may not have been held for them. In accordance to the general rules of the Sangh their conduct must have been put under examination so that the moral decrepits did not get entry into the Sangh.

Subjects of Study

At Nalanda, instruction was imparted in the Brahmanical and Buddhist religious texts as also in other important non-religious and secular subjects. Although the Mahayan sect predominated here, nevertheless the students of the Hinayan sect were not neglected. I-tsing who lived here for ten years to receive his education was himself a staunch upholder of the Hinayan sect. Heun T Sang studied the Yogashastra, telelogy, phonetics, grammar, philosophy and astronomy etc here.

The secular subjects of study at Nalanda included all these. About one thousand lectures pertaining to various subjects were delivered every day. Teaching and studying went on all the time barring the period of sleep during the night. Attendance at lectures was compulsory for the students, but they themselves did not at all want to be absent even for a moment from these lectures. The fame of the Snataks of Nalanda had spread so much that some people spuriously pretended to be students of this university and thus derived great advantages.

Methods of Teaching

Oral instruction and annotative discussions of texts, lectures and literary affrays, were the three methods of teaching in vogue at the University. According to the system of oral instruction lessons from books were prescribed to the students who studied them along with all the available commentaries, and then repeated them before the teacher. Portions which were not easily intelligible were thoroughly discussed while the doubts were removed through questions and answers. In the system of lectures, the specialists in particular subjects delivered their lectures on different topics. At the end of the lectures the students who had any doubts and difficulties put questions to the lecturer. In literary affrays, erudite scholars debated upon particular subjects. We have already mentioned the rules relating to the system of literary discussions. According to the Chinese travellers most of the time of the teachers was consumed by these literary debates and the entire day was not sufficient for asking and answering pertinent and intelligent questions.

Management

The management of the university was looked after by its Head or the Chancellor in consultation with the two committees appointed by the Sangh. The Head and the Chancellor were elected by all the monks and only those monks were suitable for these posts whose conduct, erudition and experience were acknowledged by all. The following were the functions of the Advisory Committees for the Head.

The first committee advised the Head in respect of educational matters relating to the admissions, courses of study, and the time-table of the teachers, etc. Due to the absence of printing presses libraries had great importance. The ancient libraries differed from the modern ones. The collections of books and their preservation and publication were the responsibilities of the libraries and hence to meet requirements of different students several old books had the to be given new forms and several copies of the same were also prepared. The managing committee of the library carried out all these functions. Great care in regard to accuracy had to be taken when copies of books were prepared. Copies of books were generally prepared by teachers and students although there were other workers also for this job. All the above mentioned work of the library was carried out by the first committee.

The second committee looked after the finances of the university and its general administration. Two hundred villages were attached to the university and the committee managed the affairs and produce of these villages. It was not child's play to manage the messing of ten thousand students, and yet the finances were so well controlled that every article of daily necessity was available. This committee further looked after the construction of new buildings, proper management of the hostels, upkeep and maintenance of old buildings and the arrangement of clothings and books for the monks.

In the university, there were Departmental Heads elected by the monks and these Departmental Heads supervised all the management of the university affairs. The students also had their own associations which prescribed punishments to the derelict students. In the hostels also the students, nominated by the particular Departmental Head, managed all the affairs themselves. The teacher left all those affairs to the students, the management of which inculcated in the students the spirit of self-reliance. Along with this, the ascertainment of the ability and probity of the teacher was made through the students. Thus all the affairs of the university were managed in a thoroughly democratic manner.

The old monks enjoyed greater facilities as compared with the new ones. The whole management of the university was done in a highly satisfactory manner through the mutual efforts and co-operation of the teachers and the students. Hence, although the university had a long existence of seven hundred years, yet there is no mention anywhere of any such incident which could show that even for once the co-operation between the teachers and the students had weakened or that there was a lack of dicipline among the students.

The Library

In keeping with the grandeur of the university, the library of Nalanda was magnificent. The library was housed in three grand buildings known as 'Ratnasagar' , 'Ratnodadhi' and a 'Ratnaranjak' and this section of the building was called 'Dharmganj'. Books which were extremely precious and were not commonly available were housed in Ratnasagar, which was a two storeyed building. In all probability some portions of the Nalanda library continued to exist even after the Muslim invasion on India. Foreign scholars used to prepare copies of these books and take them to their own countries. We have already mentioned that Heun T Sang had collected four hundred books to carry to his country.

Vikramshila

Emperor Dharmpal of the Pala dynasty established theVikramashila Vihar in the eighth century. This Vihar was situated in Northern Magadh on a hilly rock along the banks of the Ganga. It appears that the construction of the Vikramshila Vihar was carried out under a certain plan. A strong rampart surrounded the Vihar and in the middle there was a grand temple of the Mahabodhi. Besides, there were other temples numbering a hundred and eight. On the parapets of the buildings were pictures of the renowned teachers.

There were about a hundred and eight learned teachers at Vikramshila and six other scholars were deputed to look after the temples. Thus, there were a hundred and fourteen scholars in the university. On account of the erudition of these teachers the fame of this university spread far and wide. Students from Tibet kept coming here for higher education for four hundred years. Deepankar, the famous scholar of this university went to Tibet for religious propagation.

The Head or the Chancellor of the university was very carefully elected on the basis of profundity of scholarship and probity of conduct. The university affairs were in the hands of different persons. To get admission into the university the new entrant had to qualify at an admission test. At the main gates of the main building there were Gate-pundits who took the admission test. These gate-pundits had specialised knowledge of particular subjects and they made a very significant contribution towards the maintenance of the high prestige of the university. In the twelfth century there were about three thousand students in the university. In the library of this university there was such a huge collection of precious books that the Muslim invaders were greatly astonished.

In this university there was a special arrangement for study in non-religious or secular subjects. The sciences of ritualism, grammar, logic, mystical formulas and philosophy were the main subjects taught here. It is also gathered that diplomas were awarded to the students of this university. This system did not obtain in any other institution of the time. This is sufficient evidence for the fact that the system of studies at this university was much more organised than that of any other university. Later on the increased importance of the study of charms (Tantras) and mystical formulas in the field of education had a baneful effect, but Vikramshila continued for a long time to radiate the light of knowledge to far off places. In the thirteenth century the Muslim invader Bakhtyar Khilji destroyed this famous centre of education. The entire library was consigned to fire and all Brahmans were put to sword because the university was thought to be a military stronghold. Shribhadra, the chief protector of the university fled away to Tibet and started religious propagation there. Thus ended once and for all this highest centre (Empress) of education.

Valabhi

Valabhi, the prominent educational centre of Buddhist India, functioned from 475 to 775 A.D at the capital of Maitrak kings situated on the western coast of India near modern Kathiavad. This centre of education also enjoyed a good reputation like Nalanda and its students were as much respected as those of the latter. In the time of Heun T Sang, Valabhi was at the zenith of its glory. Here too there were grand monasteries and Vihars in which about six thousand Sramans lived. Students from every province of the country came here for education and those who had received higher education here were highly revered and were given high posts in the royal courts. Thus it may be inferred from the above that it was not only a centre of religious education but politics, economics and medicine were also taught here.

The financial obligations were met in two ways. In the first place it was given financial support and aid by the wealthy traders who predominated here because Valabhi was a trade centre. Secondly, financial aid was given from time to time by the Maitrak Emperors. As in other universities here also there was a very rich library. Guhsen in his deed of gift laid down an instruction for the purchase of books. This university served the cause of education right upto the twelfth century after which this educational centre of Western India became the unfortunate target of the wrathful invaders.

Odantpuri

Very little is known about this university. Perhaps this university had been established prior to the establishment of the Pala dynasty. The kings of this dynasty contributed to the development and expansion of this university and established a rich library consisting of the precious Brahmanical and Buddhist texts. Although this university could not acquire the fame of Nalanda and Vikramshila yet about one thousand monks lived and studied here. Usually students from Tibet came here for their education and on this basis the first Tibet Vihar was constructed in 794 A.D. Odantpuri also contributed a great deal towards the propagation of Buddhism.

Jagaddali

In the 11th century, Emperor Ram Pal of the Pala dynasty of Bangal brought into existence a new township Famvati, along the banks of the Ganga, and established a Vihar which he named Jagaddali. This remained famous as an educational centre for about a hundred years after which the Muslim invaders destroyed it. There were a number of renowned scholars in this Vihar among whom Daansheel, Mokshakar Gupta, Sudhakar and Vibhuti Chandra are worthy of special mention. Students from Tibet while living here had translated several Sandkirt texts into the Tibetan language. Daansheel and Vibhuti Chandra also translated some Sanskrit texts into the Tibetan language and earned the glorious epithet of 'Maha Pundit'. Mokshakar Gupta and Sudhakar wrote books on the Nyaya system of Indian philosophy and on mystical formulas respectively, which were later on translated into the Tibetan language.

Nadia

Navdweep or Nadia was founded at the confluence of the Ganga and Jalangi rivers by the Sen Kings of Bengal in the 11th century and was made the capital of the kingdom by king Lakshman Sen. It remained famous for a very long time due to its commercial importance. The old dilapidated ruins are still extant as mute custodians of the record of its prestine glory. It was probably accorded the unbrageous protection of the Pal kings. A number of reputed scholars were born here. Even the Prime Minister of Lakshman Sen was a renowned scholar and was reputed to be the author of 'Smriti Sarvasva', 'Mimansa Sarvasva' and 'Brahman Sarvasva'. The elder brother of the Prime Minister Haloyudh wrote a book called 'Pashupati Paddhati'. The air of this place is still resonant with the warbling echoes of 'Geet Govind' of the renowned poet Jaideva. Among the great writers like Umapati, Dhomi Shoolpani and others of this place there were those also who wrote books like 'Smriti ke Vivek' on Nyaya philosophy besides pure literature. The importance of Nadia increased at the downfall of Nalanda and Vikramshila. It remained a famous centre of Hindu education in the Muslim period of Indian history.

Here it was not permitted either to make students memorise a book or to translate it and prepare extra copies of it. The students were only given a certificate of diploma. Vasudeo Savabhom, a student of Mithila had memorised 'Tatva Chinta Mani' and he started at Nadia the study of logic. Later on, his disciple Shiromani started a new system of logic and established a new department for its study. In this way Nadia became particularly famous for the study of logic. There were several renowned scholars in the department of logic among whom Gadadhar Bhattacharya Rambhadra, Mathuranath are worthy of special mention.

Along with the study of Nyaya, instruction in Smriti was also given. The scholar Raghundandan who started the study of Smritis was renowned in the 17th century A. D. , Krishna Vageesh started a separate department for studies in the Tantras, while Acharya

Rambhadra established a department for astronomy.

The appointment of teachers in the university was made on the basis of their scholarship and ability in literary discussions. Literary discussions formed an essential part of teaching . The students listened to and took part in the discussions which were made by two teachers on any particular subject. In the university, education was given at the three centres-Navdweep, Gopalpada, and Shantipur. The period of study of certain students extended to even twenty years. In 1680 A.D. the number of students in the university was four thousand and of the teachers six hundred.

Mithila

The Upanishadic name of Mithila was Videh and it was a centre of Brahmanical education since very ancient times. In the period of the Upanishads, king Janak used to hold religious discussions here and scholars from far off provinces assembled here to take part in these debates. The importance of this educational centre continued in the Buddhist age. Vidyapati, the sweet singer and the most mellifluous of poets who worked a spell on Bengal and Bihar through his inspiring melodies was born here. Jagdhar, a scholar of this very place, wrote commentaries on Meghdut, Gita, Devi Mahatmya, Geet Govind, Malti Madhav and other texts.

Instruction was imparted in literature and the fine arts along with some other subjects. Several master logicians of this place made this educational centre famous throughout the country, from the twelfth to the fifteenth century. Pundit Gangesh Upadhyaya brought into existence a new institution known as 'Nabya Nyaya' and created a revolution in the field of the study of Nyaya by his book, 'Tatva Chintamani'. His son Vardhman was also was a great master of logic and wrote eight books on the subject. Amongst the other scholars who added to the glory of Mithila, the foremost ones were Pakshdhar Misra, Vasudev Misra and Mahesh Thakur. Mithila was reputed throughout India for its teaching in logic. Even in the time of the Moghul Emperor Akbar was very famous. Raghunandan Das, the disciple of Mahesh Thakur, had, on getting permission from the King, given proof of his knowledge and scholarship in various provinces. As a reward for this, the Emperor endowed upon the scholar the entire land of Mithila. The last examination for Snataks at Mithila was extremely tough. This examination was called Shalaka and on being successful in this, the Snatak was given the degree.

Summary

Varanasi

An educational centre of the eastern India, where facilities were available for Brahaminical education only. The system of education was strictly personal. There was no proper educational institution.

Taxila

It was the capital city of Gandhar State and an educational and cultural centre of ancient India. Numerous professors used to impart education. The fame of the centre was, due to its learned professors. It faced invasions by Persians, Greeks, Kushans and Shaks. There were arrangements for teaching in eighteen trades. Teaching facilities were also available in astronomy, medicine, grammar, Vedic studies and military science. The famous scholars who received their education there were Chanakya, Panini and Jiwak.

Nalanda

It was the capital of Bihar state and the centre of the disciples of Buddhism as well as Jainism. It was the birth place of Buddha's famous disciple Sariputt. In the names of different kings, there were many monasteries. Admissions to university were restricted by an entry examination. All the blocks of the university building were strong and attractive. There were arrangements for the boarding and lodging of the students. There were three categories of teachers numbering 1,510. Sheelbhadra was the chancellor of the university. According to Shraman Lee, there were 10,000 students at the university. Teaching facilities were available in jurisprudence, grammar, etymology, philosophy and astronomy, and in Brahamin and Buddhist literatures. The lecture system prevailed. Oral teaching was also popular. There were two committees to aid and advise the chancellor in the management of the university affairs. One of these committees used to look after the academic affairs. Libraries had more importance in those days. The academic committee was also responsible for the efficient management of the library. The other committee was to manage general and financial administration. Students had their own independent unions.

Heads of Departments were elected on the basis of popularity and merit. The famous professors of this university were Chandrapal Jinmitra, Dharmpal, Nagarjun, Sthirmati, Gyanmati, Sheelbhadra, etc.

Vikramshila

The founder of the Vidramshila monastery was Dharmpal. There were 108 temples here. The university had 114 professors. The Chancellor of the university was elected. Admissions were restricted by an entry examination. There were 3,000 students at roll in the twelfth century. The main subjects taught in this university were Grammar, Logic, Philosophy, etc. Degrees were conferred on Graduates. There was a well-managed library. Bakhtiar Khiljee destroyed this university in the 13th century. Deepankar Shrigyan spread Buddhism in Tibet and at last Shribhandra also fled to Tibet.

Valabhi

It was an important education centre of the Buddhist India and the capital city of Maitrak kings. It was also a famous trade centre. The main sources of income to the university were businessmen of repute and the Mritrak king. It also had a well-equiped library. Its monasteries and temples used to accomodate about 6,000 monks. Teaching facilities were available in political science, economics, medicine etc.

Odantpuri

There were 1,000 monks. Kings of the Pal dynasty contributed towards the unprecedented development of this centre. Students from Tibet used to come to study in this monstary. It had an incalculable importance in the spread of Buddhism.

Jagaddali

Rampal established this monastery in the 11th century. It had scholars of repute like Dansheel, Mokshakar Gupta, Sudhakar, and Bibhuti Chandra. Bibhuti Chandra translated Sanskrit works into the Tibetan language. Mokshakar Gupta and Sudhakar wrote books on jurisprudence and Tantra.

Naida

Capital city of Lakshaman Sen. Halayudh and the brother of the king wrote many books. There were separate departments for the teaching of treatise, tantra and astronomy. The education institutions were housed in three towns — Gopal Parah, Navdeep and Shantipur. The distinguished scholars of this centre were Jaideo, Umapati, Dhomi, Shulpani, Vasudeva, Sarvabhaum, Raghunath Shriswami, Gadadhar Bhattacharya, Rambhadra, Mathuranath, Raghunandan, Krishnanand Vagish.

Mithila

The ancient name was Videh. During the reign of king Janak, scholars used to come to participate in classical debates organised from time to time. Vidyapati was born here. Apart from literature and fine arts, Mithila was famous for education in jurisprudence. The famous scholars of Mithila were Jaghar, Ganesh Upadhyaya, Pakshadhar Misra, Vasudeva Misra, Mahesh Thakur etc.

Exercises

1. Describe any three universities of ancient India.
2. Compare and contrast the teaching methods at the Nalanda and the Taxila universities.
3. Write short notes on Nadia, Mithila and Valabhi.
4. What light is thrown by the ancient universities on the educational system in Ancient India ? Explain.

Chapter 11

Education in Monasteries

No definite evidence is available to prove the existence of monasterial institutions before the tenth century. The Buddhist Sanghs carried on the work of education along with the propagation of Buddhism. Probably being influenced by this, priests took to teaching in the Hindu temples and hermitages, but there is no proof available to show when this practice started. The inscriptions and gift deeds of southern India are the only proofs which shed some light on the monasterial institutions of education in south India. It is conjectured that a similar system must have existed in the North and the reason for the absence of guidance and proof is the Muslim invasion upon the temples of northern India. As a result of these inroads, all the materials from which we could gather information about the monasterial institutions of northern India, perished with those temples. We are giving below an account of the monasterial institutions in southern India on the basis of the material available.

Ennarium

Ennarium, a famous monastery was in existence in the district of Arcot in the eleventh century. We get an account of this monasterial institution in a very early writing of King Rahendra Cholai. In this school there were fifteen teachers and three hundred and forty students.

The number of students for each subject was fixed and beyond this limit no one could get admission. The subjects and the number of students were distributed in the following order :

Subject	No. of Student	Teachers
1. The Rigveda	75	3
2. The Yajurveda (Skukla)	75	1
3. Samveda	40	1
4. The Yajurveda (Krishna)	20	3
5. The Atharvaveda	10	1
6. Vadant	10	1
7. Grammar	25	1
8. Vaidhayan Dharm Sutra	10	1
9. Mamansa	35	2
10. Rupavatar	40	1
Total : 10	340	15

The school arranged for the board of the students free of charge. Each student was given one seer of rice (six Nali) every day and 1/8 Tola (1/2 Kulanju) of gold every year probably to meet the requirement of clothes. According to Radha Kumud Mukerji the students of philosphy and grammar were given 66 per cent more of rice and gold than other students. The teachers were given sixteen seers of rice (1 Kalam) every day, which was sufficient for sixteen persons. The teachers also were given 1/8 tolas of gold to meet other expenses but the teacher of Vedant got 25 per cent more in remuneration.

All these financial obligations were met by the institution out of the income from the acres of land attached to it.

Salotgi

The minister of King Krishna III of Rashtrakuta had built a temple here in 945 A.D. which also carried on the work of education. This monasterial school became famous all through the country and students from different provinces came here for education. There were twenty-seven hostels here and it can be said on this basis that the number of students must have been quite large. There were separate deeds of gifts for different expenses, for example.

Boarding	500 Nivarttan
Light	12 "
Expenses twoards the head.	50 "

The institution received financial aid from the village in other ways also, for example :

On the occasion of Tonsure ceremonies 1/1/4 rupees
At the time of Upanayan 2/1/2
At the time of marriages 5 rupees

This amount was given to the school and students and teachers were invited on all festive occasions. Thus the school went on in a smooth manner through the income from the gifted land and other collective aids from the village.

Tirubhukkudal

This school was in existence in the eleventh century in the temple at Perumal in the district of Venktesh. In the hostels here the boarding and lodging of the students was arranged free of charge. The sixty seats in the hostel were allotted to students on the basis of their subjects. The allotment was done in the following manner :

1. For students of the Rigveda	10
2. For students of Grammar	20
3. For students of Yajurveda	10
4. For students of Panchtantra	10
5. For students of Shaivagam	3
6. For Sanyasis and Vanprasthas	7

The teachers of this school got a lower remuneration compared to that of the teachers of Ennarium.

The Monasterial School of Malakpuram

We get a description of this school in Abhilekh (Rock-edict) No. 110 of 1912, according to which there was a hostel attached to the school where students were provided with meals free of charges. There were in all eight teachers of which five taught grammar, Nyaya, literature, etc. and three were solely for instruction in the Vedas. At that time in South India twenty students were under the charge of one teacher and thus the total number of students must have been one hundred and sixty.

The ordinary staff of the school was given one Putti of land for general maintenance. Whereas, the teaching staff was given double, that is, two Putti of land. The Head of the institution received hundred Nishk as honorarium. In this way the teaching staff got sufficient remuneration to keep the pot boiling.

Tiruvorriyur School

The information regarding this school is based on Abhilekh (Rock-edict) No.110 and 202 of 1912. This school was located in a temple of Shiva and 10 Veli or 410 acres of land were attached to it to meet financial obligations. The number of teachers was twenty and of students about four hundred and fifty. There were some realisations through certain taxes for the expenses of the school. This school remained in existence till the fourteenth century.

According to hearsay, Lord Shiva had appeared here before then great grammarian Panini, and given him instruction in the first fourteen Sutras of the Ashadhyayee for full fourteen days. It was in commemoration of this incident that this Shiva temple was constructed.

Other Monasterial Schools of Malakpuram

In the twelfth century there existed a school in the Praneshwar Temple of Shibhog district. Only forty-eight students read the Vedas and other subjects in this school. There was no tuition fee. Two cooks had been engaged to cook meals for the students.

In the eleventh century there existed a school at Nagayee in the modern Andhra state. The number of students in different subjects was two hundred in Smritis, two hundred in the Vedas, one hundred in Mohabhashya and fifty-two in philosophy. A library was attached to the school and six librarians were in charge of it.

There was a school in the Bhuvaneshwar Temple in Dharvar district and two hundred acres of land were attached to it. The messing of the students was arranged for by the school and the total number of students was two hundred.

A school famous for instruction in grammar was located at Punnarvaliya in the district of Tanjore. The number of students here was probably five hundred. Four hundred acres of land was attached to it to meet financial obligations.

Punidit Yogeshwar used to impart free instruction in Mimansa in a temple of Bijapur. Twelve hundred acres of land had been gifted to him for boarding and lodging, etc. of the students and ascetics who came here.

Agrahar

Information about a particular kind of educational centre is obtained from the Abhilekh (Rock-ediet) discovered in Mysore in south India. This centre of education was known as Agrahar. The localities of well educated Brahmans were called Agrahar and these remained the vanguard of educational activities. All the Agrahars were self-dependent and self-managed. The kings and wealthy citizens gifted pieces of land for the fulfilment of the economic needs of the educated Brahmans of the locality. Thus these learned Brahmans remained fully engaged in educational work. There was a committee for the management of the land etc. We describe below two such famous Agrahars.

Sarvagyapur Agrahar

This Agrahar was situated in the Hassan district of the kingdom of Mysore. There was special provision for instruction in the Vedas but other subjects like the Puranas, prosody, Smriti, etc. were also taught. All the teachers of this place devoting themselves to intellectual persuits lead a highly religious and moral life.

Kadipur Agrahar

This Agrahar did the work of education in Karnatak in the tenth century A.D. and land had been gifted to this Agrahar to meet its expenses regarding the remuneration of the teachers etc. Instruction was imparted here in the Vedas, grammar, puranas, politics, logic and prosody, etc. The destitute students were provided free boarding from the school.

Tols

Ever since ancient times Tols have been playing an important and active role in the field of education in the Northern and Eastern Provinces of India. Even in modern times some Tols exist in the provinces of Bengal, Bihar and Uttar Pradesh. The Tols also had gifted land like the Agrahars. The Pundits of those Tols which had no such land used to realise donations and contributions from the wealthy people of the localities close by, for the maintenance of the students and also for their own expenses. The arrangement for the messing of the students was the responsibility of the Pundit. On the occasion of social and religious functions the Tols used to get some money from the public. Nowadays at some places the Tols get annual grants from the State.

Summary

Monasteries

It is very difficult to establish the advent of monasterial educational system in India. The inscriptions, found in Southern India, contain some descriptions about monastery schools existing in or after the 10th century A.D. Probably such monastery schools also existed in the Northern India. The evidences of these schools were destroyed by Muslim invaders.

Principal Monastery Schools of the South

Ennarium

There were 15 teachers and 300 students on the roll. There were limited seats in different subjects. Students used to get rice and gold for their fooding and clothes. There were similar arrangements for the teachers. Three hundred acres of land were donated to the school to meet these expenditures.

Salotgi

There were 12 hostels. Separate gift deeds for the different heads of expenditures were earmarked. The school used to get fixed amounts on social rituals.

Tirubhukkudal

About 60 students lived in the hostel. There were limited seats for different subjects. The teachers of this institution got lesser emoluments than those of Ennarium.

Malakpuram

There were 8 teachers and 160 students. The teachers and other employees were given plots of land. Teaching facilities were available in Vedic studies, jurisprudence, literature and grammar.

The school was being run in a Shiva temple. It is said that Panini received his lessons on 'Asthadhyayi' (octave chapters) from Lord Shiva in this very temple. It comprised of 20 teachers and 450 students. Land measuring 410 acres was attached to the school to meet necessary expenditures.

Other Monastery Schools

There were similar schools in Bijapur, Shibhog district, Nagai in the modern Andhra State, Bhuwaneshwar Temple in the Dharwar District, and Punnarvaliya in the Tanjor district.

Agrahar

The education expansion programme of this township was in the hands of Brahamins. The learned Brahamins were given land for their livelihood. Sarvagyapur and Kadipur were famous Agrahars as these centres were called.

Sarvagyapur was situated in the Hassan district of the Mysore state. The teachers were religious and disciplinarians.

Kadipur was situated in Karnatak. The teachers used to get their remunerations out of the income of the land donated by Rastrakut kings. There were free fooding arrangements for the students. Teaching facilities were available in politics, grammar, ancient and Vedic literature, philosophy, etc.

Tols

These centres functioned in Bengal, Bihar and Uttar Pradesh since Tols were also given land for their livelihood. Brahamins used to make provisions for the fooding of students in these centres. Some Tols which are functioning even these days receive grants from the State governments.

Exercises

1. How was education spread in the South India through the monasteries?.
2. Describe some principal monasteries of the South India.
3. What was the arrangement for financing monasteries ?
4. Describe Tols and Agrahars.

Chapter 12

A Critique of Ancient Indian Education

We have already studied in the previous chapters the main features and characteristics of the educational system of ancient India. We have also got evidence of the fact that the real basis for the fame and renown which India enjoyed for thousands of years in places like Java, Sumatra, Japan, Siam, Tibet, Korea, China, Central Asia, etc. was the this educational system. We will now discuss in brief the chief merits and demerits of this ancient education.

Merits

Indian education had within its purview both the mundane and ultra mundane life of man and hence it played a significant role in the process of the internal development of man. To be successful in the mundane world this education inculcated in man the spirit of dutifulness, faith, morality and self-discipline. And for attaining the sublimation of life, i.e salvation, man was given knowledge of the Almighty God through religious instruction.

In this ancient Indian system of education the life of the student was an ideal one. The student received education in the very affectionate lap of nature. While living in the hermitage of the preceptor, the life of the student was well-planned and well-disciplined. The lesson of dutifulness was inculcated in him through the scheme of early rising, timely bathing, sleeping on the floor, wearing few clothes and eating as little as possible. His life was thus totally unvitiated by luxury and he always completely abstained from eating flesh,drinking intoxicants and attending dance parties, etc. Control over sensual appetites and desires were the chief attributes of the student of those days. Thus education helped a great deal in making the life of the individual pure, great and divine or godly.

Ancient education contributed towards social life also. A householder who had received education had a thorough knowledge of social responsibilities. He always attempted to rightfully discharge his obligations towards the family, the society, the village, etc. Ancient education did not make a student anti-social but on the contrary, made him a perfect social being. The basis of the development of ancient Indian culture was the well-planned social organization. In the ancient Indian educational system, the highest development of personality was brought about on the basis of social values.

In ancient India there was provision in the educational institutions for higher instruction in practically all the known subjects as also for specialised study. The students in these institutions acquired thorough and complete knowledge of a particular subject and consequently quite a few Indian scholars acquired fame even in foreign lands. In these institutions a particular subject was taught by the most profound scholar.

Though the ancient Indian educational system was religious in its bias, yet it afforded opportunities to persons of all the castes. After the rise of Buddhism, everyday language became the medium of instruction and as a result of this about eighty per cent of the people became literate.

For quite some time women were also provided with facilities in the field of education. In the Buddhist educational plan the women lived as nuns in the Sanghs and studied there. At that time, there were a number of learned women whose service to society are of historic fame.

Indian industries also made much progress through ancient education. Several neighbouring countires were influenced by Indian arts and crafts and there, too, we find specimens of Indian arts. Besides, the standard of achievement in the field of medical science can be judged from the fact that Indian physicians were invited by other countries. India was foremost in the field of medical science in ancient days.

This system of education produced several eminent and erudite scholars in other secular subjects. Even to day several countries of the world are influenced by the original ideas of Chanakya, the author of Arthshastra. The conception of zero in arthmetical calculations originated in India, and knowledge of mathematics travelled from India to Arabia and Europe. Panini's grammar is still reckoned among the greatest works of the world.

Defects

The progress of Indian education stopped with the passage of time due to the predominence of the religious view point. The teachings of the sages that the world is all illusion made the people indifferent to material advancement. Out of the four ideals 'material prosperity, action, religion and salvation' only the last two became the *summun bonum* of education in the later period. Consequently, education became one-sided and it remained confined to religious subjects alone. Non-religious subjects came to be neglected.

Too great an importance was attached to Smritis and Puranas in the field of education with the result that the ordinary people began to think that whatever the Shastras said was the eternal truth. It was explained by the Shastras that the false could never be true. Consequently, the imaginative power of the people was blunted and came to lack logicality. But this happened over a long period of time for in the age of the Upanishads logic had a great importance in the field of education.

As an evil consequence of the caste system, the manual labourers were looked down upon. People of high castes did not give encouragement to industrial education with the result that handicraft, dancing music, etc. came to be regarded as vocations of the Shudras and of the women. Due to this no new investigations could be made in the fields of industry and education dragged on in the traditional manner.

In the education of the Buddhist age self-indulgence developed as an under current to the principle of democracy. Consequently, the control of the Sangh began to relax. In the Buddhist education, the Sangh was all important and when the Sangh itself began to rot inwardly it was natural for education to deteriorate.

Due to the preponderence of Ahimsa in Buddhism, military education, and the arms and ammunitions industry got no encouragement. As a result of this, students engaged themselves in studying the means of deliverance from the misery of this sorrowful world, and when the foreigners invaded India the people could not successfuly face them.

Epilogue

It is evident from the above consideration of the ancient Indian system of education that the merits outweighed the defects. This system continued for about fifteen hundred years and helped a great deal in the physical, mental and spiritual development of an individual. Even the foreigners praised the moral virtues which this education inculcated in the students. We give below the opinions of some of the foreigners :-

Megasthenes

The Indians have a high regard for truthfulness and moral conduct. No Indian is guilty of prevarication.

Strabo

There is so much of mutual confidence that witnesses and seals are not needed when Indians keep deposits with others nor do they have to protect and safeguard their houses.

Heun T Sang

The character and conduct of the Indian is always above board. They never try to get illegal possession of anyone else' assets, and for the benefit of others they behave in a very polite and courteous manner. They always stick to their word and never try to deceive anyone.

Al Idrisi

The Indians always follow the path of justice. On account of their love for fair play and justice, honesty, mutual trust and faith people flock there from far and near.

Marco Polo

The Indian traders belonging to the Brahmanical class are very competent and able men. They never fight shy of the truth. They protect the goods and commodities of foreigners like their own. They do not even expect a commission for their efforts in trade and remain content with the money they receive from foreign traders.

Ibn Batuta (About the Marathas of Devgir)

They are pure-hearted, reliable and religious minded.

Thus we see how education at that time had raised high the moral strature of the Indians.

India enjoyed international reputation in the field of industry also. The textile industry, till recently had an exceptionally high standard. The Dacca muslin was unparalled as a handloom cloth in the world.

In fact the general principles of education, individual supervision, intellectual independence, morality and rectitude, the peaceful environment of educational institutions, the monitorial system, the combination of industrial and cultural education and the Gurukul ideal, etc. can be useful in modern education also.

Summary

Indian education was concerned with both the abstract and concrete manifestations of the human life. Away from all sorts of luxuries, students led a simple life. The students were, moreover, dutiful and disciplined. Education was in conformity with the needs of the contemporary society. It was beneficial to spiritual, mental and physical development. There were specialists for each subject to teach advanced students. There were equal opportunities for the students of every caste.

Facilities were also available for vocational education

The products of the Indian industries were exported to foreign countries. Indian universities produced world famous scholars, like

Chanakya, Panini, Charak, etc. In the field of Mathematics, it was an Indian research scholar who first discovered the hypothesis of zero. This system of education lasted for about 1,500 years. Foreign travellers have appreciated the Indian ethics. Some of them are, Megasthenes, Strabo, Heun T Sang, Al Idrisi and Morco Polo.

But religious dominance proved fatal to Indian education. The attention was diverted towards the salvation of the soul (Moksha), instead of the intellectual development. The unanimous acceptance of religious books proved to be a stumbling block in the development of individuals. As the result of caste segregation, persons engaged in industries were considered low. The spirit of democracy was misused and the Buddhist monasteries gradually became corrupt. The ideology of non-violence resulted in the exclusion of military science from the curricula of the Buddhist education and stoppage of weapon manufacturing.

However, some of the principles of the ancient Indian education, due to which the country ranked among the famous countries, may be useful even to-day.

Exercises

1. Discuss the merits of the ancient Indian educational system. How was India famous in the world due to this system ?
2. What were those demerits of the ancient educational system of India which impeded its further progress ?
3. How did the ancient system of Indian education influence the life of the Indian people of the period ? Discuss its impact on some foreigners also.
4. What features of ancient Indian educational system should be incorporated in our modern education in order to make it more adequate and why ?.

SECTION II

Chapter 13

General Features of Muslim Education

Establishment of Muslim Rule in India

In the seventh century Prophet Mohammand propounded in Arabia a new religion which he called Islam. Its followers came to be known as Muslims and their numbers increased within a short time by leaps and bounds. Consequently, Islam spread over a very wide area and by 711 A.D. it reached even China via the northern coasts of the Atlantic. In 712 A.D. the Arbas under the leadership of Mohammed Bin Qasim invaded India for the first time, but they could establish their sway only over the Province of Sindh beyond which they could not proceed because of the tough opposition from the Gujar King Nag Bhatt. After this there was no external invasion for about two hundred and seventy-five years.

These inroads could not have any remarkable effect in the political sphere. On the contrary the Muslims were influenced by Indian literature and culture with the result that several Indian scholars were invited to Baghdad and asked to translate the important Indian texts into Arabic. It is to be noted that it was the Arabs who acquainted the Europeans with the knowledge and wisdom of India. Thus because of these invasions Indian culture spread far and wide. Then after about three hundred years Subuktagin, the Ruler of Ghazni, invaded the glorious cities of India and after defeating Jaypal the king of the Frontier Provinces founded his own empire. His son Mohmud made several inroads upon India and carried off to Ghazni most of the fabulous wealth of India. As a result of his depredations a number of glorious cities of India rolled into dust and splendid buildings were razed to the ground. The most notorious inroad of Mohmud was the one upon the Temple of Somnath. Mohmud never had any desire to found his empire in India, his chief aim being to plunder the wealth of India and to make his own country prosperous with its help. It was for this reason that he did not bring under his control any province other than the Punjab. However, other invaders found easy access to India through the Punjab.

After Mohmud, India again remained safe from external invasions for quite sometime. In 1191 A.D. Muhammad Ghori, the ruler of Ghazni, again invaded India but was repulsed and defeated by the doughty warrior-king Prithviraj Chauahan. Ghori was not daunted by this and after a year he defeated the Chauhan king in the battle field of Tarain. He was the first Muslim invader who desired to establish his sway over India. He again defeated in 1194 A.D. Jai Chand, the king of Kannauj and thus laid the foundation of Muslim rule in India.

After Muhammad Ghori's death, Kutubuddin Aibak ascended the throne and founded the Slave Dynasty. Several other dynasties, viz. Khilji, Tughlak, Sayyad and Lodi, ruled in India. The rule of these five dynasties was put to an end by Babur, a descendent of Timurlane, who defeated Ibrahim Lodi once for all, in the first battle of Panipat. Babur founded in India the Moghul Empire which had a glorious existence for six generations till the time of Aurangzab. It is, of course, necessary to remember that Sher Shah, the ruler of Sarram in Bihar, had for some time snatched the reins of the Indian Empire from the Moghuls, but he could not consolidate his position. In the second Battle of Panipat, Humayun defeated the Afghans for the last time because after this the Turks and Afghans could never acquire power in India. The Moghul Empire was finally uprooted form India by the British in 1857. Bahadur Shah, the last of the Grand Moguls was imprisoned and packed off to Rangoon. A fresh page was thus turned in the history of India and the administration of India passed into the hands of the British people.

The Muslims ruled India for a total period of about six hundred and fifty years. We shall recount hereafter the history of education during these six hundred and fifty years. It will be seen that in the field of education the inclinations and tendencies of a particular ruler held good and hence the history of education has been dealt with in terms of the rule of a particular king. We have given below some general features and characteristics of education during the Muslim period.

Destruction of the Ancient Indian Educational Institutions

The ancient Brahmanical and Buddhist education was at its peak of glory when the administration of the country passed into the hands of Muslims. The new rulers were the upholders of a new language and culture which caused much harm to the cultural institutions of India. Due to religious fantacism several Indian educational institutions were razed to the ground and innumeral texts of Indian culture were burnt down. Rulers like Bhaktyar, Alauddin, Firoz and Aurangzeb, dealt fatal blows against the Indian educational system. Bakhtyar desecrated Buddhist schools and propagated Muslim education instead. Mosques began to replace Temples and Maktabs and Madarasas usurped the place of Brahmanical and Buddhist educational institutions.

Supremacy of Persian

Ancient Indian education ceased to get any sort of state patronage and due to lack of encouragement Indian languages like Sanskrit and Pali became dead and succourless. Only a very few Indian scholars studied these. Persian became the State language during the Muslim rule and only those who knew Persian could secure a hand in the general administration. This provided an incentive to the Indians to study Persian and Arabic languages. As a result of the efforts of the Muslim rulers and other influential persons the study of Koran and other texts of Islam was introduced in the educational system. Thus education was given a totally religious bias with the result that not much progress could be made.

Education at the Direction of the Rulers

The Muslim rule in India was nonarchial and the will of the autocrat ruler was all powerful. Due to the individual inclinations and peculiarities, the expansion of education differed from emperor to emperor. Only a few of the liberal rulers who had a love of knowledge gave serious attention to education as a result of which some progress was made on the educational front. Education could not retain one general form during the Muslim rule because of the individual inclinations and idiosyncracies of the different rulers. The State did not recognise education as a part of its administrative scheme,nor could there evolve any basic system of general education. It the absence of sound basic principles, education remained at the beck and call of the emperors. Sometimes efforts were made to render to education a purely religious bias and at others to make it general and liberal.

It must be admitted that in spite of these handicaps progress was made during the Muslim rule in several aspects of education, yet however, it cannot be gainsaid that this progress was linked up primarily with the idea of propagating Muslim education although some other aims and objects were also fulfilled in an indirect manner. Muslim education expanded in the following ways :

The Construction of Mosques, Maktabs and Madarsas

The Muslim rulers of India were staunch followers of Islam in which sufficient importance is attached to the procurement of knowledge. Hence, these Muslim rulers made commendable efforts for the propagation of knowledge. When after the establishment of Muslim rule in India, innumerable Muslims settled down here and burnt up localities and several Hindus embraced Islam, the propagation of knowledge became all the more important for the satisfaction of the religious needs of the Muslims of both the types. Consequently, a number of Mosques were built and along with them Maktabs[1] and Madarsas[2] were also opened. Thus the rulers did the work of religious propagation by means of education.

Mosques were built by the Muslim emperors in every nook and corner of India and along with this the network of Maktabs and Madarsas also spread all over the country. In these Maktabs and Madarsas the students were taught the Koran and other customs associated with Islam. Even at the higher level, instructions in Islamic religion was imparted through the medium of philosophy, history and literature. Due to this religious tendency, the construction of Maktabs and Madarsas came to be regarded as a holy and sacred duty of the ruler. Maktabs were necessarily built up with the Mosques and the religious minded Muslims treated general education as a must part of religious education. The teacher was regarded as a very holy person and the favourite pupil of the teacher was also looked upon as a holy being. But it must be remembered that it was this very strong religious sense which provided the incentive to the desecration of the Hindu and Buddhist temples and schools and their replacement by mosques.

There were some Muslim rulers also who had no touch of fanaticism in them and they built several Maktabs, Madarsas and libraries out of their heart's desire. Not only these rulers, but some respectable citizens also made a commendable contribution to the development of education. The educated persons were given a high position in the administrative machinery of the country and hence those who were keen for government jobs were all the more attracted to education.

Educational Expansion through Learned Assemblies

In the royal courts of the medieval period the presence of poets and literateurs was regarded as a source of additional glory to the patron. Hence, poets and literateurs who were the jewels and adornment of the courts were accorded great honour by the State and also huge rewards for subsistence. The presence of learned persons in the court added glory to the name of the ruler. As a result of this other ambitious and aspiring nobles and wealthy lords harboured learned persons in their courts and extended help and honour to them. In this way a learned assembly used to come into existence in the capital and other important towns. These assemblies helped in the expansion of education.

Facilities for Poor Students

The State looked to the education of the poor but deserving students. Orphanages were opened with this end in view and very often scholarships and bursary grants were given. The destitute students had ample facilities for persuing their studies.

The Main Currents of Indian Education Continued

In the preceding pages we have seen that in the individualistic educational system of ancient India, the teacher-student relation was based on affection and reverence. The teacher treated his pupil as a member of his family and loved him as his own son and the pupil highly revered his teacher. This Indian tradition continued to hold good in the educational system of the Muslims and the mutual relation between the teacher and the pupil continued to be on the pattern of the ancient times. Some renowned teachers were individually entrusted with the education of the children of wealthy persons, but other teachers also did not take under them more than ten or twelve students. As a result of this the teachers and the students could well establish deep personal contacts. This personal touch enabled the teachers to educate and guide the students fully according to their own earnest desire. In the Muslim education of the medieval times, the importance of schools was not on account of the student as it is in the modern education, but the deep personal contact with the teachers. This contact between the teacher and the student was very holy with the result that there was usually no element of misconduct and misbehaviour in the students.

Religious Bias

Religious education had a great deal of importance in the Muslim educational system of medieval India, for its very basis was religious. The Muslim rulers imbibed with religious zeal had built up Maktabs and Madarsas. In the field of education, however, the government did not interfare with the Hindu and Muslim students in their work of receiving instruction in their respective religions. Although, the fanaticism of Muslim rulers had sucked out the educational institutions of ancient India, yet those which could manage to subsist received no interference from the then government in their educational system and they remained completely free in their internal matters.

Religious instruction was given prime importance in the Maktabs and Madarsas, as was the case also in the ancient Indian educational system. Knowledge was the solution to all the religious problems and education was the bedrock of knowledge. In the Muslim period also education helped in the solution of religious riddles and enigmas.

Education did not aim primarily at providing a means of livelihood, nor were the students equipped for this in a mechanical manner. The students gained through education a knowledge of literature and other subjects, but the object of education was the procurement of knowledge and not of the means of subsistence.

General Outline of Education

Muslim Educational Institutions

The children of the wealthy persons in the society received education in their homes under the guidance of some competent teacher but that was not possible for common people. Hence, the children of the common people received education in schools.

The Maktabs imparted primary education, whereas the Madarsa was the centre for higher instruction in religion and literature. The Maktab was usually attached to some mosque and here the students were given instruction in the alphabet and were also taught religious prayers. Education in the Maktabs was essentially religious but in the Madarsas other useful subjects were taught. Some of the Madarsas of this time can compare well with the modern universities. We shall consider these Muslim institutions in detail later.

The Working System of the Maktabs

In the Muslim period the Maktabs were the institutions for primary education. A child got admission into the Maktab after attaining a certain age. The system of admission was a different one. In the ancient Indian system also a certain practice was observed at the time of the commencement of the child's education. In the Muslim system, similarly, the child had to put on a new dress and repeat some sacred sentences from the Koran. The basis of education was religious and hence in primary education the child had to memorise some portions of the Koran, the most important religious text of Islam. The students in these Maktabs were acquainted with the various aspects of religion and along with this they were taught reading, writing and arithmetic.

The education of the royal princes was arranged for in the royal places. Competent teachers were employed to give them education inside the palace, in various subjects right from the methods of administration to military training, literature and religion. It has also been mentioned at some places that the education of the princes was entrusted to eunuchs who were sent to the palaces for the purpose.

The children of the common people went to the Maktabs for primary education. Hindu children also went to these Maktabs for education and they too had to read Arabic and Persian. In the Maktabs education in Persian was started by making the children acquainted with its script and later on they were made to study some portions of the Koran. After that the students had to study other texts of Persian literature in order to be fairly well acquainted with the Muslim culture. Among the famous Persian books were 'Yusuf Zulekha', 'Gulistan', 'Laila Majnu' and 'Sikandar Nama'. By way of some practical knowledge the students were also taught how to draft applications and write letters. In this way the primary education for children was organised in the Muslim educational system.

The Working System of the Madarsas

The Madarsas were institutions of higher Muslim education. The students after completing their studies in the Maktabs joined these Madarsas without observing any practices or ceremonies. The Madarsas were managed either by the government or by some good charitable persons. But there was no system established by the government for the working of the educational machinery because the ruler established these Madarsa and gave financial assistance only for self-glroification. Sometimes 'Jagirs' were gifted to the Madarsas.

Religious education was in vogue in the Madarsas as well but here other subjects also, viz. literature, grammar, logic, laws, and prosody were taught.

Competent and able teachers were appointed in the Madarsas by the State or often by other respectable persons. Persian was the medium of instruction in the Madarsas but every Muslim student had to read Arabic. Under higher education the study of history was specailly stressed. In some places hostels were attached to the Madarsas and the messing etc. of the students wa arranged by the State.

The Teachers

The teacher was accorded a very high and important place in the scheme of ancient Indian education. The education of the teacher earned him a respectable position in society while his high moral character and conduct was treated as the basis of his dignity. In the period of Muslim education also the students had the same regard and reverence for the teachers as was found in the Brahmancial system of education.

As in the ancient Indian system, in the Muslim system also the mutual relation between the teacher and the taught was based on love and reverence. The students revered their teachers and the teachers treated the students with fatherly affection and did everything within their means for the good of the students. Thus in Muslim education also the personal contact between the teacher and the taught continued and helped in strengthening the holy ties of mutual attachment. In the hostels attached to the Madarsas the teachers and students usually lived together and took the same kind of meals. This afforded additional opportunities for deeper personal contact. It was believed that it was not possible to gain true knowledge without the blessings of the preceptor although the treatment meted out by Aurangzeb to his teacher was in flagrant contradiction of this belief.

In the Madarsas good and able students themselves managed the teaching work in the absence of the teacher. In ancient education this type of monitorial system was in vogue and in the medieval period also this feature existed.

When the Muslim domination over India was completely established a large number of Indians embraced Islam. It was necessary for these converts to have a thorough knowledge of their religion and hence they had to come into the field of education where the teachers usually made the student conversant with the principles and ideologies of Islam.

The knowledge of Persian, the State language, was essential for securing high posts in the administration. Consequently, a number of Hindus desirous of jobs and position used to join these Muslim institutions and study Arabic and Persian. None was prohibited from receiving education in the Maktabs and Madarsas. Hence, it will not be wrong to say that Muslim education which did not know caste considerations, could prove very helpful in bringing about a cultural synthesis, but religious fantacism prevented this. If the path paved by Muslim education, was trodden with the spirit of liberalism there would have been no lack of literacy in India.

Summary

Mohammad Ghori defeated Prithviraj Chauhan in 1192 and laid the foundation of Muslim rule in India. He was succeeded by several Muslim dynasties which one after another established their rule over Delhi. These are known in history as the Slave, Khilji, Tughlaq, Sayyed and Lodi dynasties. Muslim education took shape under these rulers and depended for its progress mostly on the attitude and enthusiasm of individual Sultans, whose approach to the problem was more for personal popularity and prestige in that sphere. Religion was the core of education, and it continued to be so even during the rule of the great Moghuls. Education had two distinctive forms - primary and higher.

Teachers and Taught in Muslim Education

Teachers were highly respected by the pupils and a bond of mutual love existed between them. In hostels both lived freely together and in schools the student looked after the work of the teachers in his absence. Teachers were held in high esteem in society for their character and learning.

Administration of Education

There was no exclusive department to look after education. In Muslim autocracy education was looked upon as a religious act. The State helped the poor and resourceless students and honoured the scholars. Scholars assembled around the king and the provincial chiefs. The State made the appointment of teachers for schools and Maktabs and looked after their management. At times landed properties were attached to schools. The system of education was interfered with by the State which could effect changes when necessary. The efforts of Akbar the great in that direction are noteworthy.

Influence of Muslims on the Ancient Indian System of Education

Bigots among the Muslim rulers did considerable harm to the old Indian institutions, at the very dawn of the Islamic rule. Innumerable educational centres run by Brahmans and Buddhists were destroyed by the fanatics who set fire to huge stocks of books. Despite this destructive policy, Hindus were free to receive Muslim education, and read their religious texts. The institutions, which escaped the initial warth of victors functioned freely in later periods.

Shape of Education in General

The Maktabs imparted purely religious education. The pupils were introduced to the Persian script and taught passages from the Koran.

The entrance to the Maktabs was accompanied by certain ceremonies, and pupils followed the system of learning by rote. General institutions known as Madarsas differed from the Maktabs in as much as they meted other subjects of practical utility with religious courses and the teachers there delivered lectures on various subjects. Literature, logic, philosophy, mathematics, grammar, law and prosody were some of the subjects taught at Madarsas. Education in the Madarsas was not pecuniary in its primary objective.

Salient Features of Muslim Education

Besides religion which had preponderence over Muslim education, there were certain other things that made it conspicuous. These were (a) full freedom to Hindus to read in Muslim institutions, (b) abounding love and respect between the teachers and the taught, (c) student's allegiance to teachers and not to institutions, (d) non-mechanical character of education, and (e) the urge for knowledge, rather than material gain, as the primary object of education.

Notes and Reference

1. Primary Schools.
2. Muslim centres of higher learning.

Exercises

1. Discuss the evolution of Muslim education in India. What were the basic guidelines for the same ?
2. Describe the special features of Maktabs and Madarsas.
3. Point out to the similarities between Muslim education and ancient Indian education.
4. Muslim education was entirely religious — elucidate.
5. Muslim education in India during the medieval period lacked a good system. Elucidate.

Chapter 14

Muslim Sultans and Education (1206 - 1560 AD.)

The Slave Dynasty

Qutubuddin

Qutubuddin, the founder of the Slave dynasty in India was a ruler who had a love for learning. He ruled for a very short period, yet due to his religious inclinations and love of learning he built several mosques which had Maktabs attached to them. He wanted to give impetus to Muslim education and he intensely disliked the Hindu religion. As a result of this, during his reign quite a large number of temples were desecrated and mosques built in their places. This had an adverse effect on Indian education. Bakhtyar, the commander-in-chief of Mohammad Ghori caused immeasureable harm to the Indian educational system and institutions. By playing havoc upon Nalanda, Nadia and Vidramshila, etc. he shook Indian education and culture to their foundations, built mosques on the ruins of these educational institutions of India and helped the expansion of Muslim education.

Iltutmish

Although Iltutmish also was a ruler with a love of education yet he disliked looking to the development of education. So he devoted most of his time in finding ways and means to strengthen the administration of his kingdom. Consequently, education could not make any appreciable progress during his rule nor did the government make any effort in this direction. But because of his liberalism and his love of education the learned were honoured in his court which had quite a few of them. He even built a Madarsa in Delhi but it was destroyed in the time of Firoz.

Razia

Razia herself was a scholar of Koran and had a great love of learning. Hence she also honoured the learned in her court. During her rule there was in Delhi a big educational institution known as the 'Muijji Madarsa'.

Nasiruddin

The method which Nasiruddin adopted for the expansion of education was a unique example of his wisdom and frugality. The Sultan used to earn his livelihood by means of his own pen. This provided great encouragement to the future lovers of knowledge. The Sultan regarded the development and expansion of education as the prime object of his life. During his rule of about twenty years Muslim education made good progress in Indian and Persian literature also developed a great deal. The famous historical document 'Tabkati Nasiri' was written in his court under his supervision.

Balban

Balban was a ruler who had an ingrained love of literature. In his court a large number of learned persons were honoured. A number of petty chieftains and rulers of the frontiers tempered by the inroads of Changez Khan had taken shelter in Delhi. Several of these Chieftains were learned litterateurs. Thus there was a good assembly of the learned in Balban's court.

The famous poet Amir Khusro, who had acquired fame outside India also for his works in Persian, was the teacher of Mohammad, the elder son of the Sultan. Khusro often joined his pupil Mohammad in literary functions. During Balban's rule literary assemblies were often convened. Amir Hasan Dehlvi was another poet and he also gave much encouragement to prince Mohhammad who also had an intense love for literature. He often invited foreign scholars to Delhi to enhance his prestige. He even tried to invite Sheikh Usman Toorani and the famous poet Sheikh Saddi of Siraj, but could not succeed. Balban's love for knowledge is well indicated by his instruction to his sons that no stone should be left unturned in searching out learned scholars. He thus influenced his sons by his own feelings and consequently his second son also became a lover of literature and he founded such an institution which had great musicians, dancers, story writers, etc. as its members. This cultural institution brought added glory to Balban's kingdom, and also helped in the expansion of education. Besides these efforts, Balban used to converse with the learned and reward them handsomely. Thus during his rule great educational development took place and Delhi made cultural progress. Amir Khusro has hinted at this in his poetry.

The Khilji Dynasty

Jalaluddin was the founder of the Khilji dynasty and he had a great love for learning and literature. In his court all the litterateurs and poets of the preceding periods were greatly honoured. Along with this he established a library to facilitate the pursuit of knowledge and appointed Amit Khusro as incharge of the Royal Library. His successor Alauddin, however, had no love for learning and was a phillistian autocrat. Due to his philistinism he greatly harmed the educational institutions running in his time and confiscated the land attached to the Madarsas with the result that several institutions closed down due to lack of finances.

The swelling tide of culture could not, however, be stemmed in Delhi by Alauddin's boorish indifference towards education. The respectable persons and the lovers of education tried successfully through their individual efforts to keep up the tradition and thus the assembly of the learned which was established long before was not allowed to break-up even during Alauddin's rule. The learned continued to be objects of reverence and adoration in the Muslim world. The learned of different categories continued to make progress in their individual fields and even in Alauddin's time there were a number of scholars in history, jurisprudence, dharmashastra (science of religion) and logic, etc. After Alauddin there was no ruler of the Khilji dynasty who could evince the least interest in matters of education. In that chaotic state of education only Mubarak Kilji came forward to restore to the educational institutions the land which had been confiscated by his ancestors. This resuscitated the then languid religious institutions and several schools were revived and started working afresh.

The Tughlaq Dynasty

The encouragement that the Tughaq dynasty gave to the development of education is worthy of priase. Nearly all the rulers of this dynasty were great lovers of learning and their zealous efforts for the advancement of education deserves high commendation.

Ghayasuddin Tughlaq

Ghayasuddin, the founder ruler of the dynasty, himself a learned man also, had a great love for education. He laid the foundation of such a building for cultural purposes which could be completed later by Firoz. In the court of Ghayasuddin also, the learned were greatly honoured. He used to invite scholars to his court and reward them and also extend facilities and government help to scholars living in other places outside the capital.

Mohammad-bin Tughlaq

Mohammad-bin Tughlaq was a famous scholar and a successful writer. In his court lived poets, philosophers, physicians and logicians. The Sultan had probably the knowledge of all these subjects and it was quite natural that education should take great strides in the reign of such a ruler. Education received a great impetus from the erudition, wisdom, charitable disposition and substantive co-operation of the ruler. Several scholars attracted by these sterling virtues of the ruler came to his court. Maulana Moinuddin Umrani was the famous man of letters of his time. Besides this active effort of the Sultan directed towards the cause of education, he also granted stipends and bursaries to several prominent students. The Sultan also built a number of Maktabs.

This progress of education could not continue for long and when Delhi became the target of the whims of the Sultan, several learned scholars were shoved into the jaws of death. The transfer of the capital totally destroyed the learned assembly in Delhi. The learned having lost patronage scattered far and wide and the wealth which had been accumulated for centuries was frittered away in the winking of an eye. The populace was tortured and the whole country was in sloughs of despondence. It was not possible for education to draw any nourishment from such an atmosphere. On settling at Daultabad the Sultan attempted to reorder his capital but he did not succeed at all and Daultabad could not attain the splendid majesty of Delhi.

Firoz Tughlaq

Firoz Tughlaq was not only an able ruler but also a man with a liberal disposition, wisdom and a great love of education. He is an immortal figure in the history of Indian education. His efforts in the cause of educational expansion, establishment of peace and cultural upliftment, will always remain commendable.

From his very childhood Firoz had enjoyed the protection of competent teachers and also the company and association of learned persons. Mohammad Tughlaq himself paid great attention to the education of Firoz and consequently when he came of age he became the very embodiment of art and literature. With the help of this unique excellence Firoz set aflow in the country the joyful tide of literature. By according financial aid to the learned he gave great encouragement to them. Under his own protection about eighteen thousand slave-children received education. He also built about thirty such Madarsas where the students and teachers lived together. Apart from monetary help to individual scholars, the government also extended financial aid to educational institutions. In every Maktab attached to a mosque, a permanent teacher was appointed.

The learned and the litterateurs were greatly loved by Firoz. Among the palaces the most splendid ones were set apart for the scholars. Out of the total of one hundred and thirty six lakhs of rupees set apart for charitable endownments, thirty-six lakhs were disbursed to the scholars and religious perosons.

On account of his liberal disposition he took great care about the progress of his slaves. In his empire there were twelve thousand such slaves who under instructions from the Sultan carried on productive work in various fields. These slaves had a hand in religious work also. They were entrusted with the task of reading the Koran and writing and transcribing other religious texts.

Amongst the laws operating in the well organised administrative set-up one pertained mainly to the work of educational expansion.

According to this, educational development was the responsibility of the government and the Sultan regarded it as his prime duty to keep running institutions built by his ancestors and to look to their reorientation. The Sultan has described the building up of these institutions in his autobiography 'Fatuhate Firozshahi'. In his conquest of Kangra he found a big library in which there were thousands of Sanskrit texts and being extremely fond of learning he got a very large number of these texts translated into Persian.

Firoz established at Firozabad his Firozshahi Madarsa which was housed in an exquisitely splendid and attractive building. A big garden was attached to the building. The famous scholars of the time were the teachers of this Madarsa and the students and teachers lived here together. Great attention was paid here to religious studies and the students had to participate as a rule in the daily 'Namaz'. The government bore all the expenses of the school and of the daily requirements of the students. The school also doled out charities. Since education in the Muslim religion was compulsory here, the followers of Hinduism had naturally no place. This does not imply in any way that Firoz neglected the Hindus. He had installed a Hindu on the high post of 'Khan Jahan'. Some Muslims also had a love for the knowledge of Indian languages and culture. We have some evidence of the synthesis of Indian and Muslim cultures in the reign of Firoz. The translations of various texts of Indian religion and culture testify. to this fact.

After Firoz's death there was no such able ruler who could have paid any attention towards the expansion of education. The conditions were also not propitous because a number of Subedars had sprung up and the depredatory invasions of Timurlone had sent through the country a wave of unrest. Still the efforts which a few petty chieftains made for the cause of education are really commendable.

The Sayyid Dynasty

The Sayyid dynasty did not play any role in the expansion of education, for no ruler made any attempt worth mentioning in this direction. Consequently, during the period the progress of education and the development of Delhi as a cultural centre was at a standstill.

The Lodi Dynasty

With Bahlol Lodi peace was once again established in the country. He was himself not very highly educated yet he honoured the learned. He built some Madarsas and thus cultural institutions once again got an opportunity for development.

Sikandar Lodi

It was natural for Sikandar Lodi who was a poet himself to serve the cause of education. He wrote poetry under the pseudonym of 'Gulrukh'. Sheikh Jamil was the teacher of the Sultan. The Diwan or collection of poems of the Sultan, consists of nine thousand verses. Sikandar invited to his capital city Agra foreign scholars also . A number of such famous scholars had come from Arabia, Persia and Bokhara to stay there. The Sultan also emphasised the appointment of educated persons to various posts in the military so that education was introduced in the war department also. A number of books were compiled and transalted under the patrongage of the Sultan and thus Muslim education made a lot of progress. The religious fanaticism of the Sultan, however, greatly harmed Hindu culture. A number of temples were desecrated and mosques were built of in their places and hundreds of Indian educational institutions were destroyed and replaced by Maktabs.

In the period of Ibrahim Lodi, the resplendent Lucky Star' of the Turks and the Afghan began to set and the Moghul invasion of India turned the tide of Indian history. Sher Shah, however, tried to re-establish the sway of the Turks and Afghans in India for some time but it could but it could not last long and power passed into the hands of the Moghuls.

Summary

Every Muslim dynasty that held the reins of administration after the advent of Islamic rule in India, contributed its mite to the cause of education.

Qutubuddin, Iltutmish, Sultana Razia, Nasiruddin, Balban, Jalaluddin, Alauddin, Ghayasuddin, Mohammad Tuglaq, Firoz Tughlaq, Bahlol Lodi and Sikandar Lodi, were the prominent rulers from these dynasties. The chronolgical order of the succession of the dynasties was, Slave, Khilji, Tughlaq, Sayyid and Lodi. Qutabuddin erected the edifices of Muslim education but he disamantled some Hindu educational centres. Scholars were respected in the darbar of Iltumish and during his reign he built a Madarsa at Delhi. An educational institution flourished during Razia's rule, who accorded honour to men of learning. It was under the direct supervision of Sultan Nasiruddin, that the 'Tabkati Nasrisi, was written. At the time of Balban India had a number of scholars of repute. His son, too, had a passion for learning and would invite foreign scholars for intellecutal discourses. Ghayasuddin Tughlaq rewarded scholars and founded a college. Mohammad Tughlaq himself was a good scholar but his policy of shifting the capital hampered educational development. Firoz paid due attention to education and took upon himself the responsibility of running the institutions. He wrote his biography. Madarsas were constructed and scholars were honoured during the rule of Bahlol Lodhi. Sikandar Lodi was a poet and mention has been made of a 'Diwan' composed by him. It contained 9,000 verses.

Form of Education

Elementary and higher education in the Muslim scheme of education was imparted by the Maktabs and Madarsas respectively. Emphasis was on religious education. Most of the Sultans were charitable in their dispositions towards the Hindu system of education. uncharitable in their dispositions towards the Hindu system of education. Persian was encouraged and the Hindus could not get a proper place in the educational field. Some of the Sultans took to education as a means of livelhood, but utilitarianism was not infused in the general system of education as such. A few of the Sultans encouraged music and dance also. Greater attention was paid towards enriching Persian literature. In the absence of an organised education department, the full advantage to education could not be given and certain beneficial aspects of it remained undeveloped.

Exercises

1. How was education promoted during 1206-1560 by the Muslim Sultans in India ?
2. What were the services rendered by the Muslim Sultans to Indian literature ? What was the impact of these services on

education?

3. Discuss the educational system as it prevailed under the rule of the Muslim Sultans in India.

Chapter 15

Education in the Petty Muslim States

Apart from the centre, the petty states in the Turko-Afghan period also made some commendable efforts for the progress of education, but these were not on a wide scale. The important states and petty kingdoms during the period were Bahmani, Nijapur, Golcunda, Malwa, Khandesh, Jaunpur and Bengal etc. We will briefly describe below the progress of education in these.

Bijapur Kingdom

It is said that Bijapur is the corrupted form of Vidyapur. Its founder was Mohammad Adil, a highly cultured man of letters. He was a writer of good prose and poetry and in his court men of letters and musicians were greatly honoured. Foreign scholars of Persia, Russia and Turkistan, etc. lived in his court.

Ismail Adil, the second Sultan of Bijapur, wa a great lover of art and literature and was fond of music and painting. Consequently, Bijapur was graced with the presence of artists and learned scholars. An event of very great significance that took place in his regime was that the account of the government income and expenditure began to be maintained in Hindi and not in Persian, and competent Brahmans were employed for this purpose. Yusuf Adil by marrying a Brahman girl gave an impetus to the process of cultural synthesis. He also helped other Indian languages to develop. Mohammad Qasim, the author of 'Atikhi Farishta' belonged to his court. The ruins of the government library are still found in the Asiri Palace of Bijapur.

Bahamani Kingdom

Among the prominent rulers of the Bahmani Kingdom, Mohammad Shah Bahamani was a lover of learning and in his court even foreign scholars lived. To provide education to the orphans he established a big Madarsa in which competent teachers were appointed. He opened other Maktabs also where the orphaned were looked after. Land was given to these institutions to meet their economic needs and with the income accruing therefrom these institutions managed expenses very well. On account of his learning people called Mohammad Shah 'Aristotle'. After him Firoz Bahmani also contributed a great deal towards the progress of education. He himself was a master of several languages. In his palace lived damsels of various countries and he talked with them in their mother toungue. Firoz was fond of logic, comics, science and poetry, etc. and was himself a good poet. Being particularly fond of the study of natural phenomena, he wanted to build a laboratory on a hill near Daultabad for invesigations, but due to the death of Husain Jilyani the contemporary astronomer he could not do so. He used to send ships every year to foreign lands to fetch scholars from there. He was also fond of religious studies, and used to transcribe fifteen lines of the Koran everyday. It is a matter of regret that this religious proclivity made him destroy Indian institutions of education.

Mohammad Shah II, the third learned ruler of the Banmani Kingdom, invited foreign scholars to his court and honoured them. He also established several institutions with his personal money. His famous minister Mohammad Gawan, who was a lover of education had built a grand building to house a Madarsa in which there was also a provision for the residence of students. A library was also attached to the school. In one portion of the school there was provision for the residence of the scholars and a large portion of this wing was destroyed when the arsenal caught fire. The other rulers of the kingdom showed no inclination for the development of education.

Khandesh

Nasir Khan Faruq, the ruler of this place, gave great impetus in several ways to the expansion of education during his long rule of forty years. The ruins of the Madarsa at Burhanpur, the capital of Khandesh, bear eloquent testimony to the educational development of the time. Faruqi was himself a lover of knowledge and he had extended patronage to several learned persons in his court.

Golcunda

Mohammad Kuli Kutub Shah, the ruler of Golcunda, built in Hyderabad a beautiful mosque and four turrets in which places were fixed for the students and teachers of the Madarsa attached to the mosque. A number of smaller Madarsas were also established in which competent teachers were appointed. These Madarsas which were to impart education were also beautifully decorated. Apart from these Madrasas, there were innumerable small schools in the houses of teachers.

Bengal

In the Muslim period Bengal had attained a glorious position in the field of education. The special virtue or characteristic of the rulers of Bengal was that they helped in the development of Hindu literature along with the Muslim. Bakhtyar has destroyed the educational institutions of Nadia and built Madarsas in their places. Ghayasuddin Subedar built at Lakhnooti a splendid mosque, an Inn and a Madarsa and by honouring the learned gave them incentive to work for the expansion of education. Nasir Shah to whom Vidyapati, the Sweet Singer of Mithila has dedicated one of his songs, had a particular fondness for the Bengali language and he encouraged the translation of Mahabharata into Bengali. Husain Shah also tried for the development of Bengali by appointing a scholar named Maldhar Bose for translating the Bhagwat Puran into Bengali. He also established a Muslim school in the memory of Saint Kutub Alam. One of his commanders of forces translated some sections of the Mahabharat into Bengali. As a result of the love of Bengali evinced by these Muslim rulers, the Indian kings and scholars also contributed towards the development of Bengali literature. The Bengali men of letters came to be honoured in the courts. Thus the Bengali language made great advancement during this period.

Nawab Murshid Kuli Khan got two hundred scribes to copy out the Koran and sent his own transcription of the Koran to Mecca and Medina. This is in itself an indication of his love of learning. Abdulla, a contemporary landlord of Birbhumi apportioned half of his income to the work of educational expansion. Thus the way for the development of the Bengali language was paved along with the work done in the course of Muslim education.

Jaunpur

Shershah, who wrested from the Mohgul emperor Humayun his kingdom and power, was educated in a Madarsa at Janupur. In the time of the Turks and the Afghans, Jaunpur was an important centre of education. According to 'Tazkirat Ululma' there were in the regime of Ibrahim Sharki, hundreds of Madarsas in Jaunpur to which students from all parts of the country came for their studies. In order to make the students and teachers devote themselves carefully to their studies, teaching funds and Jagirs (estates) had been apportioned for their maintenance. Shahjahan used to call Jaunpur 'Shiraj-e Hind'. The rulers of Delhi having great regard for Jaunpur helped in the development of the school in Jaunpur and being impressed by the attitude of the emperors the petty chiefs and nobles also followed their example. Nawab Saadat Khan, however, destroyed the schools of Jaunpur.

Malwa

Mahmood Khilji, the founder of the glorious kingdom of Malwa, was also a lover of knowledge and he helped in the expansion of education in various ways. The Sultan invited several scholars, men of letters, philosophers, etc. from far off places and honoured them. According to Ferishta, Malwa was at that time a very famous literary and cultural centre comparable to Shiraj and Samarkand. In the time of Ghayasuddin the arrangement for the education of the learned ladies of the harem also was made here. Seventy ladies of the harem knew the Koran by heart and the Sultan was extremely pleased to hear them recite it.

Summary

The central government of Muslims had made sufficent arrangements for the promotion of education. The provincial governors also made efforts at their level to serve the cause. Education had made a mark in the Muslim Kingdoms of Jijapur, Golcunda, Jaunpur, Bahmani, Malwa, Khandesh and Bengal. A large number of Madarsas and Maktabs were established in these states. Provincial rulers invited scholars to their courts and in many cases the invitations were extended to foreign scholars as well. The state encouraged students in several ways, grant of scholarship was one among them. There was also the practice of giving them rewards.

In Bengal, the Nawabs made efforts to enrich both Bengali and Persian simultaneously. Scholars in Bengali were given due honour in the court. Ghayasuddin encouraged women education in Malwa. Efforts were made to develop astronomy in the Bahmni kingdom. In Bijapur encouragement was given both to literature and the fine arts. Not only educational institutions but also libraries and hostels were set up in these kingdoms.

Form of Education in the Muslim Kingdoms

Education had a religious bias in the states as well. Arrangements existed both for higher and primary education. In some states, Hindi was used along with Persian as the state language. Several rulers were conversant with a number of languages. Attention was paid to the education of women and subjects of practical utility were taught along with literature at Madarsas.

Contribution of Muslim States to Literature

Even the small kingdoms made a valuable contribution to enrich the literature of the time. A number of works were completed by the scholars enjoying state patronage. The author of Tarikhi Ferishta, Mohammad Kasim was in the service of the Bahmani Kingdom during the region of Yusuf Adil. The Bengali translation of the Mahabharat was prompted by Nasir Shah of Bengal. Hussain Shah appointed Maldhar Basu a scholar to translate the Bhagwat Puran in Bengali. Nawab Murshid Kuti Kan engaged as many as two hundred scholars and got a number of copies of the Koran prepared by them. In this way, these states played a significant role in the promotion of literature.

Exercises

1. How did the petty Muslim kingdoms help in the expansion of education ?
2. What is the importance of the petty Muslim kingdoms in education in medieval India ?

Chapter 16

Education during the Mughal Period

There is a turn in the tide of the history of Indian education from the time of the Mughals. A new chapter opened in the history of Muslim education, for it had never received from any of the Muslim rulers such an impetus as it received from the Mughals. Babur the founder of the Mughal empire, has in his autobiography 'Babur Nama' talked of the indifference towards education, of the preceding Muslim rulers. Although Babur's statement that there was neither any educational institution in India nor any civilised society is not truthful and has to be taken with a pinch of salt, nevertheless, even this wrong notion of his is indicative of his fondness for higher education.

Babur

Zaheeruddin Mohammad Babur, the founder of the Mughal empire was a peculiar scholar of his time, and a gifted poet and writer. Among his various works, his autobiography has a unique excellence on account of which he has been regarded as the prince of the autobiographers. The style of writing initiated by him became known as Baburi - probably based on his own name. A copy of the Koran written in this style was sent by Babur to Mecca. He had established a separate department known as "Shohrate Aami' the main function of which was to manage new publications and to build new schools. In this way he made the work of educational expansion an essential function of the government and one of the responsibilities of the emperor. Babur, the lover of art, extended honour to men of letters, rewarded the scholars, and thus gave an impetus to capable persons to strive on. It was in this way that he contributed to the advancement of education. To decorate the library at Delhi, Babur collected the most exquisite paintings of the country. In Babur's administrative machinery great importance was attached to the expansion of education and it was regarded as a very holy function. Among his close friends were the notable scholars of the time and of these Ghayasuddin Mohammad Khudamir, the renowned historian in Persia and Maulana Sahabuddin deserve a special mention.

Humayun

Being the son of an educated and learned father, Humayun was by nature a lover of literature. He was such a bibliophile that he made ceaseless efforts for their collection even in his disturbed and unquiet regime. The royal library was adorned with these books. When Humayun went anywhere outside the country, he always carried with him the necessary books. Even when he had to flee from India he did not forget to carry with him his favourite books and also took with him his beloved librarian Lal Beg or Baaz Bahadur.

Along with this love of books, Humayun had a great regard for the learned and there were a number of these in his court. The author of 'Tazkirat-ul-wakiyat' worked under him in a very ordinary capacity. Humayun opened a Madarsa in Delhi and several others were built in his reign. On regaining his throne in India, Humayun converted Shershah's 'Shermandal' into a library. People go to the extent of saying that a Madarsa used to be held on the upper storey of Humayun's mausoleum.

Akbar

Akbar's reign is famous as the golden age in the medieval Indian history and he himself as a great Emperor. It was quite natural for education to make unprecedented progress in the glorious reign of Akbar. The extraordinary development that took place in the field of education and literature is praiseworthy. Indian culture made all-round progress in the reign of Akbar. We are giving below an account of Akbar's love for education and learning :

The Royal Court

In Akbar's court there was an abundance of scholars and men of letters. The 'Navratna' (nine gems) of the court added extra glory to the world of culture. These have won the attention and approbation of practically all the historians. Abul Fazl, his brother Abul Fayeez 'Faizi' Abdul Rahim Khankhana, Abdul Qadir and Badayuni, etc. were among those scholars who were patronised and highly honoured by the royal court. Akbar used to present himself in the court and derive great pleasure from the literary discussions initiated by him and erudite scholars like Birbal.

Liberalism in Education

We have already seen that great harm was done to Indian culture and literature by the religious fanaticism of the Turk-Afghan rulers, but Akbar exhibited extreme liberalism not only in respect of education but in every field and aspect of life. In this period both Hindu and Muslim students received education together in the same school. For the first time attention was paid by Akbar to the development of Hindu education besides Muslim education and due to this efforts were made for the rejuvenation and development of the Indian educational institutions. By introducing changes in the prevalent courses of studies in the Madarsas, provision was made to give education to the Hindu students in their own language and culture.

System of Education

An attempt was made to make the students self-reliant. The teachers simply gave certain instructions to the students and afforded them some guidance and help. It was the responsibility of the student to understand and learn anything in accordance with the prescribed courses of study. Akbar even made efforts to make the alphabet easier. The students had to memories some pieces of poetry everyday, and to gain knowledge of writing and scripts they had to write something or the other everyday. Apart from giving religious education to the Hindu and Muslim students respectively, Akbar also desired to impart some scientific knowledge as well. Hence agriculture, human anatomy and physiology, geometry, arithmetic and some other subjects were given prominence.

Literary Output

In Akbar's time many books were written and a number of Indian texts were translated. Under the umbrageous protection of Akbar, the good lover of learning, there was a great output of literature. Books were written on various subjects and Akbar himself wrote a book called 'Akbar Nama'. 'Aine Akbari' written by Abul Fazi deals with the principles of Akbar's government. Badayuni's 'Tarikh-i-Badayuni', Nizamuddin Ahmad's 'Tabkat-i-Akbari' and Abul Fath's 'Murshiyat' are immortal Persian works. Apart from these original works we also have a number of translations which were made during this time. Abdur Rahim Khankhana was handsomely rewarded by Akbar to whom he presented his transation of the book 'Waqiyat-e-Babur' from the Turkish language. Badayuni had translated from Arabic the book 'Zam-e-Rashidi' whereas Badshah Nama, Hayatul Hayvan and several other were written in Persian. Besides these texts in Arabic and Turkish languages, books in Hindi and Sanskrit were also translated into Persian under various titles. The great religious texts of India 'The Ramayana', ''The Mahabharat', 'the Bhagvadgita', 'Artharvaveda' etc. were translated into Persian. 'Rajtarangini' and 'Singhasan Battisi' were also translated under royal protection.

Efforts Pertaining to Expansion of Mass Education

Scholars were given economic aid by means of Jagirs or cash payments. Various scholars used to assemble in the Ibadatkhana at Fatehpur Sikri for verbal discussions and criticism of subtle subjects. Student from far off places came to Agra to study and they attended lectures by renowned scholars. Akbar appointed the noted scholars of Shiraza as professors in the Madarsas. In the royal library books on various subjects were preserved and in order to facilitate the readers in finding the books easily, books in Arabic, Persian, Hindi and Sanskrit were catalogued separately. Faizi, the poet and the lover of Indian Art, was its librarian. The valuable books were decorated with pictures and illustrations.

Besides education, other fine arts also attained glorious perfection in the reign of Akbar. The noted musicians Ramdas and Tansen were his court singers. In order to develop the art of painting and to provide training to the competent painters, a building for painting was also constructed.

Jahangir

Jahangir preserved the literary wealth which he had inherited from his ancestors. He built several Madarsas and the schools at Agra functioned as before in his reign also. Jahangir even revived some dilapidated Madarsas. He had a special regard for artists and men of letters and he himself prepared several copies of some of the chapters of 'Babur Nama'. He instituted a special law confiscating the property of persons who died issueless and intestate and endowed this property on the educational institutions. The art of painting was much developed in his reign. We have no account anywhere of religious fanaticism and persons of all religions lived in Agra. The Indian painters were also conversant with the western art.

Shahjahan

The emperor Shahjahan who followed the footsteps of his ancestors was in no way inferior in grandeur to Jahangir. Although Bernier has pointed out that there was a lack of education in his reign and has even greatly condemned the period on this score, yet it is not the truth. Shahjahan was himself a learned man and he respected the learned. How could a ruler who was the great builder of the world famous Taj Mahal and who was extremely susceptible to love, remain indifferent towards education? The ancestors of Shahjahan had built several schools and he zealously looked after these, and honoured and rewarded the learned. Among the gems of his court the names of Amin Qazvini and Abdul Hakim Sialkoti are worthy of mention. It is said that the emperor had built a government educational institution near Jama Masjid in Delhi. 'Daru-ul-Baqa'was a famous Madarsa, but by the time of Shahjahan its condition had miserably deteriorated. Shahjahan successfully tried for its rejuvenation and after rebuilding it entrusted it to the charge of Khan Bahadur Maulana Sadruddin. He also appointed competent teachers in the schools of Agra and Delhi.

Shahjahan had his own individual importance in the field of education. Probably, he studied systematically every night. One of his sons Dara was an accomplished and acknowledge writer, and he knew Hindi and Sanskrit along with Arabic and Persian. Dara, who was greatly influenced by Indian culture, also translated several Sanskrit books into Persian.

Aurangzeb

In the reign of Aurangzeb we find religious fanaticism in place of Akbar's religious tolerance. He was a bigoted follower of Islam in which he had intense belief. Consequently, he paid special attention only to Muslim education. Aurangzeb, rigidly following the path shown by the old respectable Prophets, did not remain indifferent towards education nor did he hestitate in helping some Hindu educational centres to develop. He appointed competent teachers in the schools at Gujarat and he started there the system of monthly tests, the result of which were sent to him. He granted a huge sum of money to revive the old schools and sent instructions to the provincial rulers to look to the expansion of education. The students of these schools were given encouragement by means of monetary assistance.

Although Aurangzeb was an advocate of religious education, yet he did not feel satisfied with the Muslim education of the time. He liked the practical form of education more and he introduced certain reforms in this field. Aurangzeb believed that education should be helpful in making an individual rely upon himself in the midst of difficult circumstances.

For the library too, Aurangzeb collected a number of prominent religious texts and he got 'Fatwa-e-Alamgir' written under his own supervision. This book was kept in the Government library.

Aurangzeb's Successors

After Aurangzeb the course of Indian history again became turbulent and mutual non-co-operation and animosity destroyed the prosperity of the Mughal Empire (Sultanate). Although all of the later rulers Bahadur Shah, Shah Alam II, and Bahadur Shah II were educated and fully conversant with the significance of literary knowledge, but these rulers did not do anything appreciable for the expansion of education in India. Foreign invasions had also started, political changes were taking place, social conditions were also not satisfactory and the pleasure hunting Nawabs were wallowing in carnal pleasures in their resorts. How could educational expansion take place in such conditions ? So only a few of the fine arts were given some impetus for development.

Summary

Characteristics of Mughal Education

Education made an all-around development under the Mughals who kept the doors of knowledge open to all and allowed religious distinctions to be no bar to intellectual pursuits. Study was carried beyond the sphere of religion to other branches of knowledge. Mughal emperors themselves produced literature and left an indeliable impression of their scholarly aptitude. A remarkable thing of the age was the introduction of the script in the system of education by rote. Due attention was paid to the practical aspect of education.

Scholars

Every Mughal emperor had the good company of scholars at his court. Learned persons from abroad were also invited and sometimes they were appointed as teachers in schools. The presence of scholars in the court spoke of the greatness and literary taste of the Mughal emperors. Gifts of land and cash rewards were given to scholars by emperors. This almost kept them free from pecuniary worries. These persons showed a great liking for the translation of standard Indian w' ks on culture and literature. Indian scholars were also among the favourites of the Mughals.

Important Scholars of the Mughal Period

The important scholars of the Mughal period were Ghiyasuddin Mohammad Khudamir (Babar), Lal Beg (Bumayun) Faizi, Khankhana, Badayuni Adi (Akbar), Abdul Hakim Sialkoti, Amin Kazvini (Shahjahan).

Efforts for the Expansion of Education

Almost all Mughal emperors set up schools and appointed competent teachers. Students would stay in the boarding houses of schools and the poor among them received financial help from the State. Learned persons were appointed to high administrative posts.

Books on different subjects were available in the royal libraries, which were classified on the basis of language. This made the search for a book of one's choice easy.

Development of Literature

Immense work was done in literature during the Mughal period. People got inclined towards writing history. The poets wrote a number of books and many of the emperors penned their life-sketches. Outstanding original works of Hindi, Arabic and Turkish were translated into Persian. Some of these original and translated works are the Babar Nama, Akbar Nama, Aaine-Akbar, Wakayat-e-Babar, Tabkat-e-Akbari, Zem-e-Rashidi, etc.

Exercises

1. What efforts were made for the expansion of education in India during the Mughal period ? What was the importance of religious education during this period ?
2. The Mughal period in India is a golden period of the history of education during the medieval period. Elucidate.

Chapter 17

Some Centres of Muslim Education

The earlier Muslim invasions upon India were made with the object of plundering the fabluous wealth of the country, but later on with the establishment of Muslim rule several Muslim localities came into existence. In these localities the education of the children began in the Maktabs attached to the mosques and higher education was given in the Madarsas. The religious proclivity of the Muslims led to the establishment of mosques in every nook and corner of India but Madarsas were built only in big cities which were important either for being the capital cities of any one of the Provincial rulers or for being their resorts. The importance of the capital of the central government is self-evident. In religious places also a town was regarded as important if a large number of Muslims lived there and in these towns majestic institutions were built to raise the level of higher education. We are giving below an account of Delhi, Agra, Bidar, Jaunpur, Malwa — some of the then important centres of education.

Delhi

The earlier Sultans raised the prestige of Delhi by making it their capital and the Mughal emperors also preserved its high position. Nasiruddin built the Naseeria Madarsa in Delhi during the regime of the slave kings, while in the time of Alauddin there used to be a sort of a regular big-meet or get-together of scholars in Delhi. Several renowned scholars were working in the various Madarsas. In the Madarsas bulit by Alauddin there were more than forty great scholars of Muslim religion and Islamic laws working as teachers. The learned enjoyed great honour in the reign of Mohammad Tughlaq for the Sultan was himself a lover of education and made efforts for its expansion. At that time, education developed a great deal in Delhi and it became a prominent centre of education. But education received a set-back from Mohammad-bin-Tughlaq's scheme of the transfer of the capital. Firoz Tughlaq's efforts and his love of education, however, restored Delhi to its earlier dignity. Firoz had built a separate palace for the reception of the learned people. About fifty new Madarsas were opened in Delhi at that time and several of the old ones were revived. He made arrangements for the education of his innumerable slaves and also took their help in literary work.

The downfall of the Turko-Afghan Empire did not have any effect upon Delhi in the field of education, because the love for education of the new Mughal emperors was greater than that of the preceding rulers. Humayun introduced new subjects of study along with his new Madarsas. A Madarsa was established in Delhi for the teaching of astronomy and geography. Sheikh Zanuddin Khafi also built a Madarsa and it is said that this learned scholar was buried in this very Madarsa. In the reign of Akbar several Madarsas were built and the one in which Badayuni received his education was built by Akbar's nurse. Jahangir also did not allow the standards of education in Delhi to fall and he looked after and well maintained the schools which had been built by his ancestors. Shahjahan built a Madarsa near Jama Masjid and himself appointed the teachers. Efforts in the cause of education continued to be made even in Aurangzeb's time and Delhi remained a prominent centre of education where scholars and students remained busy in teaching and learning.

Agra

Agra was founded by Sikandar Lodi, a poet and the disciple of Sheikh Jamil. Sikandar Lodi who wrote a 'Diwan' of nine thousand verses, built several Madarsas in Agra and made it an important centre of education. After him Babur, the founder of the Mughal Empire, also built several Madarsas here but after the enthronement of Akbar, Agra became a very prominent centre of not only education but of culture as well. Scholars and students from far off foreign lands came and assembled at Agra and the Emperor himself entered into literary and religions debates with them and rewarded them. During the reign of Akbar several Madarsas were built in Agra which had become a centre of various arts. Education in various subjects like literature, arithmetic, agriculture, astronomy, medicine and commerce etc. was given in these Madarsas by highly efficient specialists of particular subjects. There was a good arrangement for the residence of the students and students from distant lands came to Agra and lived and studied there.

The glory of Agra was at its zenith during Akbar's reign and Jahangir and Shahjahan preserved it through their individual efforts. A few Madarsas were built by Jahngir and Shahjahan also. The bigoted Aurangzeb also gave impetus to religious education and by paying attention to Maktabs, etc. he tried to develop primary education. Later on, the splendour of Agra rolled into dust with the downfall of the Mughal Empire. Even today while we recount the saga of its past glory, we find in Agra a few Maktabs existing and functioning on traditional lines.

Akbar had built many Madarsas in Fatehpur Sikri also which is adjacent to Agra. In the Ibadat Khana of the Palace several scholars used to deliver learned discourses and have intellectual intercourse through mutual discussions and debates. Thus Agra was a prominent centre of education where foreign teachers and students lived.

Bidar

Mohammad Gawan, the able minister of the famous and learned ruler Mohammad Shah II of the Bahmani dynasty, had built a Madarsa at Bidar. There was a grand Mosque in the courtyard of this Madarsa which was built after the ceaseless labour of three years at a cost of several lakhs of rupees. It had an attached library consisting of three thousand volumes. In practically every village of the Bahmani kingdom adjoining Bidar, Maktabs were built. Prior to this Alauddin Ahmad had also built several Maktabs and Madarsas. Bidar became an important centre of education in the areas around the then Bidar. Great contribution was made also to the development of literature. The rulers also propagated the principles of religious education to satisfy their individual inclinations and also to gain fame. We find in the field an all absorbing influence of Persian and Arabic languages. Thus due to this educational centre of South India, education there reached quite a high level. There were a number of Mosques in places around Bidar, with attached Maktabs where primary education was imparted.

Jaunpur

Jaunpur, the city of education is worthy of comparison with the Paus or Shiraz of the middle ages. It had great importance during the Muslim period. Students of different countries came here for their education. In the Madarsas military education also was given along with that in history, politics, philosophy, etc. Ibrahim Sharki built several Madarsas for whose management the kingdom had granted Jagirs[1]. The royal order (Farmans) of the Emperor relating to the successful students and the situtation of the schools , testifies to this. Shahjahan had enhanced the glory of Janunpur by giving it the epithet 'Shiraze Hind'. Shershah the founder of the Sur dynasty was educated here. At the time, the handicraft and workmanship of Jaunpur were at the acme of perfection and remained as such even later on. The learned were greatly honoured here and financial aid was also given for their maintenance. The number of schools in Jaunpur at that time was very high. This attitude of the Delhi Emperors towards Jaunpur continued right upto the time of Mohammad Shah and became a very prominent educational centre of the country. Twenty schools were opened here in the regime of Mohammad Shah. The Mosques built by Ibrahim Sharki still remind us of the pristine glory of Jaunpur.

Malwa

Malwa was a very famous centre of the art of music when Akbar reigned in India. According to Ferishta Malwa could well rival Shiraz and Samarkand, the famous educational centres of East Asia. There were many schools in Malwa and one was built near the Mosque of Husain Shah.

The learned of different parts of the world were attracted by the prosperity of Malwa and were often invited here. Malwa made great advancement during the reign of Mohammad, the founder of the Kingdom of Malwa.

Muslim education expanded in the places around Malwa and several

Maktabs and Madarsas were opened in the adjoining provinces. We find here the glorious example of female education. Several of the damsels of the harem of Malwa knew the Koran by heart.

Besides these prominent centres of education, there were several others in the country. Among the centres of Muslim education Bijapur, Khandesh, Golcunda, Lucknow, Lahore, Jullundhur, Multan, Firozabad and Sialkot, etc. deserve special mention. At these places Muslim education made an all round progress and these remained centres of education during the whole period of Muslim rule in India.

Summary

Wide Field of Education

In spite of inadequate means of transport in medieval India, education had spread fairly over a large part of the country. In different provinces the local rulers had associated themselves with the development of education. Even the lesser rulers took interest in the field of learning and paid due respect to scholars, among whom were the invited scholars of foreign countries.

The central ruler was fully aware of the conditions of education in different provinces. The subject-matter taught was mainly religious, but other subjects were also included in the curricula.

Love for personal popularity, inspired the provincial rulers to set up Maktabs even in far off small villages. It was customary among the rulers to have a Maktab attached to a mosque which they liberally got constructed as a part of their religious duty.

Importance of Educational Centres

Educational centres, spread all over the country, brought the advantage of learning at the doors of persons, who in those days of undeveloped communication could not swiftly and too frequently move from one place to another. The centre provided shelter to men of learning and made the responsibilities of the central government less burdensome. The race of making a name in the field of education resulted in the extensive development of education. The provincial chiefs vied with each other in setting up a greater number of Madarsas, Maktabs and mosques. Every part in the country had its own cultural feature. The centres played a commendable role in promoting education in the country and in the course of time many cities came to be known only because of their education centre. Even the foreigners made a point to visit these cities and centres.

Shape of Provincial Education :

Though Islamic education, had no prescribed form, yet it maintained a uniformity at all the educational centres. The centres taught some other subjects as well. Mention has been made of arrangements for women and military education. Encouragement was given to the fine arts and handicrafts. Th personal liking of the rulers had a distinct effect on the shape of education.

Notes and References

1. Landed estates.

Exercises

1. Describe any two centres of learning during medieval India.
2. 'During the Muslim period in India it was not possible to expand education through central administration., Explain.

Chapter 18

The Organisation of Education, Special Type of Education, Literature and Culture during The Muslim Period

General Introduction

Religion was the main spring of Muslim education. According to the Prophet the pursuit of knowledge is essential and the followers of Islam must discharge their duty by propagating their religion. Hence, with this object Maktabs were necessarily built along with the mosques. By such efforts the Muslim religion was widely propagated in India and those Hindus who had embraced Islam due to certain circumstances were made conversant with Muslim traditions. Later on, the liberal emperors of the Mughal period included within the scope of education subjects pertaining to every day life. In this way Muslim education had two forms; firstly, primary education and secondly, higher education which were respectively given in Maktabs and Madarsas. The working system of the Maktabs and the Madarsa has already been described in the thirteenth chapter, yet even at the risk of repetition details are being given for the facility of readers.

Maktabs

The wealthy citizens made individual arrangements for the education of children, but the children of the common people received primary education in Maktabs. In Maktabs children were taught religious prayers, but along with this they were taught the alphabet and pronunciation as is usually the case even with the modern primary schools.

Commencement of Education

In the Brahmancial system of education the entry of a student in the school was regarded as a sacred ceremony and a more or less similar feeling seems to pervade through the educational set up during the Muslim period. On attaining the prescribed age the child had to go through the 'Maktab ceremony'. Out of joy over the commencement of his education, the child was dressed up in new clothes and to start with he was made to repeat some portions of the Koran, the sacred text of Islam. The teacher recited lines from the Koran and the child repeated them. If the child could not do so, he simply said 'Bismillah'. On a particular day the child was made to write something. The relatives of the student would be present on this occasion. Muslim education commenced in this way and the student was admitted into the Maktab.

Courses of Study

At the primary stage, the child was given education in the three R's and portions of Koran were taught to a few students. It was not necessary for the students to understand those selections from the Koran, only memorising them sufficed. Besides Muslim children, the Hindu boys also had to read Persian. After getting acquainted with the Persian script, the student had to memorise Persian grammar. Ethical education was also taken account of and the famous Persian poems like Laila Majnu, Yusuf Zulekha etc. were also taught. The students were taught to write letters, applications and also arithmetic.

As against this, the primary education of the royal princes commenced in the palaces. The prince received his education in the Harem through some competent teachers, under the protection of his own father. The princes were given political education also along with elementary knowledge of Arabic and Persian. In order to equip them to solve the complicated problems of the state easily and efficiently, they were taught the principles of equity, jurisprudence and law. They were also given military training because they were the future rulers and administrators of the country. And to build up a benign government, it was necessary to give them a knowledge of the Islamic religion. Thus through primary education, the student gained some practical knowledge also along with the knowledge of some subjects.

Madarsa

In the Muslim period, the Madarsas were centres of higher education. The supervision and management of these Madarsas was entrusted to some highly educated and able persons who along with other scholars carried on the work of teaching. To meet the expenses of the teachers and the schools, the State sanctioned some monetary grants and some Jagirs (landed property) as well. Some of the respectable and munificent citizens also took part in the management of the Madarsas and their co-operation and monetary aid helped in their development.

The students got admission into the Madarsa after having completed their education in the Maktab. The working of these educational institutions was never inspected and supervised by any particular department of the central government. Although Babur had made this work the responsibility of the government, yet the management of the Madarsas was controlled by managing committees and respectable citizens. The teachers were also often appointed by these. The government, of course, gave some fixed financial aid.

The emperor helped in the expansion of education either because it enahanced his own prestige or because he regarded it as a religious work. Akbar's reign was an exception to this. There was a provision for hostels also in some Madarsas and students and teachers lived together.

Courses of Studies

The object of Muslim education was to impart religious instruction, nevertheless, in the scheme of higher education in the Madarsas, subjects pertaining to secular and practical knowledge were also taught. Akbar introduced certain changes in the educational system and thereby made many reforms and laid great stress on the practical utility of education.

Both Hindu and Muslim students received higher education in the Madarsas. In the beginning every one was necessarily given instruction in Islam but in Akbar's reign the Hindu students were taught the texts of their own religion and culture. The Muslim students had to make a deep and serious study of the Koran. The students were also given instruction in the principle of Sufism, and in the discourses of the Prophet Mohammad and other significant elements of Muslim religion. Impelled by the desire to secure high posts in the government, the Hindus themselves studied Persian and they did secure these high posts. The primary aim of this kind of religious education was to propagate the Muslim religion and to acquaint the new converts to Islam. It would be needless to say that this education did not equip the student for the practical purposes of life.

Hence, Akbar for the first time realised that this religious education had no practical utility and he introduced in higher education, subjects useful to everyday life. The Emperor laid down instructions that the needs and demands of the country and the time should always be kept in view. Consequently among subjects of practical utility economics, philosophy, law, medicine, agriculture, mathematics, history, geography, astronomy, mensuration and field studies, principle of government and domestic sciences etc. were taught to the students.

During the reign of Akbar the Muslim students studied Persian, while those who read Sanskrit had to study Nyaya, Vedant, Patanjali, etc. We find a description of this in the 'Aine Akbari'. Aurangzeb had snubbed his teacher Sheikh Mulla Shah Saleh because he had not given him any knowledge of practical utility but had taught him only words and grammar. This incident which Bernier has described shows well how important secular and worldly knowledge was in the mind of the Emperor who was himself a bigoted follower of Islam. The Emperor, in spite of this, regarded it as improper to waste the precious time of youth in the study or teaching of literature. He therefore, laid particular emphasis on equipping the student through education, for practical life in this world. But this experiment of Aurangzeb's remained confined to the royal princes only and knowledge which had practical utility could not be given to the children of the common people.

As in modern days, several subjects were taught in the Madarsas. Literature, grammar and metrics predominated. In keeping with the instructions of the Emperors, the study of history was given a great impetus. We find the presence of historians in the royal courts of all the rulers of medieval India which was not the case with the Hindu rulers of Ancient India. The Emperors also wrote their autobiographies which automatically incorporated the historical events of the time. The study of law was based on religious principles. The study of music had a place in the curriculum of some Madarsas.

Methods of Teaching

The instruction of primary education did not have any particular system of teaching and here mainly religious education was given. Hence, after the child had learnt to speak he was made to memorise portions of the Koran 'Kalma' (confession of Mohammadanism) and religious prayers. Instruction in the Maktab was usually oral and the very ancient 'practice of parrotting' obtained in the educational system of the Maktabs also. The students were also taught simple writing and some accountancy, but most of the time of the students was taken up by the practice of pronunciation of words and the study of the Koran. With a view to stopping this system Akbar laid down that the students should be taught to read and write the alphabet within a prescribed time limit, and when he had acquired proficiency in this, then only should he be asked to memorise prose and poetry selections. He also laid emphasis on the fact that the students should be trained not to depend only on the teacher, but should become self-reliant. He gave a scientific basis and system to the education of the day by introducing the method of graded studies viz. knowledge of the alphabet, words and their meanings and prosody etc.

As a part of oral instruction, the teacher had to adopt the system of delevering lectures, although the students also read books. Every student learnt his lessons in different subjects in his own individual way and on account of this free choice the weak student could also keep progressing. Again this method of learning, reading and writing separately also saved much of the time of the student from being wasted.

We also find in this system the existence of the monitorial method prevalent in India during the Buddhist period. The students of higher classes did the work of teaching in the absence of the teacher — with his permission. We find a sort of practical system in the education of music, medicine and handicrafts. In the study of these subjects some physical labour had to be done along with the intellectual. Thus contrary to the cramming system, the method of practical education was started in the Muslim period.

Examinations

At that time no examinations were held, nor were the students awarded any diplomas and degrees as is the case in the modern system, because then education was important for its own sake and not for being a means of earning one's livelihood. Education at that time was for the development of the personality. Hence, to attain a particular level no time limit was prescribed nor was there any physical standard for any sort of categorisation. The teacher himself examined the whole class and promoted the students to the next higher class. This does not mean that all the students at that time had similar abilities and that good and competant students were not awarded medals, scholarships, stipends and other rewards, but there was nothing of the modern system of annual, quarterly and half-yearly examinations.

The greatest test of the abilities of the learned person was made in the courts of the rulers where several scholars used to assemble and enter into mutual discussions and literary affrays. The poets who could succeed in winning over the hearts of the people in the 'Mushariras' (gatherings of poets) were able to get both wealth and fame. One could gain the favour of the king by virtue of his learning and be amply rewarded by him.

Teacher-Student Relation

In the ancient Indian system of education the teacher was accorded a very significant place. Some ancient devotional writers accorded to the teacher a place higher than that of the adored God. In the Muslim education of the medieval age the teacher was revered much in the old manner. He was honoured not only by the students, but also by the society and the people believed that true knowledge could not be possibly attained without the teacher. Hence, the commonly revered teacher became an object of adoration for the students and the result of this reverence for the teacher was that the student never showed any laxity of discipline. The student automatically became polite and dutiful.

No distances were maintained between the students and the teachers. In the hostels they lived together. This mutual co-operation between them did not only develop intimacy but also inculcated in the students the spirit of rightly discharging their obligations. But the students who read in the Maktabs were denied this happy state because they could remain in contact with the teacher only during the day.

The teacher also loved the student as his own son and treated him as a member of his family. The teachers were always men of ability and learning and this fact greatly influenced the students who by rendering service to the teacher learnt to respect the learned. The teacher was also responsible for the functioning of the Maktabs and the Madarsas. In some places the students went to the residence of the teacher and in this way the teacher was also an educational administrator.

Yet, in spite of all this, the students in the Muslim period did not have that spirit of sacrifice for the sake of the teacher which we find exhibited on several occasions during the period of ancient Indian education[1]. By rebuking his teacher in the presence of all his courtiers Aurangzeb demonstrated that the proud rulers regarded themselves as higher in status than the teacher.

Discipline and System of Punishment

The students in the medieval period were very well behaved although it does not mean that all had the same proclivity. Students of different proclivities did different kinds of work. There must have been in them some natural lack of restraint. The science of psychology and psycho-analysis had not developed till then with the help of which the real tendencies and proclivities of the children could have been found out. Hence, an attempt was made to crush the rude tendencies through corporal punishment.

No system of punishment was prescribed by the Government. The teachers inflicted punishment on the student according to their own will which depended on their temperamental characteristics. Often some teachers in anger got the student wrapped up in a piece of cloth and suspended from a ceiling. Generally, for minor misconducts the students were punished with a cane or a lash or whip. Other bodily punishments were also inflicted, e.g. making the student stand for the whole day or asking him to bend down and hold his ears with his hands passing through his bent legs (assuming the position of a cock), etc. were common forms of punishment those days.

Awards and Prizes

In human nature there is a mixture of humour, choler and affection. While in the educational system of the medieval times, the teachers inflicted harsh corporal punishments on the students, they also, pleased with the intelligence and abilities of the students, rewarded them with prizes and thus gave them impetus for future life. On attaining knowledge up to a certain prescribed standard the students were awarded certificates or degrees and medals, etc.

Apart from the educational institutions, the students were also given rewards by the royal courts. The students of Madarsas were given high posts in the various departments of the Government. The respectable citizens of the society also encouraged the students by giving them some rewards and thus created in them the spirit of emulation impelled by which their thirst for knowledge became keener and acuter and they tried to outshine or excel one another.

The Hostels

In the old Indian system of education the students had to live with the teacher in his hermitage. Thus a number of students lived jointly in a place and carried on their studies. The students were trained in the hermitages to become self-reliant. The use of luxuries was tabooed and they lived in secluded places and themselves arranged for their maintenance.

In the medieval period the hostels were usually attached to the building of the big Madarsas in the famous centres of Muslim education. In these hostels the arrangement for the boarding and clothing of the students were made by the Government. Ibn Batuta has, in his description of a Madarsa, mentioned that there were three hundred rooms attached to it for the students to live in, while regarding their meals he says that they were given good food. Along with fowls, meat-curry and spiced rice with meat — the main dishes of Muslim food — they were also given sweetmeats. Ibn Batuta usually stayed in these hostels during the course of his travels. In the hostels the students were also provided with carpets, books and stationery, oil etc. by the Government. We find in some texts of the medieval period the mention of hospitals and tanks for swimming being attached to some Madarsas.

The students were also provided health-giving articles of diet like fruits, milk and green vegetables so that they could develop their minds and intellect. Allama Shirvali has described the system of monthly monetary grants being sanctioned to the Madarsas at some places, to give pocket money to the students. Jafar has described the exquisite decoration of the Madarsa of the time of Firoz.[2]

In these hostels there were arrangements for the abode of teachers also. The teachers and students were put on the same plane in these hostels and were given the same treatement. The students derived several benefits from close contact with the teachers in these hostels.

Some Special Types of Education During the The Muslim Period

Mllitary Education

The lack of military education among the Rajputs who were the very embodiments of the courage, bravery and valour of India, was responsible to a certain extent for the founding of the Muslim Rule in India. The military organisation of the Muslims was far superior to that of the Hindus. They made several invasions against India and in due course succeeded in establishing themselves in this coundry. Hence, military education was of great importance to them and the earlier Sultans made particular efforts for the expansion of military training. In the primary education for the princes military training was compulsory.

They were given this training in the palace from their very childhood and later on they were taught horse riding and the use of sword, spears and bow and arrow. They were also made conversant with the various tricks and ambuscades of war and were trained in beseiging a fort and in various military operations and war diplomacy.

In the Moghul period a greater fillip was given to military training and the science of warfare because the rulers of the centre kept under their subjugation various far off provinces and were always desirous of the expansion of their Empire. Consequently, a good military organisation was a necessity.

Fine Arts

The Muslim, attracted by the wealth and splendour of India of those days, became desirous of capturing it. In fact, India was dubbed as golden bird. The Muslims, though occupied with innumerable wars ultimately succeeded in establishing their empire in India, whose culture and civilisation had gained a high place in the world. Although most of the time of the reign of the Muslim rulers, was taken up by destructive activities, nevertheless, some of the rulers succeeded in establishing peace and order. At that time literature along with some fine arts made much advancement. Some of the Muslim rulers are notorious in history for their luxurious life made up of indulgences and rounds of pleasure. It was quite natural for them to become like this because they had become the masters of the fabulous wealth accumulated by the Hindus. Thus in the prosperous reigns of these rulers, it was natural for the fine arts to flourish and develop. Huge amounts were spent to enhance the grandeur and splendour of the royal courts for worldly opulence and flourish had become an essential part of the life of these pleasure-hunting rulers. Music and painting thus made great strides. A number of musicians lived in the royal court, Tansen the royal singer of Akbar's court was non-paralleled in his time. The art of dancing was also well patronised by these rulers. Besides, dance and music were common features of the daily life of the petty fief-holders and chieftains. Ustads (teachers) used to impart training in music and dancing.

The palaces of the Emperor were decorated with beautiful paintings so much so that the libraries, schools, etc. were also well decorated. The painters also enjoyed an honourable position in the royal court and good painters of high abilities used to win over the regard of the Emperor through their excellent paintings and be rewarded. Thus music, dancing and painting made much progress during the Muslim period.

Handicrafts

The Hindu handicrafts that had been existing since ancient times were patronised in the Muslim time. The production of goods for the requirements of the daily life of the grand and opulent monarchs gave great impetus to the handicrafts and helped much in the development. The exquisite ornaments, the ivory work and the superb muslin and embroidery work are symbolic of the acme of excellence attained by the handicrafts at that time. Training in these handicrafts was given to the youths in the traditional manner in their families for no institution of industrial education was established by the Government.

The production of war goods also helped in the development of handicrafts. Boats, ships and chariots were being manufactured on a very large scale. Art did not exist for art's sake but also for providing a means of livelihood.

The Taj Mahal of Agra, the Red Fort of Delhi and the Buland Darwaza of Fatehpur Sikri are excellent specimens of the highly developed architecture of that time and also eloquent testimonies of the Muslim rulers tendency to construct huge buildings.

Female Education

In Muslim culture the vogue of the Purdah system is particularly important. In spite of having been in contact with the Hindus for such a long time, the Muslim ladies are still seen adhering to this system much in the old manner. The women in the medieval times must have still more keenly observed the Purdah system. Consequently, girls did not go to the Madarsas, like boys, to receive education. Sometimes and at some places very young girls went to the Maktabs attached to the Mosque and by way of primary education simply learnt some reading and writing. Still, it cannot be maintained that there was a total lack of female education during the Muslim period because a number of women were learned and fond of education and they even made their contributions to the output of literature. The name of empress Nurjahan can very well be mentioned in the society of learned women for she gave abundant proof of her abilities by playing a very efficient role in the administrative system of her husband.

This example of Nurjahan is a testimony to the fact that arrangement for the education of the ladies of the royal family was made in the palace and that probably along with literature they were also given education in religion and domestic science. The daughters of the gentry were also educated individually at home like the royal princesses. The Hindu girls must also have been included in this system.

Some of the girls of the royal families, who had an artistic bent of mind also learnt music etc. through 'Ustads' who went to the palace regularly to impart instructions. But female education during the Muslim period was not as much in vogue as it is today.

Among the learned ladies of this period Sultana Razia was well educated and she honoured the learned. Princess Gul Badan, the daughter of Babur, the founder of Moghul Empire, is famous in history as a good and successful writer and the book 'Humayn Nama' is a famous book. Aurangzeb's daughter Zebunnisa possessed a good knowledge of Arabic and Persian and she wrote good poems in these languages. Among the educated women Sultana Suleema, Mumtaz Mahal, Jahan Ara etc. had a wide knowledge of art and literature. Thus education was in vogue among the Muslim women, but only women of high families could receive it. No separate arrangement for the education of girls was made either by the Government or by the society and hence it had a very limited scope.

Development of Literature During the Muslim Period

The Muslim literature of this period indicates in itself the literary progress that had been made those days. We get to know from this literature how it developed under the protection of the rulers and through their efforts. The muslim rulers had a great desire for prepetuating their glory as a result of which a number of historians were writing during this time. Secondly, there was no dearth of the aesthetic sense in their life of grandeur. Hence, the presence of the learned in the royal court was symbolic of the majesty of the ruler. Thirdly, belonging to a different religion, they had to propagate their own religion and they also wanted to gain knowledge of Indian culture. For these three reasons, a number of books were written during the Muslim period and much progress was made in the field of literature. We are giving below a short account of this progress from different points of view.

Love of History

We find that in the reign of practially every ruler some texts of history were written. Ziauddin 'Barauni's 'Tawarikhe Feroz Shah, and Yahis Abdulla's 'Tarikhe Mubarakhahi' written during the Turko-Afghan period are worthy of mention. There was a prolific growth of this type of work during the Moghul period. Babur wrote his autobiography under the tile of Babur Nama. In Akbar's time also a number of historical works under the name of the Emperor were produced, of which Abul Faz's Aine Akbari and Akbar Nama, Dau's Tarikhe Alfi and Badayuni's Muntkhabut Tawarikh are very well known.

Love of Art

The Muslim rulers had a great love of art. Although the earlier Muslim rulers did not flinch from destroying the excellent specimens of Indian Art, yet the Persian men of letters and Muslim Artists were given great honour in their royal courts. Persian Poetry of a very high quality was written during the reigns of these Muslim rulers. Amir Khusro was a great scholar during the reigns of Tughlak and Khilji dynasties. During the time of Mohammad Tughlak, Mir Hasan Dehalawi composed his 'Diwan' (collection of poems) which was applauded even outside India. Babur himself was a Persian and Arabic poet and his style is known as 'Baburi'. Abul Fazel an Abul Fateh were among the gems of Akbar's court, while the renowned Persian poet Faizi was the incharge of the government library.

During the Muslim period education in the art of music was also given and the musicians were greatly honoured in the court. The famous musicians Tansen and Ram Das were the gems of Akbar's court. In this way the aesthetic sense of the Muslim rulers helped in the development of art and literature.

Cultural and Religious Tendencies During The Muslim Period

Nearly all the Muslim rulers attached great importance to religion and even political administration was based on the principles of religion. Hence, literature shot with religious lines made great advancement during the Muslim period. The men of letters prepared copies of the texts of Muslim religion. Firoz had directed his slaves to copy out the Koran and Babur also had made a copy of the Koran in his own style and sent it to Mecca.

During the reign of Akbar, the most liberal of the Muslim rulers, a number of Indian texts were translated from Sanskrit and Hindi into Persian with the purpose of widening the cultural knowledge. Among these were the religious texts, the Ramayan, the Mahabharat, the Bhagwatgita and others like Rajtarangini and Singhasan Battise. Albaruni, the erudite scholar of Sanskrit, had come to India before Akbar, in the tenth century and he had translated into Arabic many of the Sanskrit texts on Indian astronomy and philosophy. In the time of Firoz Tughlak also the translations of Sanskrit texts had become widely known under the appellation of 'Dalayal Firoz Shahi'.

During the Muslim period Hindi literature also developed along with Persian. During the time of Akbar a new language known as 'Urdu' was born and a lot of literature was written in this language also.

Summary

Educational Institutions and System of Education

Primary and higher education during the Muslim period was given by Maktabs and Madarsas respectively. Educational institutions were run by the State or by citizens who were financially well off. Mostly the residence of the teacher served the purpose of a school where, he was both the manager and instructor. Some of the schools, had the facilities of a hostel as well. Students were kept in these hostels at State expenditure or on donation by the Amirs and Sardars. Schools were decorated and made attractive. Boys in their early ages finished primary education and sought admission to Madarsas. Primary education consisted mostly of learning by rote the religious books. Students during this period picked up some knowledge in reading and writing.

At the higher stages of education, the student would get acquainted with many subjects. The educational system which Akbar, introduced laid greater emphasis on making the student self-dependant and perfect in his practical dealings. The teacher and taught lived in an atmosphere of complete freedom in the hostels. Besides literature, subjects helpful in earning a livelihood were also given a place in the syllabi for higher education. The relationship between the student and his teachers was ideal — on the pattern of Brahamanic educational system. Monitorial system had come in vogue and the students, by order of the teacher, would look after his work in his absence.

Unlike the modern system, examination had no place in the scheme of education of that era. The teacher would promote the student to higher classes after being satisfied of his ability. The real yardstick for measuring the educational achievement of a student was the successful display of his knowledge in public. Students of outstanding merit were rewarded both by teachers and rulers. A man with marked ability alone could get an honourable position and high cash reward in royal courts.

Forms of Education

Education was of various types to suit the needs and requirements of different sections of the society. A prince would have to undergo compulsory military training and learn the art of statecraft. Women education was not prevalent but private arrangements were made for teaching princess at their residences. Razia, Nurjahan, Zebunnissa, Mumtaz Mahal, Sultana Saleem and Jahanara occupied top-position among the educated women of that age. In the period of Muslim education, fine arts, handicraft and sculpture had wide popularity. Special attention was paid to the teaching of music and dance. Embroidery and engraving on ivory were the most popular forms of handicrafts. Artisans were the products of there own families. There existed no arrangement for institutional training in the crafts. Besides the Taj which has won universal popularity, Delhi Fort and Fatehpur Sikri Palace also enjoy an enviable position in the domain of sculpture.

Discipline in Education

No psychological analysis of punishment was made during these days and corporal punishment was resorted to in order to enforce discipline among students. The filial affection with which the teacher treated the taught, played a tremendous role in the character formation of the students. They were mostly humble and obedient. Arrangements made by the State to give a nutritious diet to the students living in hostels, is an evidence of the awareness of their duty on the part of Muslim rulers. Meritorious students were awarded certificates and medals by the kings.

Literary Progress

The Muslim rulers' love for fame, and art and their religious disposition helped the creation of literature in that age. Biographies and autobiographies of the kings were written during the period. Kings, displayed their poetic talent and composed standard verse books. A number of literary and cultural works originally in Hindi and Sanskrit were translated into Arabic and Persian. The important works of that period are Tarikhe Feroz Sahi, Tarikhe Mubarak Shahe, Aiene Akbar, Akbar Nama, Tarikhe Alfi, Muntkhabut Tawareekh. The translation of works like the Ramayan, Mahabharat, Atharvaved, Bhagwad Gita, Rajtarangini, Singhasan Batteesi and several other books of astronomy, medicine and Tantras was also done during this period.

Notes and Reference

1. Eklavya, who had learnt archery from the statue of preceptor Dronacharya, which he himself shaped, cut off his right thumb and gave it away to Dronacharya when he asked for his Dakshina. Ek Lavya thus destroyed for life the utility of his knowledge of archery.
2. Jaffar S.M. , Education in Muslim India, published by S. Mohammed Sadiq Khan, Kissakhani, Peshawar, 1936.

Exercise

1. Describe the nature of primary and higher education in the Muslim educational system.
2. Describe some special features of education in Muslim period in India.
3. Give some evidences of the growth of literature during the Muslim period in India.

Chapter 19

A Critique of Muslim Education

Discussion of Merits and Demerits

Education which developed and expanded during the long period of six hundred years of Muslim rule in India, had several merits as well as demerits. This educational pattern, good in patches and bad in patches like the curate's egg, cast a lasting influence on Indian culture. The vestiges of that old educational system nurtured by the Muslim rulers are still to be found in the form of Maktabs etc. Although these Maktabs, the dying echoes of the old system, had no utility for the masses, yet we do get an idea of the religious significance and the peculiarities of those times from these Maktabs which have tenaciously continued to exist in spite of various politicial upheavals. We shall discuss below separately the merits and defects of this significant and lasting educational system.

Merits

The Compulsory Nature of Education

The pursuit of knowledge has been treated as a sacred duty in the Islamic religion for devotion to God is not possible without knowledge. The precepts laid down in the Koran do well show that knowledge was regarded as the truest friend of men, the giver of real

happiness and the sole means of enhancing one's prestige and glory. The educational pattern built against this background of the religion was given much impetus by the religious minded citizens and rulers and the expansion of education was regarded as a religious performance. In this way its scope kept increasing and education came to be deemed essential for the procurement of mundane happiness. Muslim education was thus compulsory from both the mundane and ultra-mundane points of view. According to Prophet Mohammad, knowledge gained through education had the capacity of endowing man with immortality.

Personal Contact

As in the old Indian system, the relation between the teacher and the student in the Muslim educational pattern was also based on personal contact and mutual feelings of reverence and affection. This personal contact greatly influenced the student's life and rendered particular help in the development of his abilities, understanding and intellectual brilliance. In both primary and higher education the teacher paid individual attention to each student, while the students studied the various lessons in their own independent and individual manner and won the admiration and love of their teacher and of other persons by the sharpness and brilliance of their wit and intellect. Thus, it was due only to this system of personal contact that the abilities of both the teacher and the students were recognised and honoured by the sovereign as well as the common people.

The Practical Aspect

Muslim education was undoubtedly religious, nevertheless it did not totally neglect the mundane world. The ideal of education was not simply to impart knowledge, but also to equip the student for the practical life of the every day existence. In spite of the great influence of ethics and morality in the field of education, its scope was however not only to bring about spiritual upliftment. Hence, the student who had received Muslim education was well fitted for future life. The Moghul Emperors, Akbar and Aurangzeb, laid great emphasis on the practical aspect of education and by discarding the method of unintelligent cramming introduced some necessary changes. The way in which education was expanded in order to make the royal princes perfect in all respects, serves as an illustration. The predominance of action in Muslim life had made them the Emperors of the vast Indian continent. It is therefore no wonder that education suitable to the practical spheres of life had so much importance for them.

The Combination of Religious and Secular Education

It becomes evident from the above that in Muslim education great emphasis was laid on the harmonious combination of religious and secular education. This was the main characterstic of the Islamic educational pattern. It was essential to give accent to the religious element in education in other to facilitate the expansion of Muslim culture even after coming into contact with the culture of India. Religion was the chief source of inspiration in the expansion of Muslim education. Every Muslim regarded the attainment of education as compulsory because of the commandment of Prophet Mohammad.

Since there was no theory like that of the transmigration of soul or ultra-mundane existence in Islam, all their attention was riveted on the worldly splendour, and the utilitarian aspect of other glorious objects of mundane life. The result was that great stress was laid on the practical utility of education in human life and the individual was given the knowledge of the world by means of this education. The need for suitable and capable persons to carry on successfully the work of general administration was easily fulfilled through these men who had been educated in the Madarsas, and these students were appointed as commanders, ministers and other officials. The pleasure hunting rulers of the Muslim period were also inclined towards the development of the fine arts.

The teaching of medicine, agriculture, commerce and handicrafts in institutions of education is in itself a proof of the fact that the aim of education was to harmonise religious education with the secular. Even in primary education, which had a religious bias, worldly education was given an important place.

The Development of Ardent Literature and History

The Hindu rulers were never desirous of gaining any permanent fame in history and consequently barring the Purans, etc., no material pertaining to the history of Ancient India is available. No ruler ever tried to get the real events recorded . Contrary to this, the Muslim rulers themselves wrote their memoirs. This tendency of the Muslim

rulers brought a number of historians in the field and quite a large number of events and occurances that took place at that time were fully recorded in books. We have already seen that a number of historians lived in the courts of the Muslim rulers.

The daily life of the Muslim rulers of that time was made up of rounds of sensual and carnal pleasures and of the enjoyment of artificial beauty. This led to the development of ardent and passionate literature and in that field, excellent prose and poetry embodying the fine, tender and delicate human sentiments was produced.

Free Education

In the educational system of the Muslims the students did not have to pay any kind of fees. All the expenses of the educational institutions were borne either by the Government or by some committee so much so that in the hostels there was arrangement both for boarding and lodging. The students were provided with nourishing meals which was so essential for their mental development.

Other Special Features

Apart from the above mentioned characteristics of Muslim education, we find that the Muslim educational institutions were built in peaceful surroundings far away from the maddening din and turmoil of the world so that the students could study with greater concentration. The students had no other work besides their study and they were encouraged in their work by awarding them stipends and other rewards. The criterion of success was not examination but intrinsic capabilities and as such the tendency for building up good moral conduct and character was automatically developed in them.

Thus through the assessment of Muslim education we find that it contained several such elements which the modern system glaringly lacks.

Defects

Predominance of Arabic and Persian Languages

As the medium of education was not the mother tongue but Persian and Arabic, the development of provincial languages totally stopped. The Hindus also, impelled by the desire of securing high government jobs, studied Arabic and Persian. Primary education commenced with the cramming of the Persian alphabet. The medium of higher education also was Persian because it was the State language and its study was essential. Akbar, through his liberal policy tried to develop Hindi along with Arabic and Persian, but this could not be followed in practice and remained only a principle. Aurangzeb gave impetus to Urdu and pointed out the grave defects of the cramming system of Arabic and Persian. Still Persian and Arabic predominated in the field of education and Hindu culture did not benefit. A large section of the public was neglected.

Disproportionateness between Writing and Reading

In the Muslim educational system, writing and reading were taught separately. The student first had to practise the reading of words, and after having knowledge of reading he was taught to write. This led to the double wastage of time and also hindered his development to the same level. Akbar realised this and he issued a royal directive that the student should be taught both reading and writing within a prescribed time, but the king could not eradicate this defect completely and we find this defect subsisting all through.

Predominance of the Worldly Viewpoint

Religion played a significant role in Muslim education but the Muslims were more attracted towards worldly pelf, because Islam recognised only the visible reality of this broad physical world. Consequently, ideas of gross materialism and worldliness entered into the field of education. There was a total lack in this education of that spiritual and transcendental content of ancient Indian education on account of which India was deemed as the teacher of the old world. The aim of education was confined to the procurement of material comforts, worldly splendour and honour and position in this world. For the satisfaction of the intellect this education had little or no value, and thus Muslim education could not reach the depths of the philosophy of life for which Indian education was renowned in ancient times. Thus, we find that Muslim education was mainly based on the demands of the time and circumstances and was not geared towards intellectual development.

Impermanence of Institutions

The institutions of Muslim education depended solely on Government support. In the sphere of education there was no such administrative department which could do the inspectoral work on a permanent basis. Often many institutions closed down because of the lack of sustenance. Several teachers gave education to some students in their own houses according to their own inclinations. This was a serious defect of the system.

Education not Extensive

The educational institutions had the stamp of religious fanaticism. Consequently, the Hindu masses could not derive any benefit from these, because, although they could get admissions somehow. The absence of complete freedom deprived them of real benefits. Among the Muslims also it was the upper class which profitted by it. The children of the common people were not in a position to gain education because the Maktabs and Madarsas were built in those localities of the big town where Muslims predominated or where the Muslim nobles or chieftains lived.

Neglect of Female Education

The purdah[1] system is very important in Muslim culture. Hence only ladies of the royal family were able to receive education because arrangements for their education were made in the harem. It was not possible for the ordinary people to make private arrangement for the education of their daughters. There was no arrangement from the Government for female education. In some places some girls went to the Maktabs for their education. Thus, no attention towards female education was paid in the Muslim pattern of education, on account of which except a few girls, the daughters of the ordinary people could not be educated. As exceptions to this defect, we find the mention of some erudite royal princesses who had made a place for themselves in the field of literature.

Other Defects

Besides the above mentioned defects, other demerits of this educational system was the almost inhuman form of corporal punishment, oral system of instruction, the luxurious life of the students, and the lack of any philosophy of life.

General Remarks

The Muslim educational system having both merits and demerits led by its religious practice to the destruction of the old ancient Indian educational institutions. Nevertheless, it also helped the expansion of Indian culture to Europe and central Asia. This educational pattern was a veritable boon for preserving unity among the Muslims. It was also helpful in strengthening the ties of equality and brotherhood among the neo-muslims of India who were Hindu converts. Thus, this education while propagating Muslim culture succeeded in unifying into a complete unit the whole of the Muslim society. Consequently, Muslim culture went on developing in spite of being in close contrast with the culture of India.

The knowledge of Urdu and Persian gained by the Hindus with a view to securing Government jobs influenced Indian literature also with the result that the Hindu poetry was infected by the Masnavi style of Persian poetry[2].

Summary

Education System

The system of education of the Muslim period no doubt had many good points in it, but there were certain flagrant shortcomings that cannot escape a critical eye. If the education system of that age could take pride in the affection and regard between the teacher and the taught, self-dependence of students, the peaceful environment of educational institutions, various means of encouraging students and integration of terary, 'useful' and religious education , it would necessarily admit that severe corporal punishments, religious bigotry, waste of time in learning reading and writing separately, supremacy of Arabic and Persian, aloofness of students from the realities of life, the temporary character of institutions, and lack of arrangement of education for women and people at large were the major defects of the system.

The Effect of Muslim Education on Hindu Society

The religious bias of Muslim education did not make it wholly acceptable to Hindus, though some of them were installed in high positions under the kings for their knowledge in Arabic and Persian. The translation of Indian literature made it reach European countries, but Hindu culture as such did not receive any encouragement or patronage under this system.

Stability of the Muslim System of Education

Despite its defects the Muslim system of education flourished for about six centuries. The Maktabs, still existing, here and there in the country are reminiscent of the old system. The religious content of education, was alone responsible for giving the Muslim system a durable form. It was this religious aspect of education, that inspired Muslim citizens largely to take up the cause of education.

Notes and Reference

1. Veil.
2. The 'Padmavat' composed be Malik Mohammad Jayasi is an example of this.

Exercises

1. Discuss the special features of Muslim education in India.
2. Hint at those qualities of Muslim education in India which even today may be considered as good.
3. Discuss the merits and demerits of Muslim education in India.
4. Draw a comparison and contrast between the Muslim and ancient Indian education.

Chapter 20

Hindu Education during the Medieval Period

Education was much in vogue prior to the Muslim domination over the country. The Brahmanical and Buddhist system of education were in a highly developed state and there were many such institutions to which students came from foreign lands to receive education. But due to the religious fanaticism of the Muslims several renowned institutions of education were destroyed and innumerable books were consigned to the ribbons of the blue flames. Nevertheless, it is to be noted that Indian culture was so old and so well-grounded and organised that it was nothing short of a Herculean feat to destroy it in toto. The Muslims left no stone unturned to scatter to the winds the social fabric of India, but they came out a cropper in their attempts. The ancient Indian system of education was not in the least affected by the Muslim rule although the educational centres were verily destroyed. Hindu education went on progressing even in the medieval period. Muslim influence was confined to those big cities where the Muslims were in large numbers or where any Muslim ruler lived. The villages which were the real cultural centres of India remained clean of Muslim influence and the tide of Hindu education continued to flow from these villages to the hermitages located in the solitary sequestered places. Besides, the Indian saints and sages and other leaders of Hindu society remained opposed to the superficial culture and made commendable and zealous efforts towards the development of their own culture. Consequently, Hindu education continued in its old manner and literature of high intrinsic quality was produced at that time. The Muslim invaders could not do anything more than material damage to the Hindu educational system. Marwar, Mathura, Kashi, Patna, Nadia, Ujjain, Dhar, Vijaynagar and Pondichery can be counted among the important centres of education in the medieval period.

Form of Education

In this period the Indians were faced with the question of the preservation of their own culture with the result that the religious and social leaders attempted to awaken the masses. Till this time literature was uninfluenced by the Prakrit language, but now Hindi, orignating from the Prakrit language, became the medium of everyday speech and thought. Books were written in other prevailing dialects of Hindi and the religious and social thinkers made the community conversant with their views. There were some such saints like Kabir, Nanak, Tulsi and Surdas whose importance in the field of literature cannot be regarded in any way as inferior to that of the other in the religious sphere.

By the medieval period both the Buddhist religion and Buddhist education had disappeared root and branch, but Brahmanical education remained intact. In places where Muslim influence could not reach, Hindu education continued in its old religious form. The preceptors continued teaching the texts of Hindu religion, viz. the Vedas, Puranas, Upanishads and Smritis, etc. to the students in their hermitages. Due to this personal contact with the preceptor the students lived in a disciplined manner and observed all the rules and regulations of the hermitages. The students recognized it as their prime duty to revere their preceptor.

The Subjects of Hindu Education and the Level of Achievement

Hindu education in the medieval period received no government aid whatsoever, but the spirit of self-denial in the preceptor, and self-immolation in the students, inculcated by the Hindu education system is really worthy of high commendation. Hence, Hindu education although devoid of any extraneous support reached and remained at a high level. The Indians could never admit and acknowledge that

Muslim culture and education was in any way superior to their own and as such in the medieval period along with the expansion of Hindu education, literature of high quality was also produced.

Books were particularly written on subjects like, philosophy, history, music, dramaturgy, dancing, grammar and logic, but along with this impetus was also given to architecture and painting. There was also, besides this, a prolific growth of religious literature.

Education and Languages in the Medieval Period

Sanskrit is a very ancient language of India, and in the medieval period also it was studied by the students because its knowledge was essential for the study of the religious texts. Several other provincial and regional languages besides Sanskrit had entered into the field of education. The Rajasthani, Gujrati, Marathi and Bengali languages also were becoming the media of instruction. Pali and Prakrit had achieved their sublimed form in the Hindi language. Some Jain literature was written in the Dravidian languages like Tamil and Kannari, and in some provincial dialects also. Tulsi wrote his monumental epic poem 'Ramcharit Manas' in this very period in the 'Avadhi' dialect and Surdas wrote his 'Sur Sagar' in Braj Bhasha. Thus various provincial dialects made great progress during the medieval period.

Expansion of Education, Literature, and Literary Productions

In the medieval period, Hindu education had expanded from North India down to the South where Vijaynagar was an important centre of this education. Kushnadev Rai, the king of Vijayanagar had extended his umbrageous protection to poets and artists in his court and he did commendable work for the expansion of Hindu education. The Shaivists made a great contribution in the thirteenth century to the development of literature. In North India the religious and social leaders worked for the expansion of education. In the hermitages of renowned ascetic sages located at holy places of pilgrimage, a large number of pupils received education. The students those days went particularly to Kashi, Ayodhya and Mathura.

The number of Indian literattures in the medieval period was larger than that available even in the ancient period. Kabir, Dadu, Nanak, Jayasi, Kutban, Tulsi, Sur, Nanddas, Bihari, Bhushan, Kalhan, Sayan, Madhav, Nidyaranya, are a few of the names to be reckoned with in the field of literature.

A lot of literature was produced in the medieval period. An idea about this can very well be formed by looking at these texts, viz., Padmavat, Akbravat, Ramcharit Manas, Sur Sagar, Shivraj Bhushan, Chhatrasal Dashak, Kavipriya, Rasik Priya, Raj Tarangini.

In this period commentaries on the Vedas were also written and innumerable texts were written on the various systems of Indian philosophy, viz. Yoga, Nyaya, Vaisheshik and Vedant along with those on Jain and Buddhist philosophy.

Epilogue

In the medieval period the domination of the Muslims over India was fully established and the Muslim rulers engaged themselves in the propagation of Islam. In order to impose Muslim culture upon Hindus the cultural centres of India were desecrated and ceaseless efforts were made to strengthen the foundations of Muslim culture in India. Even at such a time India's culture could keep its head high and succeeded in preserving its identity. Along with this, Hindu education also advanced although it was denied royal patronage and government support. The expansion of education went on with the help of social organisation. Thus, we see that Hindu education could survive even in those unpropitious and calamitious times and it gave birth to such men of letters whose works have given immortality to Indian literature.

The deterioration of Hindu education commenced after the advent of the British in India who in order to enchain the Indians with bonds of slavery, attempted to change the culture of the country through the medium of their education. They, of course, could not desecrate the culture of India but the educational system died away once for all.

Summary

Educational Affluence of Medieval Hindu Education

Hindu education during this period maintained its traditional high standard. Emphasis was laid during this period on religious education, and the system of education was traditional. Hindu education prospered mostly in the places away from the Muslim influence.

Remarkable progress was made in the sphere of Hindu literature. Books were written on almost all topics, even in regional languages, like, Gujrati, Marathi, Rajasthani, Bengali, Kannari, Prakrit, Pali, etc. Commentaries on Sanskrit works were also written. Regional languages were being adopted as the media of instruction. Inspired by the idea of forging a religious unity in the country, some of the Muslim saints, also contributed towards the enriching of the Hindu literature. Writings of Kabit, Jayasi, Kutban, Raskhan are precious possessions of Hindi literature. Students had to learn their regional languages and also Sanskrit to study religious books. The relation between the teacher and the taught continued to be on the old pattern.

Exercises

1. What were the difficulties before the centres of Hindu education during the medieval period in India ?
2. Discuss the special features of Hindu education during the medieval period in India.
3. Point out some evidences of the promotion of Hindu literature during medieval India.

Selected Bibliography

Ancient Period

Altekar, A.S : 'Education in Ancient India, Nanda Kishore & Bros., Banaras 1948.

Balmik : Ramayana.

Bohil, V.P. : The History of Education in India.

Chhandogya Upanishad.

Das, S.C. : Indian Pandits in the Land of Snow, Calcutta 1893.

Das, S.K. : Educational System of Ancient Indus, 152, Panchanontola Road, Howrah, Calcutta, 1930.

Dharmshastra.

Kautilya Arthshastra.

Mookerjee, R.K : Ancient Indian Education, Macmillan & Co, 1994.

Keay, F.E. : Indian Education in Ancient and Later Times, Humphrey Milford University Oxford Press, 1942.

Mahabharat : Adi Parva

Manusmriti.

Mundak Upanishad.

Maxumdar, N.N. : Education in Ancient India.

Muneshwar Prasad : Bhartiya Shiksha Ka Itihas.

Padma Puran.

Panini.

Raja, C. Kunhar, : Some Aspects of Education in Ancient India.

Sacred Books of the East, Vols, XIII, XVII, XX Vinaya Texts. (Translated by Rhys Davis and Oldenberg.)

Sankalia, H.D. : The University of Nalanda.

Sarkar, S.G. : Education Ideas and Institutions in Ancient India. The 1925-26 Readership Lectures, Patna College, Patna.

Shatpath Brahman.

Yajnavalkya.

Medieval Period

Aini-i-Akbari (Traslated by H. Blochmann)

Barnier : Travels in the Moghal Empire (Translated by A. Courtable).

Barnier : Travels.

Combridge History of India, Vol. IV.

Ishwari Prasad : History of Medieval India, The Indian Press, Ltd. Allahabad.

Jaffar, S.M. : Education in Muslim India, Published by S. Muhammad Sadiq Khan, Peshawar, 1936.

Keay, F.E. : Indian Education in Ancient and Later Times.

Law, Narendra Nath : Promotion of Learning in India during the Mohammedan Rule.

Maulvi, Abul Hasant Nadia : Hindustan Ki Qidim Islam (In Urdu).

Moreland, W.H. : From Akbar to Aurangzeb.

Muneshwar Prasad : Bhartiya Shiksha Ka Itihas.

Nadavi : Muslim Thought and Its Source.

Sufi, G.M.D. : Al-Minhaj (The Evolution of Curriculum in the Muslm Educational Institutions in India) Shaikh Muhammad Ashraf, Kashmiri Bazar, Lahore.

Waheed, A : Evolution of Muslim Education, Ferozsons, Lahore, 1937.

Glossory

A

Abhilekh	-	rock - edict
Abhyasa	-	practice
Acharya	-	Brahmanical teacher
Adhvaryu	-	priest of old Rigvedic religion
Adhyayana	-	study
Adhyapana	-	teaching
Agnihotra		worship of fire
Adivasis	-	primitive people
Agrahara	-	settlement of learned Brahmans
Ahimsa	-	non-violence, Buddhist doctrine.
Ahmkara	-	empincal ego
Amurta	-	aspect of Brahma without form
Anasuya	-	wife of Rishi Arti
Anna	-	food
Apara	-	all knowledge except the highest.
Aranyaks	-	forests portions of Brahmans
Asana	-	posture
Ashkara Purusha	-	Eternal Being
Ashrama	-	a stage of life according to Hinduism, such as - Brahmachary, grihasth, Vanprasth and Sangas
Ashtanga Yoga	-	loss of consciousnessof external objects
Asuras	-	non-Aryans
Atharva	-	Vedic samhita
Atma	-	the absolute
Avidya	-	ignorance
Ayurveda	-	Indian medical science

B

Bhikshu	-	monk
Brahmachari	-	a general term for a student in ancient India
Brahmacharya	-	celibacy
Buddhi	-	intellect
Brahman	-	God

C

Chitta	-	mind
Crore	-	equivalent to ten million, i.e, 10000000

D

Dandaniti	-	science and art of government
Darsana	-	pursuit of truth
Dharmashastra	-	the science of religion
Dhyana	-	contemplation
Dikshant Samaroha	-	convocation ceremony

G

Grihastha	-	householder

H

Hinayan	-	a Buddhist sect

J

Jagir	-	landed property granted by Muslim kings in India to persons rendering unique service to them.
Jagat	-	world

Jatak	-	stories relating to pre-birth of Lord Buddha
Jnana	-	realisation of atman
Jyotisha	-	astronomy

K

Kala	-	arts & crafts
Kshatriya	-	the second Hindu caste in hierarchy

L

Lac	-	an Indian technical term used in calculation. This is equivalent to one hundred thousand, i.e. 100,000

M

Madarsah	-	the centre of higher learning according to the Arabic and Persian traditions.
Maktab	-	the Arbic or Persian primary school
Mahabharat	-	the great Indian epic
Manu	-	the law giver, one of the sons of Brahma according to Indian mythology.
Manthas	-	indigenous Indian example of educational organization.
Mekhala	-	girdle of students at Upanayana.
Mimamsa	-	Two philosophies out of the six philosophies according to Hindus.
Mukti	-	emancipation
Murta	-	aspect of Brahma with form.

N

Nai Talim - new education, a word used for basic education

Nighantu - collection of Vedic works and synoyms.

Nai Talim Sangh - An association for furthering the cause of basic education.

Nirukta - cultivation of Vedic speech.

Niyama - self-restraint

Nyaya - justice

O

Om - A mystic syllable

P

Pabbajja - first ordination

Pancha-Mahayajnas - hierarchy of five yajnas.

Panchayat - a committee of the representatives of the common people.

Para-Vidya - supreme or highest knowledge

Parishad - academy of learned men.

Prajna - discriminating insight

Prakriti - nature

Prasna - question

Pratyahara - suppression of organs of sense

Puranas - the eighteen religious stories (mythologies) of Hindus written by Vedavyas

Purohit - family priest.

S

Samkhya	-	the Indian philosophy propounded by sage Kapila. It is realistic in epistemology and dualistic in Metaphysics.
Samadhi	-	absorption
Samavartan	-	a Buddhist sect
Sangh	-	association
Shreshthi	-	the head of a guild
Shraddha	-	means of attainment of absorption.
Smriti	-	the Hindu science of religion.
Sraman	-	the Buddhist monk
Snataks	-	graduates
Sreni	-	guild
Sudra (Shudra)	-	the lowest Hindu caste in hierarchy.

T

Tahsildars	-	An officer appointed by the Government over the affairs of a sub-division of a district.

U

Upanayana	-	the thread ceremony of high caste Hindus
Upsampada	-	final ordination
Upnishads	-	the sacred texts of Hindus embodying the great Indian philosophical thoughts.

V

Vedas	-	The original sources of the philosophy of life in ancient India. They are still regarded as one of the scriptures of Hinduism.
Vinaya	-	discipline
Vaishya	-	the third Hindu caste in hierarchy.
Vihar	-	The Buddhist seat of learning, a place where Buddhist monks dwell.
Varta	-	discussion, debate, seminar

Y

Yama	-	Abstention, of various types as an aid to Yoga

Index